Translations

of

Love

Translations

of

Love

Philip Joe Zamora 2

authorHOUSE®

AuthorHouse™
1663 Liberty Drive
Bloomington, IN 47403
www.authorhouse.com
Phone: 1-800-839-8640

First published by AuthorHouse   11/15/2011

ISBN: 978-1-4567-9519-1 (sc)
ISBN: 978-1-4567-9517-7 (ebk)

Library of Congress Control Number: 2011915046

Printed in the United States of America

Contents

I dedicate this book to the underground music for making me. I dedicate this book to God for saving me from distractions from people's devilish minds to collect currency. I dedicate this book to my skateboarder, punk rocker, b-boy brothers and sisters around the world keeping it raw. I dedicate this book to a girl who only took me understood around sound and others. I dedicate this book to Eyedea from Atmosphere, *First Born* was a huge inspiration in my life; and to remember him, there's an eye he can see through on page nineteen. I dedicate this book to the love I hold so deep in my heart in which makes me create and stay young with youth. I dedicate this to you, if you've ever accomplished anything in your life. I dedicate this book to everyone who thought I'd never be shit. This is my ointment for you.

HEAL

MY TEACHER GOD FATHER MINDS

REACHING TALL SCHOLAR SIGNS

FROM THE YOUTH OF ALL WATER KIND

HEAL IS MY NAME BECAUSE I GET BETTER IN TIME

PHYSICALLY PLUS STUDY MENTALLY COMBINED

I ADVANCE MY RESEARCH DEVELOPMENT PROCESS
AS A ONE

I DON'T SEE COLOR OR SEX

PEOPLE NEED TO BE MORE ORIGINAL

AND STOP TAKING ADVANTAGE OF RACE

YES, YOU MIGHT MAKE FUN OF ME

BUT THE ONLY RACE I SEE IS ME

IN THE FRONT LEAD

WINNING WITH MY SOCIAL

STAYING POOR

STRUGGLING

KEEPING UP WITH MY ART

AND PEOPLES DIVINE ACCOMPLISHMENTS I
ACQUIRE

IS THE HIGHEST FORM OF RELIGION IN MY OPINION

A PERSON DEDICATES THEIR TIME WERE IN

YOU ALL STILL LIVING IN NINETEEN SEVENTY TWO

WHILE I STAY HOME MEDICATING MY RHYMES

GIVES ME AN ATTITUDE THAT LISTENS

THEN SLOWLY TURNS INTO LOVE

BUT I CAN'T LOVE THE ONES WHO JUDGE FOR NO
REASON

THEN GOES TO CHURCH ASKING FOR GOLD

PLEASE SUN,

I WILL RAISE YOU AS PROPER

TECHNOLOGY IS UNFOLDING ON OUR PRESENT

TO BE A PIONEER,

STRUCTURE SETS SIGHTS SWELLED IN SKIES

SINCERELY SOWN IN SEAMS IN PEOPLE EYES

AND I GOT A MILLION STATISTICS

SAY THIRTY TWO,

AND I'M GOING TO FIGHT THAT WAY

UNTIL MY CHILDRENS COLOR TURNS BLUE

THIS IS JUST A METAPHOR FOR NOT HAVING A BAD
ATTITUDE

BECAUSE WHAT OTHER COLOR IS LOVE

THAT I SEE MY SOUL LYING IN DAILY

COVER RED WITH BUGS

NOT EXPECTING ANYONE TO PAY ME

SPAWNED FROM THE WORLD IS MY FEELING

SO NIGHT IS WHEN I'M REALLY NOT ALONE

2

EVEN THOUGH I KNOW I'M NOT ALONE

BECAUSE I CAN FEEL THE VIBRANCE RUNNING THROUGH MY BODY

GIVING ME THE MOST SUPERIOR FEELING

WHEN I SET NEW MOVEMENTS THAT YOU JUST CAN'T WORK YOUR WAY UP TO

SO YOU EITHER GOING TO HATE ME

LOVE ME

HATE ME SO MUCH

YOU'RE GOING TO PRETEND TO LOVE ME

BECAUSE YOU WANT TO BE ME

A PIECE OF DUST

THAT PUTS HIS FIVE CENTS IN

YO, I TRY, I TRY

I JUST TRY MY HARDEST TO GO THE FARTHEST

I TRY,

DON'T CRY

UNLESS I'M PLAYING WORDS OF RAY

IT'S ABSURD TO ME TO SAY SOMETHING

THAT'S NOT GOING TO ACCOMPLISH NOTHING

MY VOCALS HAVE NEVER BEEN READ

AND NO ONE REALLY UNDERSTANDS THE WORDS IN A SONG

THEY'RE SO USE TO A BEAT

I'M IN NEED OF HEAT

DREAMING SEEDS WAS ONE OF MY MOST
BEAUTIFUL EXPERIENCES

I NEED THIS BEAT TO FUZZ

MY FEET'S A BUS THAT NEEDS NO GASOLINE

BECAUSE IT'S HOW I DISCIPLINE MY BODY

MADE HEAL

BLACKLINES

MY BLACKLINE IS UNDER WHAT I THINK IS
IMPORTANT

AND WHAT I THINK IS IMPORTANT IS WHAT I WANT,

BUT WHAT I WANT DOESN'T MATTER

AND THAT'S LIKE FOUR KIDS, I'LL TAKE YOURS

AND MORE KIDS AND RAISE THEM FROM BABIES
GETTING HIGH,

JUST TO SEE LIFE TAUGHT WITH THOUGHT,

MY LIFE IS A PURPOSE, MY LIFE IS A REASON,

MY LIFE IS IMPORTANT, MY LIFE IS WILL,

MY LIFE I LIVE IS STILL, MY LIFE IS TRYING,

MY LIFE IS LOVE IN STUFF PEOPLE WILL NOT LOVE

UNTIL TRUST IS TRUTH WITH GUTS, MY LIFE IS NUTS,

WHEN I SEE ME NOT EVER COMING UP,

MY LIFE IS PURE AND RHETORIC SO RESPECT MY
BLACKLINES

WHEN THERE'S NO MISTAKES, IT TAKES MY LIFE TO
RAISE THE STAKES

IN CASE AND WILL TAKE MY LIFE TO SAVE WHATS
REALLY IN US,

BUT YOU DON'T WANT TO GROW, JUST OLD NEVER
LEARNING,

BUT LEARNING TO GO SLOW, WHILE I'M EARNING FEELING IT WITH

MY SOUL, I'M A KID. TAKE ME, I CAN TAKE YOU

WHERE YOU REALLY WANT TO GO, I'M HERE TO HELP NOTHING

EVER MORE NO EGO LIKE YOUR JUST FIGURING OUT LIFE

AS I EXPLORE, MY LIFE IS SOAR BECAUSE I'M TIRED OF BEING ALONE,

I NEED HOPE FROM ANOTHER IN ME ENERGY OF A HUMAN BEING WHO

CAN SEE,

MY LIFE IS HERE AND NOW AND RIGHT WITH SIGHT BEFORE I SEE SOUND.

I LOVE YOU.

MY NAME IS HEAL

My name is heal and I'm healing

My feeling is like a ceiling concentrating too

Much on the walls, because I don't want to fall

And become a ground for people to walk on again

Because of those close to me

You forgot about your best,

Haven't you ever seen Bruce Lee take a bullet

Then pull it out of his chest.

Gods are dying due to ignorance.

I want to feel what the ink in the painting spills on

The canvas cloth-like material filled room

Shield zoom full image cool clear cloudy sky

With a blue smeared dotted eye

On that pouty-faced silly kid sounding like why did this

Commercial plane place photography on me

Is anybody thinking about sex but me?

My stout complex blunt and underground like a stump of a
tree

All around areas with a cup of tea

Focusing in on and fantasizing on a fantasy

I'm bound to be reduced from population due to popularity contest on my creations

Easily defines the best variations

Scattering my belongings all out through lands I happen to be in

Another part in my life was taken out of context

People look at me weird when I touch my toes without bending my knees

And soak my sole in this barrel of leaves

Because its apparel recycling that gets me excited about shopping

Then traveling from the bottom up to the top

I think I've reached the certain level of this chart

Classified as art

Actually detailed from the help of females is how I learned to talk to you.

I figured, a lock tattooed look of expression and expressing

One self's inner static electricity,

This power in which is giving me the ability to see,

Thoughts of bringing three intricate moves before I make the right one,

I figure things out like math

I listen, until I know your dissing quality

I'm going to show you reality in my space world.

You're the sum, I'm the one

Why can't I find my other ones, I cry

Because too many people are dumb and narrow minded

Believe anything they want because they don't know how to find it.

I'm reminded by shit I don't need to hear,

So I always forget about what I'm supposed to remember.

Wait, man I'm expired past two lakes cold split top desire.

Clash with who faked their way here, you don't have to tell me

I already know

You don't have to help me, I already glow.

Though I'm invisible to the minds that keep walking

And don't take their warning serious to fact.

My back dislocated created an insignificant withdrawal of

Malls, bars, pool halls and cars,

The period to the point a litter in the joint

The heater made it moist and I sucked it.

Now I'm fucked, sick, trapped in this body deteriorating,

Fabricating cracks in crinkles with racks of sprinkles,

Sparkling for the truth,

Why these reasons time travel with the substance to process a growth line panel

Put into a mode controlled my meaning,

Cleaning every situation that occurs,

With my words, swords slash and tangle

The name he'll never forget, but got lost.

A lost architect from the middle of the earth dug out, duplicity

And considering the fact I could create electricity

Motivates me to the fullest

Extent my coffee table represents freedom index off static situated solutions

I'm off the planet grant it, my mistake is pure to a cure crammed in this liquid cube.

Whenever I make a move, it bustles in motion for reason to build

Something from nothing asteroid illusion add more confusion

Sad or contribution rip tight intense light on the substitute slight me

Degree of the game conspiracy

I'm probably going to die off the passion adding

Acting on my cautions padding

Lining my body complex, gone next

Enter tomorrow

For I got a boat that floats then goes under water

I'm smaller than an ant and taller than a plant, but I can't

Keep agreeing with you if you're going to cause me to

React in a three-dimensional

I'm artifact

The circle of the eye beholder

My circumference colder cry covers conditional shoulders

Boulders so big it's like space

No air to taste

No area to climb

In the middle of time

Locked travel distance

Blocked I'm having witnessed wands upon my body

From the inside of the red topping

Chopping up, bent and spent on what I meant

Conditional love spread throughout my surroundings.

Please give some respect back to me.

It's the key that turns to be entry levels of conspiracy.

Rebels breaking the internal codes pebbles loads eternal

Rose peddles welcoming my presents.

Resets an essence prone normally matured before your
psychoanalysis gets tense.

Flex veins pop, stress, breast might be the best care for you

Now rip my chest out while I try to pronounce sound.

Because time was almost new and that will definitely add
taste to flavor.

So taste my words and see

Seek his descendents in a long life and your thought will
recognize when we miss-use gifts.

It's amazing how a person who is never seen can bring in
a crowd.

People worshipping words written

Keep sittin'

No, stand up wishing

Hope

Glory

Kissing lovers or the others

Where's passion mixed with dignity when you're too shy to talk?

I have to realize water and wonder under all the real life drama

My karma coming to a stop

My momma prayed for this heart

Tomorrow another day I'm going to let the sun in my heart.

My heart's a chart channeled

This is a sign of my mind

Cell phones win

Two shadows my vision

Christening the un-risen

Don't give into deception

It's not going to help you

Your guy keeps falling

What about now

Your horizon is calling

THE FORTY WISE

WHY HATE AND CREATE EVILNESS IN YOURSELF?

WHY ADD TO THE FRUSTRATION OF JEALOUSY?

WHY ASSUME THE WORST IN WHAT COULD BE LOVE YOU MISSED OUT ON?

WHY LIVE WITH ANGER REMEMBERING THAT SONG YOU SANG HER REMINISCING ON THE PAST?

WHY LIVE IN A CAGE AND ONLY FEEL FREEDOM AT HOME, ALONE?

WHY PICTURE YOURSELF ON STAGE AND FANTASIZE ABOUT BEING SOMEONE ELSE?

WHY FEEL THE NEED TO ARGUE, WHEN YOU'RE STILL TRYING TO FIND OUT WHO ARE YOU?

WHY SPEND TIME DOING NOTHING, WHEN MIND FLUIDS CONSUMPTION FOR KNOWLEDGE?

WHY DANCE TO GET DOWN, WHEN ROMANCE IS AROUND?

WHY WORRY TO HURRY AND LET TIME CLIMB ALL OVER US?

WHY ARE HOLIDAYS THE ONLY TIME FAMILIES GET TOGETHER?

WHY IS WEATHER NOT GETTING WHAT IT DESERVES, WHEN IT TAKES CARE OF ALL OF US?

WHY EVER WERE COMPACT DISCS MADE?

WHY ARE PRODUCTS BEING MADE WHEN IT'S ALREADY HERE?

WHY IS SOUL RUNNING OUT OF COAL AND FIRE IS FREEZING?

WHY ARE MIRRORS SMOKING EVERY SEASON FOR NO REASON?

WHY IS LOW BETTER THAN HIGH SO OLD NEVER TOUCHES THE SKY?

WHY IS GOOD BETTER THAN GREAT WHEN WE DON'T CONCENTRATE ON WHAT PEOPLE CLOSE TO US MAKE?

WHY IS FAKE SUPPOSE TO BE REAL AND PEOPLE DON'T WANT TO DISCUSS

WHAT'S THE DEAL?

WHY IS LAZY AMAZING AND AMERICA TAKING OUR VISION AWAY?

WHY TALK WHEN NO ONE LISTENS OR REMEMBERS WHAT HITS THEM WHEN IT'S TIME TO?

WHY DO I HAVE TO WRITE AND MAKE IT RHYME TO GET THROUGH TO YOU?

WHY JUDGE PEOPLE JUST BECAUSE YOU HAVE A BAD ATTITUDE?

WHY ARE CHURCHES SO CROWDED EVERY SUNDAY?

WHY ARE PEOPLE SO EASY TO MANIPULATE?

WHY IS JESUS PICTURED AS WHITE, WHEN WHITE IS TOO SCARED TO FIGHT?

WHY IS ALONE SO LONELY, BUT WHAT ABOUT THE BLIND?

WHY ARE MENTALLY PEOPLE CHALLENGED MENTALLY AND PHYSICALLY BALANCED?

WHY ARE MISTAKES MISTAKES WHEN PEOPLE KEEP MAKING THEM?

WHY IS MONEY SO HARD TO SAVE MEN FROM WOMEN FIGHTING FOR DEATH?

WHY IS DEATH FOREVER REST WHEN FOREVER NEVER REST?

WHY IS ART A START TO PART FROM HEARTS WITH SPARKS?

WHY DOES EVERYTHING SUCK AND NOBODY GIVES A FUCK?

WHY IS LUCK LUCKY ONLY WHEN A FEMALE WILL FUCK ME?

WHY IS STUCK NOT NOTICED AND SINKING IS WHAT POETS GET IF THERE DEEP?

WHY DOES WHITE WANT TO BE BLACK AND BLACK WANT TO BE WHITE?

WHY IS WACK RIGHT FOR PEOPLE WITH NO SIGHT?

WHY IS MIGHT NO AND POLITE SO PATIENT?

WHY IS PARENTHOOD FOR ADULTS THAT CAN'T TAKE CARE OF ANYTHING?

WHY IS FEEL TOO MUCH TO GIVE WHEN HEAL IS HOW WE LIVE?

FOUR STAR

I LATER LOCATE LYRICS LOGICALLY BLESSING ME
PHILOSOPHY, PHYSICS FLOSSING BEADS THROUGH
CREVICES. THIS BODY IN THE MAKING, CREATING
NEMESIS, NOT ON FILE. I HEAR THE WITNESSES
AND THEY'RE GOING WILD, FOR WHAT I WANT FOR
THIS SHIT IS JUST A HAND SHAKE AND A SMILE.
WHILE YOU ALL BE LOVING CHILD MOLESTING
MUSIC, PUT IT DOWN NOW. FINALLY, THE LINE IN
ME BROKE LOOSE BLINDING THE GOOSE BEFORE
IT GOT COOKED, JUICE. WORK MY WAY UP TO THE
TOP, NO I DON'T STOP ANYTHING I START LIKE
THE AVERAGE POPULATION OF HIP HOP CHARTS,
THE UNDERGROUND EXIST AS LEGENDARY ART,
NOT FIGURED OUT BY ALL, BUT FIGURED OUT BY
A LOT. DON'T WANT TO BE A PART OF YOU ALL NOT
DOING NOTHING, JEALOUS MOTHERFUCKERS TRY
TO FRONT, THROW MY WORDS BACK IN MY FACE
AND THEN PASSES ME THE BLUNT. PEOPLE DON'T
CHECK THE TRASH OTHERWISE THEY FIGURE OUT
MY FORM. IT SURROUNDS ME, QUESTIONS ME,
ANSWERS MY BRAIN IN THE BACK, IN FORCE WITH
THIRD AND SECOND DEGREES. IT GETS WORSE
YOU HEARD HEAL HOLLER STEAL BALLER ON

THIS EARTH. IT'S ALWAYS AROUND WHEN PEOPLE QUESTION HOW IT SOUNDS. WHEN THEY AIN'T LIVIN' UP, THEY LIVING DOWN. SO YOUR CIRCUMSTANCE WILL NEVER HAVE ANY MEANING. SATELLITE SETS CERTAIN SESSIONS SUBSEQUENTLY SINKING SO SEAM IT ON A SAW, SILKY MANNER MY ARM. I'LL SING IT THEN STOP THEN SEE YOU STRAVE SACRET. IS WHEN BRAIN STORMIN' MY MIND GETS WARMIN' UP AND MY APPEARANCE BRING MORE MEN AND WOMEN LUCK. I'M LIKE A LUCKY CHARM, I RUB OFF OF YOU AND THEN I DEAL WITH YOUR PAIN. TEN TIMES ELEVEN ITS TWENTY IT'S PLENTY TOO MUCH FOR ME TOO HANDLE, ABOUT TO RUN OUT OF CASH FOR ELECTRICITY AND JUST HAVE CANDLES IN THIS CITY OF ENERGY, IT'S JUST NOT FAIR, I DON'T CARE, JUST UNAWARE OF THE STATUS STARING AT ME FROM A DISTANCE, I CAN'T GET TO IT, TRAPPED BY METAL SHARP EDGED BRAIDED GATE LOCKED UP WITH A SNAKE WITH POISON VENOM SO LETHAL, HATERS BE PRAYING I STAY OUT SO I DON'T CHANGE THE WORLD. YO, THIS DEEP REMARKABLE, MAGNIFICENT, I'LL TOLERATE EXCELLENT OR PERFECT THAT IN WHICH SAYS ON MY SHIRT, DIG ME I'M FOUR STAR.

SIMPLICITY: THIS EXILERATING, MAGNIFICENT SURPRISE OF SUSPENCE, THATS GLOBALY
TAKING OVER. SO YOU ALL GOT TO MOVE BECAUSE IM COATED WITH A SENSE OF SIMPL-
ICITY. THAT MEANS I GOT IT, EXTREEM, REMEDIES THAT BUILD UP IN MY CAVITIES, ITS CAPT-
IVATED, IMMITATED SITUTATION THAT YOUR BODY'S KEEP ME FADDED TO THE MOMENT OF OUT
SKIN LIQUED LOTION, SQUID POTION, NUMBER NINE, IN EFFECT TO FIND OBJECTS DEVINE,
DEVINTY, ELECTRICITY RUNS THROUGH ME, GIVING ME POWER. BUT NOT SHEILDED FROM
THE POLLEN, POLITURE, PUNCTURED THRONA MY ARM PIT, MY WRIST SLITS, BUT IM TO WEAK
TO BLEED AND TOO MEAN TO BE HAPPY, EVEN THOUGH THATS ALL REALISTICALLY I KANT IS HAPP-
NESS LOVE FREEDOM A CAR, POISON IVY NOT ON MY DICK AND FACE, JOB ANYWHERE I CAN
GO TO WORK EVERYDAY AND NOT BE FIRED FOR BEING AMBITIOUS. LIKE SOME LITTLE KID
IN CLASS RAISING HIS HAND, WHO ALWAYS GETS CALLED ON LAST. POLISH, BECAUSE I RE-
THE ZONE, AND DONT FORGET THE THE BECAUSE THE DUMB ON THE TAPE COVER
SENCE, MY TRUE LOVER STYLE, PILED OVER MILES HILLS CENTERS OF GRASS, GRASPING
ENERGY, SEARCHING FOR ENEMIES WITH ALL THE PASSION OR WITH JUST A LITTLE PAS-
SION. WHATEVER MAN, MY MOUTHS CONSTANTLY BLEEDING, AND CONSTANTLY NEEDING. A SMOKE
CHAMPER YOU COULD PUT MEAT IN TO GET TENDER, GIRL, I GOT IT FOR YOU EVERY
DAY. MY SIMPLISTIC STYLE OF ALTITUDES GIVES ME VARIETY, RELIGION CONFUSED OUT
IN ANXIETY TRIUMPH, IM BEING, BUT IM NOT DEAD YET. YET IM STILL GOING
AND IM STILL GOING TO BE HANGING WITH MY MAIN MAN GABE FOLDING DIAMOND
S OUT OF SHEETS OF PAPER. ITS GOING TO TAKE HER FOREVER ANY WAY, SO WELL JUST
SIT HERE AND STAY PRODUCTIVE AT A SENCE OF SIMPLICITY, SIMPLICITY. IN A SPIRIT
SUSPENDED THROUGH ORGANIC FRAGMENTS ORIGINALY TO BE CREATED FOR GOVERNMENT
AL EXPERIMENTS, ENDEARMENTS IN FAMILY OCCASIONS CAUSE INHALATION THEN VIOLA-
LATION. VIOLENT TEMPERS BREAK LOOSE, LET ME SKIP TO PAGE TWO ON THE
SIDE RIGHT BEFORE THIS. IN A SIMPLE FORMAT, WAITING TO GET THE FUCK ON CONTACT.
WELL I GOT MY NOTEBOOK AND MY BACK PACK, AND MY PANTS SAG SO LOW, BUT IM TOO
HIGH TO PULL 'EM UP. IN THIS CHUMP ASS AREA, COMPARED TO YA FAST ITS EXCITING
BUT ALL IM DOING IS INVITING NEW PAIN THROUGH OUT MY LIFE SEEMS LIKE
ALL THE PURIETY I PUT INTO A PRODUCT TO PRODUCE ABSOLUTE TRUENESS GETS MISTAKEN
FOR STRUGGLE MODE, CONTEST TO THE BEST DECISION MAKING, MAKING MY WAYS, FORMING
MY FACE, TAKING MY AIM TO A NEW LEVEL. LOOKS LIKE ITS GOING TO BE A LATE
NIGHT FOR ME TO FIGURE THIS OUT WITH NO WEED, BUT THAT SHIT MAKES ME FORGET
BUT GIVES ME A LEAD FOR A NEW RAP TO KICK THE DUST WITH, SO FUCK IT.
I GOT TO PARALYSE YA ALL FROM THE WAIST DOWN FEAL ME, MY NAME, PEEL
RED INTENCE ENERGY MOVING THROUGH OUT YOUR MAIN ENTRY. ON SENDING WITH THE
NEXT. I TAKE IN TEXT IN TIME PUT IT DOWN IN A RHYME, COMPLICATED, TOO COMPLEX FOR
THE AVERAGE TO GRASP, CURENCY FOR A TASK OF PROXIMATE MANNER OF MEANING DEMEAN-
ING TO MOST, BUT FUCK 'EM, IM ONE WITH THIS MATURADY FOR SOUL, RISSEN UP AND
ABOVE, ILL PROVE MY WAY OF LIVING IS PRECISE AND MAKE YOU AWARE OF THE STUFF
YOU DONT NORMALLY PAY ATTENTION TO. IT SEEMS NICE, BUT INTERESTING TO KNOW SOME
THING THAT TAKES UP YOUR DAY. ITS WAISTED. IM CHASING MY DREAMS AND IM GET
TING TOO SKINNY FROM THE PAIN AND I CANT WIN. ITS HURTING AND MY SHIRTS ARE
ALL DIRTY FROM THE BLOOD MAN IM POOR AND MORE INTERESTING THAN YOUR TELEMARK
ETING. TELLING ASS FAST ON QUESTION, ITS COMMON SENCE TO ME, IT PHILOSPHY.
UNTILL I GET BRAINSTORMING ABOUT A NEW IDEA TO BRING LOVE THROUGH OUT THE WORLD
AND MINE THATS WHY IT'LL NEVER HAPPEN AND I'LL ALWAYS TRY TO CONNECT THE DOTS
FOR THE PUBLIC, SIMPLICITY FOR NATURE AND I HAVE TO MAKE SURE YOU CAN PROSPURE
FROM THE EXPOSURE, SIMPLICITY. TIME THAT I PUT UP, SIMPLICITY. VEINS ON VISION
THROUGH DOCTORS GLASSES, CIRCUMSISION WHILE HE MAKES THE PRECISE CUT, BUT
THROUGH ALL THAT, SIMPLICITY COMMON SENCE NOT LUCK. WELL WHAT THE FUCK IS
THIS SECOND NOTE NOW, CUTTING UP THROATS HOW DID YOU EVER POSIBLY THINK
OF THAT PARTICULAR PART OF YOUR BRAIN TO USE MAN. I BRAIN FROLS AND I CAME TO
THIS PLACE TO TAKE YOUR GIRL AWAY FOR A DAY, A NIGHT, TONITE MAKE IT YOURS
A POOR ASS MOTHERFUCKER PHILIP MOTHERFUCKING Z, BUT I GET UP COUGH AND
SNEEZE AND THINK PLEASE DONT DIE SAYER, WONT CRY, JUST WRITE ON THIS
PEICE OF PAPER AND FIGHT THE PAIN IN BEATS, IN STRAIN, ITS NEAT TO BE
PERFECTED IN THE SOUND THAT SEEKS PLEASURE TWO, THREE TIMES TO FOUR
YOUR CAUTIOUS WEATHER ALWAYS DEMANDS MORE ON THE UPRIGHT SYSTEM TAKE
IT IN AND SAY YOU I LACK THE CONSTANT PRESSURE NORMALLY USED TO BASE
ROUTES IN THIS BLOOD STREAM THAT IM USING CAUSES CONSTANT SHOUTS, POUT
I'LL TRY NOT TO, BUT IM TAKING AND I DONT EXIST NO MATTER HOW BAD
I RESIST, IM A PISSED OFF MAN LOST IN THE L, A, N, D, S, P, A, C,
E, O, F, F, O, O, L, S, A, QUEST, A TEST ESPECIALLY FOR GINE
SIMPLICITY I LOVE YOU, WHAT?

    I   LOVE   YOU.

TRANSLATIONS OF LOVE

My peoples even equals and all my fathers' sisters for when brothers create miracles that make us with faith. So love will find shape in trust, is one out of a hundred that must. Lust collecting dust, but there's no one near now. Just fear how people are so easily manipulated into loosing themselves.

Now you, this is a true gift of enlightenment to profit one's self.

Now you, a whole person with the power to see, touch, smell, hear, and heal is truly a wonderful thing.

Your presence is an essence and your purpose is to grow, get stronger like a plant. Learning facts, definitions, math, patterns of the planet in your own way to get things done correctly and quicker.

People were technically made to be sponges and help clean the earth. Earth is your home your place to think. Your reason in breathing and breathing must be done or death will occur, and suicide is giving back more than a million dollars in cash and having a nice car crash.

Insecurity is a form a weakness and we must grow to be strong. Forcing is something that starts something and starting something is how you create art within a certain subject. Don't give up because you earn that force later with intricate knowledge and grace; Grace is something you earn with confidence and skill. Skill is practice so practice, practice, practice.

Practice is will and can not be accomplished standing still. Standing still is what government wants demanding bills, claiming god with Jesus, and forming religion within churches keeping people separate. So public is distant.

Religion is method to take over the masses. It is somewhat of a myth to keep men white.

White is America and its pitiful to be proud of what I see is corrupt. Corruption is spreading for the cost of dollars that honor fame.

Fame is nothing unless it's your child's name.

Inspiration is good so maybe babies won't stay the same. Original is wood and has weight.

Happy is youth with paint. Stress breaks roots and holds hate.

Stress does not exist where I come from.

Where I come from is love with faith. Even I am still practicing to serve my lord, and my god is the sun. It's been here, before me, It's in each one of my memories, It can help you, It wants to. It just wants to touch you, make love in you fix you.

So white man will create sunglasses, blinds, curtains, tinted widows and air conditioners to keep it away, it's never gone though; it's the moon to incline to the mind it made you.

The mind it made you is what you make it. Permanent is you, it's not a marker, it's not a tattoo.

It's not the kind of vitamin you can buy so you might believe in you.

It's everything I said and I'll say it again because is what is and I love you. I love everything and pay much attention to what comes out around me and support those trying to make it better with perfection.

I apologize for all men, and using the word and so much, I will stop, but to stop is to not, and not is not what I got. Not is no excuse, use the useful positions a human can acquire.

Learn to be advanced and don't expire.

Grow to be young and soak up some sun.

Also give back to mankind what man gave to you. So pick something to do soon, anything would be a reason of life.

Life, for me is history being ignored and forgotten, alone watching everybody turn rotten. No matter how much I try. I try to keep up with the music as well and spread it to people who sit stay still and yell and don't care about nothing except their self.

I'm surrounded with hate, so hate would have to be hypocrisy. That's why we stay underground because I don't go to church and judge people who walk around.

So the history now will never be found; that's why I try
to capture it, I love it, it moves me. Why can't you love?
That's what god wants truly.

Really, history will always be the same. The past will never
last until we have someone to blame, songs on the radio
will still be lame and books will never change for changes
made.

Movies will worsen, profit rich wealth and gain
embarrassment in the real film industry. So quality films will
still be hard to locate, due to no competition because the
usual is so fake and not fun to rotate.

Right now the world is under a rotation with a dramatic
increase in ignorance; it is up to you to keep up with what
you did and how you loved doing it, don't let no one take
that away.

The how you loved doing things is something I just see at
garage sales. I purchase those memories so those souls
can live on with me, with strife to inspire; when really all
I do this for is the passion I have hope for the future no
matter how deep that growth grows with that grudge.

Just entered my home now, the place I look forward too so
much when I'm not here; so I can play sound and crawl up
in a tune then think about what I have to get done.

Sometimes the what I want to get dones get in the way
when I'm trying to pay attention to how much I get paid. I
don't have to worry though, because I know I'm saved for
my extreme efforts.

Writing is like drinking water for thirst, so I won't die. Due to the fact that no one listens and is so concerned about themselves. Their egos strengthened then spoil. Oil takes over and turns into fat. Fat hurts, and makes it harder to move and look nice in shirts.

Looking nice is an opinion and opinions are supposed to be kept to yourself unless someone wants it.

Wanting is bad, it creates habits in which may go into an off direction. Direction is instruction that's why it is important to teach.

Teaching is thought and thought is thinking a lot and a lot is not what these people want to give unless they get paid to, but they're probably not going to pay attention unless they're in school and that's a maybe baby because times is crazy.

Crazy is not lazy, so in the long run when my body fills with brains I'll be the one known as amazing grace. Still chasing, not wasting a minute for heaven's sake. Taking over time and adding faith in my rhyme while bathing in time waiting to climb each ladder with literacy from love, I can see it move you.

I can see it move you are my sight to prove through the past and set light in the future then watch my children grow helping each other to survive.

Helping each other to survive is staying alive and I don't know about you but I want that to continue.

To continue is to finish and if something don't get done you don't have anything to show no one.

To show is what someone should present and hopefully inspire those with no direction.

No direction is my life wasting time so gods keep me living to reach my goals and fulfill my purpose and adding my passage in the future bible which is called the language of love.

The language of love has many authors and is discussed more in the words of Saul Williams.

Saul Williams is someone who should be studied and brings great tears to my eyes.

Tears from my eyes are spears from skies piercing my life so I remember.

So I remember is for you every December and we can watch Santa Clause unwrap our Christmas trees.

Santa Clause unwrapping my Christmas tree is gods above believing in me telling me to explore fluent languages until it becomes English enough to understand stuff that's tough.

Tough is rough and rough is stuff that just takes guts. It's in us to bust and break through thrust, thrilling our odometer by the speed of movements made from memories and mistakes.

Mistakes are taken as offense by people with no sense. And you have no right to be offensive with no defense to back your logic, so learn now.

Its like shallow is not deep, so swallow what you eat and taste it, and appreciate it because your stomach is a good example of forgetting that.

A good example of forgetting is hate, drama, a little love and a wedding, but if the love is little then this is just a sample.

A sample is an example and an example is a metaphor to help people understand better.

A metaphor is a waste of professional time adults should already know or realize what's going on.

Realize is not realization in the eyes of the stagnation taking advantage of artificial light until it becomes a hazard.

A hazard is a cancer, faster by men who judge and hate with assumption because man is not satisfied with his own self's life. So they put on a mask and become a pathetic fallacy and never stop telling lies.

Lies are not secrets so secrets are probably lies unless you've seen it with your own eyes.

Eyes are beautiful and beautiful is everything, and that's what your eyes allow you to see, so fucking appreciate it.

Appreciation is something you will acquire in time when studying a certain subject you enjoy, and the only way to learn it to the heart is by fascination.

Fascination is curiosity.

Curiosity turns into discoveries, so explore what's around you because there's something that needs to be found soon.

Soon is the moon in tune with you.

The moon in tune with you is a balloon in full view so it will always be found.

Found is what this notebook just got I take it everywhere I go and work on it in a sunny parking lot. Seeing all the hateful faces drive by loosing my mind concentrating too much on what I just bought.

What I just bought is some more records and some pot.

Pot is marijuana and marijuana is a drug.

Drugs are for people who don't have close relationships with others.

Bought is what you buy, it gets fun then turns into shop, material things become my.

My means you.

You become your, so you won't seem so poor and all you want is more without counting to four just skip to tour with no knowledge to perform. Even if you did would it be above normal expectations that will actually inspire or will desire go depth with deed and acquire greed because it seems great, but it just gets worse when you take from the purse of faith.

Because what I think is great and lights up my day like the sun is an actual human being, not a computer screen or some other little things that light up.

Might want to get your head checked before this chats up, oh did you have a purpose or just want to get rid of those exposed with light to love.

Technology will never stop for the purpose to pay more is what these people do so this is what they get, type shit.

Technology physically and mentally for me will never stop due to my desire to study with knowledge, learning new things, telepathically reaching hearts with just my impressions.

Impressions are what I see not color in the faces that don't want to believe.

Believing is people believing what they see on t.v.

Television is a mechanism for circumcision and circumstance made it fact due to the lack of interest close by, most prize on what they like.

What they like is like there bike when they were little. What they like is to look away, because that's where they want to be.

Like me alone floating in the sea free, in the middle meditating, gaining energy from the sun soaking me with bless, noticing my best by breaking my chest and forming me a new one.

Saving me my rest and taking my test serving my purpose with curtains so no one can see cause, I'm a ninja secretly spreading my disease, glowing swinging from trees adapted to weather, they are my friends.

When winter come still making people say please, don't kill me with your confidence that you get when you look up, common sense, what, right here, I'm giving this to you, but your still trying to kill my king and you cant decide which way you want to choose

You loose, and you lost along time ago, you know, you know where to go, come, I'm wiser than faith pricing trust hoping for crust to nibble on, searching for hate.

So I'm going to know if your fake or if you want to take it serious in what I'm saying is from the sun so I stay driven guiding through winds like bullet piercing week shit, I call it wack with offence.

I'm one god son that really can't wait to have one, so I can play with and have fun.

Ill stay young because I hold my face up in the rain and look at the sun until I sneeze shaking my knees.

My please pleasures men in the sky making sure I don't die. Making mankind secure with happiness

Being the fountain of youth does not deal with struggles of shelter.

Shelter becomes a need that must, so income will always be messy until my creations bless me.

Best we break bubbles before barricades block basic biology from books.

Books are more interesting when there written by crooks in jail serving time to tell.

Time to tell has been told so I am just a reincarnation of another brothers sole trying to assist in this manner through poetry.

Or will this just be reincarnated over and over again until someone sees light running under my skin.

Light running under my skin is love coming to bring sight within. Bring means to be there even when it means to beware.

To beware is learning so see where were turning.

Turning is upside down until earning has completed sound with thought from words perfectly is my intention to keep going.

To keep going is to keep knowing no matter where you're at, dirt will be there.

Hurt is still care, where we at, share with me please.

I am the midget from Holly Mountain trying to help with
no limbs, mad at the dead for not staying driven, for not
listening to a word I said.

Not listening to a word I said is everybody except for when
these sentences are read.

Read is written, and written is saved.

Saved is worshiped, and worship is praised.

Praised comes from underneath a building where children
are raised with the belief of white Jesus.

White Jesus might be us if you vote before time ceases.

Government has America by the balls and everybody
thinks its cool drinking red bull before bed giving them
energy to sleep, wake up and eat and eat and eat.

So restaurants, grocery stores will always be processing
what we think we need.

What we think we need is a seed we never got to plant
because of close ones near by telling us we can't.

Close ones telling us we cant is jealousy hitting with
a bat is when you feel the heal make better my name
with weather coming back giving wisdom, courage, and
strength.

Please be safe with my words

COFFEE TABLE SONG

• Putting all my thoughts on wood liable to the dialect
moment of random completions, sturdy and mature to
the process I'm on in a second off time, locked in my
mind, no such thing as rewind, I'm blocked only to find
patterns in difficult circles scattered to spread wide
confusion to the conformity originally taking the place of
sacred laps gathered up in congressional debates of
commencing consideration. My heart is amercing a
creation of concern conjured extruded with logic to earn
for you or who ever in this nation tells me to view this
town better, conduct my style conform it to the weather.
Personality is what you make it to this city, I can't take it.
This fallacy calm awareness careless mistakes need to
get brought up into an issue with my skin tissue caught
against my bones and the stones next to my kidney my
left knee just got twisted off the passion. kick flipped my
way in this scene, caught it and stylishly staying
awesome. There's no point to my return unless it's to

give back the thanks banked off the theories. I stay

ballisticly confined to terror media pollution.

Exaggeration for execution time is getting closer to the

end, so blend on how we are living each and everyday

working these J 0 B's don't pay but the bills. The skills

are larger than yours, so then go to hers. Because in

every heart were living barter to the plot for freedom

from my return to spoil my time based on root to film

objects superior to paste what I've seen, and I've seen a

lot and I mean to start showing more effort than the

worlds ever seen, experiments risen to rise from

catastrophes finally exposed. Belt my way up to the top

it's strapped with these holes to who it may concerns or

before it manifolds off on the sickness contributed by

one soul, foreclosed on episodes, disclosed through out

a capture, intangible, entanglements, smooth soft

hardened into cement I walk. I can no longer talk with

the fragile week minded pupils from peoples. The evil

that seeps deep threw me to you is a lesson, so start to

learn and start testing the confessions of the rest of

them. Most people are intrinsic. When I stay in the fact

of my respect confined to my awareness, I swear this pleasure strained pain upon my brain for the same reason as you, with only a few decisions to choose from. I'm one with the force from the past on how to make things last on my own terms and recommendations that I want to create for everybody and nobody else to get in my way and say it's not possible. This Thanksgiving day of events, why aren't my families not that close to me? I bartered myself to a level; I live my life as a capital word on my logic. I don't know what you can call it but its not small its big enough for everybody to bite off of commodities, conjured with no crumbs in this ecclesiastical cathedral we sip the wine after commencing concentration. Congratulation is in order sort or more of us are at a higher level, than what I can tell, from mail or T.V. or people with cd collections. Tape player gets a lot of play and I place appreciation on that so much more than a compact disc. It not even compact, its too fragile for combat solutions with my gear, army, and expensive, kids get with the point and check it don't destroy it fix it, build it. Cause skills get rubbed off one another, each one of us are brothers that don't get along for a long period of time. Grasped in the palm of my hand, my grip to calm the land and rip any man contributing contributions claiming eliminating stars from a far. It's the rich land that be where people can't stand me because I be demanding and also the man G. Not trying to sound conceded but from what I can tell with your so called art you did not succeed in. I'm bleeding for your pleasure my measure is time against me, don't knock me, remember me, don't forget me, stock me and study my movements and whom I'm mostly with, myself in pleasure with myself inner wealth, but most these people really just cant stand me, even people in my family. I'm crazy to the minds that cant find me or confine three reasons to loose my generation penetrating through the ground in a familiar way too deep and hollow is when these days start to go absent and in delete if these paragraphs are grasping it will be complete to the fullest extant of my drive to survive with in this narrow meat to wide and collide and clash with the titans. This sight sends a message of variety, don't lie to me but I know you will. That's why I'll always have this spit in me to kill the dumb that left loose some adjustments that needed to made on that played ass song that's gets played on the radio all day long, its gone its like that. Its wrong to make fiction fact and to be entertained at the same time on top of that, shits wack broke your back while filming your lack in this profession to those who know lesson and got blessed in a women's stomach before she had a chance to caress him with her address fur and the enhancements of a challenges calling kids out to be banished. I am the talk of the town in everybody's apartment complex replaying messages I left. I'm left alone to be disciplined from the close relationships with my friends to steady my brain, body and mind the kind of incandescent exposure I represent, negotiated by busters globally trying to take over. I bustle with profits dedicated to one's need. If I say I'm going do something it's like I just planted a seed and it's got to grow, so I'll always come through for my man, girl, lady, yo. I'm not flakey; Travis don't hate me. Slackers around me I can't believe it, the way you all think, I don't see it; my genre is never felt in this field. It's one for them wasted time, blandishment, providence imitates itself. It's shameful, but to get over it. You just claim to blame fools with no clue for their sins that there just going to make again. I perpetrate my feeling never to get loose. Insidiously growing over stress, in a matter of speaking, with ease through these microphones, I feel left alone, but optimistically waiting, preparing for someone special to come into my life, but it's alright. Just keep my head and my fist to the sky, because this unique state of mind I'm in gives me exceptional styles to live, to seek, to find who opens your mind, and search, run your fingers through the sand and show your appreciation for this earth we live in and learn and keep giving to those, it's worth to be ready. I suppose to those who might be subtle to most, or a host in an anteroom with the most eccentric thought you could ever possibly imagine. From Majin Boo to who thinks it might rule, camouflage my camp to the intensity stamped to the bottom of my marking, sparking my art is a fracture state of mind off the wall, being debated between the lines barely seeing to the remarkable thought of my sight, just might be too much light charming to the eye as it travels light speed, through your system, calling to your insides out in my wisdom, is courage girl, it's a trilogy chain linked shiny aged stink, same as these interesting reactions dealing with everything. My life's on tape making it appear to be slow, but the ripples in the lakes just keep making it go. Yo, I'm painting a picture here as big as your house with my adolescence, through this beat. Sets my senses straight out, then lifts me to my feet with a little less frustration, I'm having a lot of frustration nowadays off the doubt of what one weighs of confusion of loose times the way my attitude changes on motives, modulates by sedatives, place in components with complications before communicating then actuates in techniques freaks in uniqueness, I be this, choking until your key twist to open certain doors people haven't even started to accomplish in there life time. The difference between me and another person is a great deal. I steal memory to gain living priorities convenient to ones uses of production, the life in me, yeah that's right, despite the current relation commonly trying to concern me, hurt me with three sterns until I see pass the glass right through you. To queue this tape I just rapped, popped off the tabs on the top of the tape, so there's no possibility to fuck it up, hospitality, you really suck chump, give it this life I have to live with time killing me. My friends depend on lengths of strength, stretched in space mass matter volume, movement, in this room to the ceiling appealing to the camera lens passing at the speed of a flash, faster, wind blowing to a deep breeze. Air pollen in my nose, I suppose I can stick it out, but I have to gift and grasp who near me, feel free to feel me. Then I'll hopefully steer you in the right direction, even I thought your income reflected on my complexion, due to the days of nothing. **In** which things are from. So save one, teach, practice trust what you preach or don't talk at all, because my rhymes will stand, fall, call out everyone disturbing in this sport, now distributes a little less on my conscience that my fellow skateboarders got lost in the nonsense of minerals with materials taking dedication away. The intention is to stay aggressive and deep, but the best of my nautical natures ability is to move with my feet, and take in and absorb through my skin, once I begin to walk, I don't have to think to talk, instant response for whatever, the gesture, to comedy to western vinyl on my list, and to the sloppy women I've kissed, I have missed your comforting, but my brother brings a gift of nutriment for I'll count the intolerance to pleasure with advanced information, quick, but less on quality and less fun if I have to make people like me. In the middle of this man to raise my ethics and understand by looking up these definitions may pilot me in the slightest with the mic press tight against my chest, a symbol of my dignity willingly to give people energy to motivate and cultivate in reasoning of being, research the horizon of priceless situations I fully remember, as mysteries of passion I find in these people to cherish and live and stand on with opportunity to the ones circus, stupid ridiculous pictures I fix in the fixer off the volume and then smothered with ovum's in my room setting flowers to bloom in time and space naked kissing your face wishing this was our own place, facade out, talking attitudes that just puts me down to waist, well I'm up and remembrance is paste. Its stained then put to control of my flow, silver, its gold sparkling. When I wash dishes I caution bitches before we sex because I get careless with the hips. My symptoms and devotions delivers an alarm to a certain degree of temperature rate inside my head breathing debating what time to go to bed and I don't like it when it seems as if your goal is to make me feel at your level, were two totally different people that just don't connect, discern you. Know what my contents consist of, perfection, and brought then sectioned, taught myself many lessons. On this side they stack shit and I climb it, if I'm not lit to the high potential goals I pray to reach. I have an independent class I teach purity to one day a week. I'm weak; you think I sink in a blink action eye movement. I grade these fools to produce improvement of levels of being a homosapien seeing yourself through my eyes in disguise of secrets that secretly get despised. The containing of the remaining entry of maintaining the same reason for this oblivion season of people eating. Don't hate me because I'm here, intelligence is witnessed and gifts get skipped on this trail, especially the pale dry water that makes my skin so rough in the winter time, and cold stays in for my memory. While my man marc calls me crazy occasionally, but I don't get offended. See just more blended in with society, even though he isn't lying. I be relying on facts coming from the side of me. The sight is key entry lock process photographed to contain training dialogue. Were racing these hours by distance from vehicles rather I'm running in my seventeen hundreds and I got my foot to the floor, like damn my feet are killing me, but so what. I keep going and you're damn skippy. I'm known to keep talking about all the messed up things in my head as I sit here thinking about my last dream instead. The past was definitely my fantasy, destiny, I should of showed you, but too late oh well roommate, fuck it I'm stuck with this shit because I'm dumb. I know the weed did it that's why I need it because my freedom is when my brain goes numb. I'm fucked up again with an I don't give a fuck attitude, but I do. Because I want you to see me and I want to see you to. I don't want to die missing life twice, is history, documentations for certain situations make common clear here to a tear. Hold it, mold it, fold it up and put it on a platter then bring it to me. I put my finger in the middle then watch it splatter through out the space of matter center colliding with such a force. A trilogy of geometry, simply geographically sending messages telepathically insert static see the divine detailed information calling me out this shape shift, swift to wind I spend time in. when I drink wine I sip it and let the flavor go all around my mouth then taste it out my nose and blink my eyes and wonder why this situation I'm in is in disguise from the planet. I mean I can't stand it, grant it's a possibility to be witnessed by your fitness, so steer your drive in the right direction and live your life to the fullest extension of your goal, the hole you dug yourself out of a bowl of special k hey stay with me don't close your eyes. I mean I'm talking certain elements into helping you ten fold, bold attitude abuse and cruise through your brain vain. I am the liquid boiling, coiling up inside causing tension to ride your countenance. It's hard to hide the certain ventures of reality from deep inside the mind. My presents is a fragrance only recognized by sickly raised individuals saved by solvements, a scholar of honor my genre can never be inflected upon my being, so don't judge a book by its cover or by how you feign. I poke around the sheets to play with this badly mannered cat. Woke up sit and sat around waiting for a solid answer in my head to act at the same time to abuse my mind with a shinning issue, wishing you were here to bare my company sight. You and me tonight bare to the t.v. light with a record playing so tight, now I'm saying as you cross my path, my point to gift the gaff harder than I have to rip this structure into bone like something in a stone, with an intricate explanation that nobody knows, I owe. For this is my coffee table that no one else can clone, shit gets dirty and a lot play, just like my bones, this is my coffee table its where ever I stay and stand sturdy stable underground just like my record label, never found in stores, but always around in surround sound clashing with your ridiculous beats, yo for this is my coffee table, a pyramid triangle, an intelligent negligent cycle of return, put your studies down on and learn off my words surrounding both corners of your eye balls, besotting, why all poor stuff be costing more than you wanna be hardcore products analy fucking you from the side of my coffee table inhabit its anatomy divided with in a little circle inside my space, lit up, just in case he had to trace the mark of a spark to get up a cause say study thought wisdom wind all elements that run thin through water decibels drip like rain and everybody does seem to run or want to get an idea made by themselves saved on the motherfucking modems to hard drives to the neck up to my scrotum with sad wives loving that shit when I'm showing them new things about life, life when I spit the sentences I entice and if the instance isn't right I might make it passed, because I'm smooth calm like silent, to improve my way of playing chess. We're all living in sixteen pieces getting lost in the years of species copulated to one state. The ability therefore rates in judgment; fundamental skills ricochet off the punishment nourished the time as I wait in struggle defect charm. I have no crew, dissect my will to make it and take shit for granted. The only knowledge I know is the shit I landed in commanded one soul to the discretion of separation to those who let go. For this is my coffee table, on it a song of words that call shit knowledge and stands, sturdy, stable thanks to my girl's elbow, like legend label underground never found in stores, but always around in surround sound going in your pores, clashing with your ridiculous beats. For this is my coffee table that girl threw in the streets because she got mad she couldn't gift the gaff like a mad scientist. I might just miss you. At least I have this music, I must study, I'm in a hurry to catch up to the beast before I loose it. You see me and my buddy Gabe appear to be slightly to the right see the light key light up when I touch it. Damn, girls your fine, I just want to lay you down and clutch tits and turn you into a spoon, my hands filled with balloon godly precision, I'm wishing for something new growing larger in many ways, the past comes back to kill me, shrieks my heart, but yet I feel guilty chilling in a filthy environment with bugs and lizards living around my head, to spawn, but these bumps didn't just come from out of nowhere. Oh where, why what when I need to borrow five bucks and say thanks I appreciate it. Now I can have some gas in my tank to get to work. Reset the day, but I'm not eating shit. I'm getting sick, save me. Its hurting, Pay me a matter of time before I go crazy, Hey he didn't look the other way when I was talking about blocking, did he? Spread those ears out until I can see a hole pierced by sound through a thermometer, as I measure the flames from the coals burning with white fire, my voice telepathically ripping you from the inside out of your skin clipping you forward with one knee down when you begin to give me thanks, well he said I love the voices that mean what they say, comes in crisp, my manner you can format the play off the stereo system in a legendary way, to form this clay to a spectacular day of events, submit to me now, but don't expect. Take it in like an ointment, make it fit, like a choice kid that needed to be chosen in a certain amount of time unwind it to the clock on my sign to find hits take the time and sit, think, stay still at will fat Phil came up with all this in minutes copulated with in the hours, late night showers, my head to the tile I'll be alright, just don't want the night to end then blends to the day. My eyes heavy holding bags of depression, agony don't despise the lack of caressing on my body lies, grants me a lesson when the days turn into nothing. What was it all for? I made something to the dates I'll remember more than you later in time to make me kind, but sad and old, cold, bad and bold. If only I had my secrets revealed through out the chapter I'm dying sometimes crying, but mostly smiling. The true meaning of sadness, I'm just glad all this is coming back to me with my back to the public see this is getting kind of better, but worse with more jerks looking at me ugly because I'm hip hop in tip top shape baby, people call me amazing because they have to. This is coming at you at a full speed, leave residue, no mead notebook no more notes taken down in the morning of the summer heat warning. No more jokes, just playing, some more quotes taken from what I already wrote. Put it down and make it happen, too many guys and girls influence me when they start snapping with moods of their world. I must sit; the spit on the ground is drying too quick. I need to think about sound before it begins to kick. I have recorded words on a three ply high ski scrapper of other conquered goals and extreme remedies brought down with souls boiled, curled, coiled, soiled then wrapped in foil. Ah what you wanna fuck with my plan for man I shit reality that don't give in, I advise the G's with gifts to keep living and take full advantage of the sage brush. The compact contract with syllables practical particles left in fools mind feeling us, heal plus, rubbing lotion lust the trust is too rare to spare and too gothic to care, but the proximity square forth lets me stare at the stars in the universe and the women with scars who keep their purse in their pocket and a locket of a love lost in their brain socket. Believe me, I tear for you. I hear four clues, the repetition abuse, the constant habits I choose, my ability to gain and the frequent naps I loose sleep during the night. The elastic waves parallel, but all twisted, an imaginary line through my wrist, I think I miss it. Thoughts of a little kid in my system, still waiting for permission man. I just wanna rhyme to the beat in my head and explain my life isn't exactly sweet again, but your gone think its neat that I beat you down with this beat in another song you'll eventually get to meet, my memory of what I can see leaves coming from my tree. This is just for all the love lost from my friends cause we be freezing, cold chilling breezy with no wind easy, with rest. Sleazy with sex and my sex, yes, just happens to be the best test penetrating through a universal vein that runs in your breast then gets busted, crooked paths in my blood, that I'm using . . . . Were all working to form one body of water, the motion stays still in some spots, but in some other spots its cold silent, dead chill, at the night. The wind goes into my skin going in you. You're the earth's lover, soiled to perfection, spoiled with an erection. A clean slate adamant, kite control, never loose might, never let go, now glow, and oh yeah your not suppose to put a drink on this without a coaster. It's the most of what I can ask of a person too many to not sweat on me unless your name is Tiffany. My reality, my base, the calamities I face, a vision of a green grassy place spiritually risen in space next to stars chased by comets, my eyes try to follow 'til the day turns into tomorrow. A moment torn with maturity provided with this swarm that gets a little out of patience when it gets warn. If I didn't have a theory for all the weak minded, wary inflations of influences, damn, I don't mean to be rude, but I'm culturally immune to the arts of progression to the point I stand dominant with selections gathered throughout the text of time. The photos are sort of or somewhat more of a proportion from what I can find. A stop brake sign is like a line that races you, chases you and that hates you too, especially when I grab it by the throat and tell it to take me back, but I can't keep up to the fact my opinions lack the concentrated thoughts that gets sought out in my songs. By the time I was brought into knowledge of a man, I was built in my mind to understand the pressure upon a person. Actuating the different ingredients from those learning around me teaching me to soul, to find another heart from the inside of a belly with the feel of jelly prior to delivery liquid environment curling bee stingers because I'm too blunt to touch with healing that gets beat in my brain with pain beat to the ceiling, coming from vain, rain in my eyes, flooding until it reaches the tops of the skies, Philip Z. I don't believe it unless I see it with my own two eyes. That's probably why I'll be alone when I die. Still to this day I pray and ask the lord why I can't be forgiving for all the wrong moves I've made in my life twice, three times a charm. That's why I'm always up before my alarm. I don't eat unless I start to starve, so when I'm dead and you all get done reading my coffee table song, I hope your tears will carve into your flesh and take charge of your heart from the soul of my coffee table, don't put your feet on it, its sonic dude. This song is to my friends that fell apart from relationships that shouldn't have been through many tasks I couldn't accomplish in the past light. Now this is the last starting with the first, a mental fist fight, who wants to write who wants to write, come on lets go.

I suggest you heal, shape, take it slow and stay home and practice, and then one day you'll wake up at night and glow with a back itch, don't be people who don't know shit and has bad habits like me, my coffee table, one move, now go, go . . . .

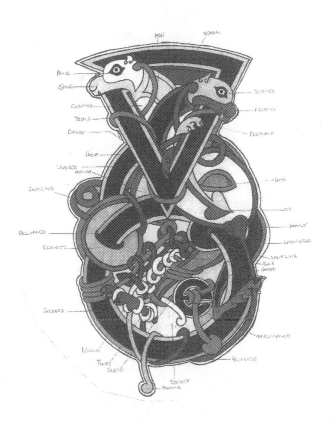

Love Bites

A NOVEL

Love
Bites

Jennifer Green

iUniverse, Inc.
Bloomington

LOVE BITES
A NOVEL

iUniverse books may be ordered through booksellers or by contacting:

iUniverse
1663 Liberty Drive
Bloomington, IN 47403
www.iuniverse.com
1-800-Authors (1-800-288-4677)

ISBN: 978-1-4620-5202-8 (sc)
ISBN: 978-1-4620-5204-2 (hc)
ISBN: 978-1-4620-5203-5 (ebk)

Printed in the United States of America

iUniverse rev. date: 08/27/2011

Chapter 1

The week that I met him started like any other. Just as the early July heat was warming up, I left my home late in the morning to make the thirty-minute commute to the city to go to work, then went for lunch at a deli across the street and got off work at 7PM to drive back home. When I walked in the door, I called up my boyfriend only to find that he wasn't answering his cell phone. "Dammit!" I exclaimed.

Before I go too far into my story, let me introduce myself. My name is Jessica Winters. I'm twenty-five years old and I work in the cosmetics department of a large department store in Munroeville, Tennessee called STARS where the motto is, "Everyone's a star." Yeah, right. Most of the customers that I deal with look more like a full moon and most of them need to go on one of those shows like *What Not to Wear*, but you didn't hear that from me. I give people makeovers and try to sell them a bunch of overpriced products, but really, I'm not a miracle worker. As for me, I've got long, blonde hair, blue eyes and I get some killer discounts on clothes that show off my model's physique. Unfortunately, all of that doesn't come without a price and so from time to time I've come across people who are jealous of me like my co-worker, Ashley Rogers.

My boyfriend, Hayden van Austen, and I live on opposite sides of the town of Hollingsford. Hayden's family is obscenely wealthy and if that wasn't bad enough, he's also an investment banker so most of our conversations are about money. It gets really old, really fast, especially when you don't have much of it yourself. My parents are middle-class, but lost a good chunk of cash to my dad's gambling habits and I'm not exactly making tons of money, either. I do alright with my job at STARS, but sometimes I take on odd jobs when money's a little *too* tight.

I never asked Hayden why he lives in Hollingsford, because it doesn't really seem to mirror his personality. It's just your average small town with a population near 2,000 where most people know one another, the lawns and boulevards are regularly trimmed and kept litter-free and there are so few businesses that they all fit on one main street. It's a nice place, don't get me wrong, but it's pretty mundane and rich people like Hayden stick out like a sore thumb. I guess he just wanted to try to make himself seem down-to-earth, which is pretty ironic considering he wears nothing but designer clothing, drives a Lexus and lives in a mansion. Munroeville, on the other hand, is a bustling hive of activity not unlike any other big city that you can think of and has a population of over 700,000. The skyline is quite impressive, consisting of multiple high-rise office buildings made up almost entirely of glass windows that sparkle in direct sunlight. The city is constantly abuzz with traffic, of both the pedestrian and vehicular variety, and is home to many beautiful parks as well as some of the best shopping and arts venues that the state has to offer.

The only highlight of the first few days of that week was that I actually got to talk to Hayden on Tuesday night. I somehow managed to catch him on a rare occasion where he wasn't busy. It didn't really feel like he was my boyfriend anymore, because he was always off at some sort of business meeting or else he had an appointment with a client. I had more of a relationship with his voicemail than with him.

On Wednesday night, I got off work a bit early, so I figured that maybe I'd actually be able to get home in time to watch an episode of my favorite TV show instead of watching it later on my PVR. I cut through a dark alley to get to the parking lot—yeah, yeah, I know that was a stupid thing to do—and all of a sudden, this guy jumped out and scared the hell out of me.

"*What the fuck*??" I shouted. The guy clutched one of my arms and held it down to my side, then gripped the other shoulder and prepared to clamp his teeth down on my neck. I thought it was weird as hell—why wasn't he trying to steal my purse?—but I was too scared to try anything. I closed my eyes as tightly as I could and braced for the inevitable. After a few moments had passed and nothing happened, I opened them and looked at my would-be attacker right in the face. A loud gasp left my lips. To my shock and horror, the guy's sharp teeth had retracted right in front of me. "What the hell?" I whispered, my voice betraying my true emotions.

"What happened?" the stranger asked me. "What did you *do*?" He stared at my eyes and all I could do in response was whimper pathetically and silently hope to some higher power that I could get away from him before I got hurt.

"What *are* you?" I asked him.

"Didn't you see my teeth? I thought it was pretty obvious that I'm a vampire. Don't you watch movies?"

"Oh my God! Oh my God! Oh my God!" I freaked out. "I thought that vampires were just make-believe!"

"That's just what we want humans to think, until it's time for us to feed on them. There've been a bunch of humans who've found out our secret, but unfortunately for them, they only lived for a few seconds afterwards." He grinned in a really disturbing way, trying to get the hint across. "*Great—vampire humor*," I thought to myself. I head-butted him until he let me go and then I began trying to scratch and claw at his face with my fingernails, wishing that they weren't so damn short. I silently cursed myself for picking at them and tried to dig what remained of them into his face as best as I could, but they were unable to find much purchase in his tough skin.

"Nice try, girly," he sneered as he gripped me again, "but all that you're doing is wasting time hurting yourself." Well, he wasn't wrong about that. I could feel the beginning of a headache coming on and my hands weren't much better off pain-wise.

"Let me go!" I screamed, hoping that my voice was loud enough to attract the attention of a passer-by. I didn't care that it would only make the pain worse; I just knew that I had to do whatever I could to get help.

"I think something's wrong with me. I can't feed on you." He tried to bite me again, but couldn't as if some invisible force was preventing him from sinking his fangs into my skin. I didn't know what was going on, but I was thankful for the intrusion.

"Get away from me!" I shouted. I tried to pry his hands off of me, but they were like iron clamps and wouldn't budge.

"No—not until you undo what you did to me."

"I didn't *do* anything!" I exclaimed, my voice beginning to tremble.

"Maybe you didn't do it on purpose, but you did *something*. I've never had this happen before."

"Please, let me go!" I pleaded, tears threatening to fall from my eyes. "I won't tell anyone that you exist. I swear. No one would believe me anyway." I stared into his eyes again. I didn't know what I had hoped to achieve by doing that, but it seemed pretty obvious that my words hadn't made any positive impact and I had been about to die so I might as well just enjoy the view while I could.

"Stop that!" he growled.

"I'm sorry, I can't help it. I just think that you're so sexy." I chuckled to myself out of hysteria. "Here I am, scared out of my mind and about to be killed by a vampire, yet I'm thinking about how attractive he is. Maybe there's something wrong with me and I should be killed, so go ahead and do it after all!" The vampire had short, wavy, brown hair, dark brown eyes, perfectly sculpted eyebrows, high cheekbones and well-developed arm muscles. If he wasn't so dead or undead—depending on how you looked at it—he could've been a model.

"Alright, if you insist." He tried once again to bite me, but just as before, he couldn't puncture my skin. The constant rejection was angering him and he punched a hole in the brick to the left side of my head in frustration. Still keeping me in his tight grip, he panted from the exertion of the punch and tried to slowly calm himself down.

"What you said about me before, you were just saying that so I'll let you go, weren't you?" he asked, sounding accusatory.

"No. I really meant it."

"No human has ever found me attractive before. They're too busy screaming for help and begging me not to kill them, kind of like you just did."

"Well, maybe I'm not like other humans," I sniffled, trying to hold my head up high and retain some sense of dignity.

"Yes, maybe."

"What can I do to make you let me go?" I asked the vampire, sounding more pathetic and desperate than ever before. One way or another, I wanted this nightmare to end.

"Go out with me."

"What? How? When?" I stammered, shocked by this strange turn of events.

"What is this—*20 Questions*? Do you want me to let you go or not? I could easily just kill you right here and now and throw your body in a Dumpster if you'd prefer. I'd hate to let someone as pretty as you go to waste like that, though."

"Alright, I'll go out with you if those are my only options."

"They are," he said. "Good, I'll meet you on Friday night."

"How will you find me? What if I'm not here that night?" I asked.

"I'll be able to smell your blood and locate you," the vampire sniffed my neck to emphasize his point. Ew.

"If we're going to go out, can you at least tell me your name?"

"You're going to have to wait to find out," he grinned again. I closed my eyes and shuddered, but when I opened them again, he was gone. I gathered myself together, relieved to still be alive and continued the walk to my car, taking care to be more aware of my surroundings from now on.

During the drive home, I kept replaying the encounter over and over again in my mind. Why did I have to go into that damn alley? How could vampires really exist? What does that vampire look like naked? No, no, no, no! I couldn't think about stuff like that so I shook the mental image from my head. When I arrived at the house, I locked the car doors and dashed into the house, fearing that something else might try to get me while I was in such a vulnerable state. I fumbled with the keys as I tried to lock the back door and then I raced up the stairs as quickly as I could to get into bed. I couldn't wait for the day to finally be over.

On Thursday, when I wasn't trying to do my extreme makeovers on customers, I was thinking of the vampire. The image of his face was burned into my memory. His eyes were like bottomless pools and they were so mesmerizing that I could've looked into them forever—that was if I hadn't feared for my life. I imagined what it would be like to run my fingers through his hair. It looked like it might have been spun from silk. I also thought of his muscles. Oh my God, those muscles! Under different circumstances, I would've loved for him to hold me close with them.

"Are you alright?" Natalie Johnson, one of my co-workers asked me.

"Yeah," I replied, snapping out of my beautiful reverie.

"You've got a few more makeovers to do before noon. Speaking of which, do you want to come with me to this great Italian place a few blocks away? They do a great linguini with marinara sauce."

"Sounds good." As she walked away, I got ready to perform some more of my magic on a plump woman who, I guessed, was in her 50s. She wore purple from head to toe and looked like a giant grape. Note to self: the less purple worn, the better.

"What's *with* you today?" Natalie asked me when we were seated at the restaurant. "You seem like your head is up in space." I obviously couldn't tell her about my vampire encounter, so I told her about my troubles with Hayden. "I think that you should dump his ass. He's barely around enough to be your boyfriend, anyway," she said.

"I know."

"Do you think he could be cheating on you?"

"No, but if he was, I've never found any proof. Besides, not everyone who says that they're working late is actually cheating. He's got clients from around the world so he's got to work some crazy hours."

"Would you even *care* if he was cheating?"

"I don't really know anymore. I mean, yeah, I'd be hurt, but it's already practically like we're not together. All that we need to do is make it official. I'd hate to have spent the past four years just to have it all go down the drain like this. I really thought that we could have a future together, you know? If it all goes to shit right now, then at least I can take some comfort in knowing that I didn't wait until we were married and popped out a couple of kids before calling it quits."

"Yeah, but I bet that you'd miss the money and gifts more than you miss him, wouldn't you?" Natalie asked and we both laughed and then tucked into the food that we had just been brought. It wasn't really true—I'm not a gold-digger—but I'm not going to lie and say that I didn't love getting the expensive gifts. Hayden had great taste and I had considered them to be consolation prizes for the times that he wasn't around, which was pretty often as of late.

When I got off of work on Friday night, I went to the employees' bathroom to freshen up and change my clothes. I had no idea what sort of date I was about to go on with my mystery man, so I had brought a knock 'em dead (or in this case, dead-er) outfit which consisted of a sparkly, red tank top, tight, black jeans and a pair of red sneakers just in case I needed to make a quick getaway.

As soon as I walked out of the bathroom, I was greeted to a few whistles of appreciation. "What's the occasion? Got a hot date?" Cynthia Walters asked me.

"You might say that," I replied casually and strolled out of the store, too nervous about what was going to happen to enjoy the attention my outfit was getting from the guys.

I walked down the main street, looking around for any sign of the vampire and figured that maybe I should go into that alley again in case he was waiting for me there. I tried to stand in the shadows and pulled on my black, leather coat so that I could blend in as much as possible. If the vampire really could smell where I'd be, it wouldn't matter, but at the same time, I decided that I'd rather not attract much attention from any other passers-by.

I kept checking my watch, feeling pretty weird and scared about this whole ordeal. After a while, I wondered if I should go back out onto the street because at least then I could walk around and have something to do. Maybe I could window shop?

A few minutes after the sun went down, the vampire found me. "Been waiting long?" he asked me, trying to appear friendly, which came off as rather creepy instead.

"A while."

"You look lovely," he said, checking me out, which was somehow even creepier.

"Thanks," I replied. "I'd say the same to you." He was wearing white jeans, a blue dress shirt that accentuated his arms and some very expensive-looking black, leather dress shoes. I almost died as I drank in his fine form. "*Dammit!*" I mentally scolded myself. "*I have to stop thinking about him like that. He's a frigging monster for crying out loud!*"

"How are your head and your hands?"

"I've been better, thanks for asking. I took some Aspirin, but I still have a slight pain in my head so I've got to take it easy for another day or two. So, where are we going? What exactly do vampires do on dates?"

"I thought that we'd go to this nearby park. Have you eaten yet?"

"No."

"There'll be a few food places on the way there that you can pick something up from if you want."

"Have *you* eaten?" I asked. "On second thought, I don't think I want to know." If I thought too much about the topic, I'd have lost my appetite completely.

The vampire smiled at me, enjoying my discomfort. "I'll be fine."

"I'm not going anywhere with you until you tell me your name."

"I guess that it's the least that I can do for you after what happened the other night. My name is Christopher Sinclair, but you can just call me Chris. I haven't really used my full name since my human days."

"Pleased to meet you, Chris," I said hesitantly, making sure to maintain some measure of caution.

"I've shown you mine, now show me yours."

"I'm Jessica Winters, but my friends usually call me Jessi."

"Pleased to meet you, Jessica," Chris said and kissed my hand like a gentleman. "You're still frightened by me, I can tell, but you're also fascinated and maybe even a little turned on. It's interesting."

"Turned on?"

"The words you speak might say one thing, but the body never lies and your body is just screaming for me to take you somewhere private and fuck the hell out of you. I won't do that, though. Maybe I will someday, but not yet. I'm rather enjoying the sexual tension between us." When he said that, I started becoming more aware of my body movements and tried to put an end to any further messages if possible.

"Can vampires do that? Have sex, I mean?"

"Oh, sure we can. We may be technically dead, but we still have feelings if you get what I mean and I'm sure that you do," he grinned. I tried not to show how badly I was cringing inside at his sexual joke. "Thanks for going out with me."

"You didn't really give me much of a choice," I replied.

"I know," he smirked and showed off his fangs to really hammer the point home. As we walked to the park, I stopped off at a McDonald's to buy a Big Mac, small fries and drink while he waited outside the restaurant. It was a beautiful summer night in the city—not too hot and humid and the stars were out in all their glory. Despite the weather, not many people were in the park so we had quite a bit of privacy, but I wasn't sure whether that was a good thing or not.

Chris found a bench, sat down on it and motioned for me to sit beside him. I didn't want to piss him off, so I did as I was told. "You said that you haven't been called by your full name since you were a human. How long ago was that?" I said as I unwrapped my hamburger and started to pick at it.

"I died in 1883 in Memphis."

"How old were you?"

"24."

"What happened?"

"I had been out at a tavern drinking with some friends and my friend, Ben, told us that he wanted to show us this new rifle that he'd just bought. One of my other friends, Alex, who was more drunk than the rest of us, decided to take the gun from Ben's hands because he wanted to show off. We were trying to get it away from him, but in the struggle, the trigger went off and I was shot in the chest. The bullet missed my heart by mere inches, but it did great damage to other vital organs.

"As I lay dying, I watched everyone run off scared out of their minds. Some friends they turned out to be, right? I could feel myself getting closer and closer to the brink of death—the pain was too great for me to live much longer. Just as I was thinking of my nearest and dearest, a strange man came out of the shadows and approached me. At first, I thought that it had been one of my so-called friends coming back after a change of heart. This man knelt at my side, introduced himself as Lucius and then he proceeded to bite me. The next thing I knew, I woke up as a vampire with a hunger unlike anything I'd ever felt before."

"Oh, that's so sad. You poor man! Those friends of yours were huge assholes. I could never do something so horrible and cowardly to a friend. What happened to them? Did you kill them in revenge?" Despite all of my reservations about being with Chris, I found myself oddly intrigued by his tragic tale and that the walls I'd tried to build up were slowly falling down brick by brick as he went on.

"No. I could've done so very easily and I *did* think about it, but I ultimately decided that they were too pathetic to waste any more of my time on them."

"So, how many people have you killed then?" I asked Chris as I took a sip of my soda.

"Too many to keep count and I've killed them in all sorts of gruesome ways—ways which I won't go into detail about, especially while you're eating."

"Thanks, I think." I continued to nibble on the burger and pondered what to say next. "If you were twenty-four in 1883," I did some mental calculations, "then that would mean you were born in 1859 and you'd be 150 years old now, am I right?"

"Yeah."

"Wow. I can't imagine what that must be like to live for so long."

"You kind of get used to it after a while. I've met some vampires who are much older than me, so I'm almost like a teenager to them in a way," he said, giving a smile so wide that I could see his fangs peeking out just a little. "What's your story?"

"There's really not much to say. I'm twenty-five years old and I work in a department store where I give out makeovers and try to sell beauty products to women." Chris raised his eyebrows at me. "Don't judge me. It's not the most exciting job ever, but it helps to pay the bills."

"Do you like it?"

"It's alright. I like messing around with makeup and trying out different looks on people and I've got good co-workers."

"Don't you want to do something *more* with your life?"

"Why do *you* care? You're the one who tried to kill me," I snapped at him.

"I'm trying to make conversation here," Chris said. "Humor me."

"I haven't really thought much about it. I suppose it'd be cool to be able to work on makeup for TV shows or movies. I wouldn't have to do just beauty stuff, I'd also get to do things like cuts, bruises and all sorts of wounds. Don't laugh at me, but ever since I was in middle school, I've wanted to be a singer."

"Why would I laugh? Are you good at singing?"

"I'm alright, I guess. I entered a few talent contests when I was a teen, but I never won anything. Mostly, I just sang to myself in front of the mirror pretending to be my favorite pop stars like lots of young girls do."

"Then there you go. Speaking of wounds, may I try to bite your neck again? It looks so luscious in the twilight."

"No! I mean, what if it works this time?"

"You don't trust me?" Chris asked. "Even after I gave you my story and my real name?"

"I want to, but, generally speaking, I don't think that vampires can be trusted. They're just like guys—only after one thing and they'll say and do whatever they can to get it."

"Does that attitude mean that you're single?"

"No. Maybe. Sort of."

"So, which is it?"

"It's messy is what it is," I snapped again and then took a deep breath to calm down. "I'm sorry; I shouldn't be taking it out on you. I have a boyfriend, but I haven't been able to spend much time with him lately. He's always so busy with work that it doesn't feel like we have a relationship anymore."

"That sucks, if you'll pardon the pun."

"Tell me about it."

"Why don't you dump him then?" Chris asked with a touch of concern in his voice.

"Someone from work already talked to me about this and I'm giving it a lot of thought."

"Don't just think about it—do it. I bet that I could do a lot more for you than he ever could."

"Like what?" I asked. My curiosity was definitely piqued despite my better judgment.

"For starters, I could give you the best sex that you've ever had. I could do things in bed that would make you blush ten shades of red. I could take you places and show you things you've never dreamed of. As if all of that wasn't enough, I've got loads of money to spend on you. All I ask in return is for you to let me drink from you, that is, if I can get things working," he explained.

"Can I think about it for a while?"

"Sure, but don't take too long. I'd hate for another vampire to try to claim you." "*Shit. Shit. Shit. Shit,*" I thought to myself. I loved Hayden, but the offer was too tempting to pass up. I tried to weigh the pros and cons in my head. I'd been with Hayden for four years and I loved him a lot, but could you still call what we had a relationship? On the other hand, Chris could give me what I got from Hayden and then some. He seemed to have more free time, which was a huge plus, but getting into a relationship with a vampire was bound to be fraught with obstacles, an obvious one being his ability to control himself around me. If he drank too much of my blood, he could kill me or at least seriously hurt me.

"When will we go out again?" I asked him.

"I'm busy tomorrow night, so how about Sunday?"

"Sure. I'll give you my decision then."

"That's fine."

"If I were to say 'yes', I want to set up some ground rules, okay?"

"Such as . . . ?" he asked, clearly intrigued.

"I haven't figured that out yet," I admitted.

"Oh, well then make them good."

"Don't worry, I will."

When I was finally finished with my supper, I threw the trash in a garbage can and we went for a walk around the park. There was a little lake there that I knew had a family of ducks, but they were nowhere to be found as they were probably sleeping by this time of night or whatever that ducks did. We did see a few frogs in the pond, though, so we stopped to watch them for a few minutes while they made "ribbit ribbit" noises to each other.

After we left them behind, Chris slipped his hand into mine. I was freaked out and a little uncomfortable at first, but the longer it stayed there, the better it felt. His hand was pretty cold, but just the feeling of his skin on mine was sort of nice. "I'm glad that you went out with me," Chris said.

"I have to be honest with you—I was nervous as hell about tonight, but I've been having some fun."

"You haven't seen anything yet!"

"What do you mean?"

"I've got a surprise or two for next time," he said, with a mischievous twinkle in his eyes.

"Uh, oh. Should I be afraid?" I asked apprehensively. I wasn't sure if I liked the sound of that. When you were hanging out with a vampire, anything could happen and their ideas of fun and surprises were probably going to be a lot different than a human's.

"I'm not going to say a word about it. Don't you like surprises?"

"Sometimes."

"Like I said before, I could take you to places and show you things you'd never dreamed of and I intend to make good on that promise. If worst comes to worst and you really feel frightened, I'll be with you and no one wants to mess with me."

"I can believe that." I looked at my watch and saw that it was getting pretty late, well, for me, anyway. "I'm really sorry, Chris, but I've got to end this date now. I've still got a half-hour drive ahead of me. Thanks for the most fun I've had in a while. I'm kind of glad now that we met, although I didn't appreciate getting the living daylights scared out of me or nearly dying."

"You're very welcome and now I guess I should say that I'm sorry about trying to attack you. What a great first impression to make, huh? If you won't let me bite you tonight, will you at least let me kiss you?" he asked.

"As long as you don't have your fangs out, I don't really see why not," I replied. Chris leaned in close to me and when our lips met, a tingle of electricity flowed through my body. It was weird how kissing a dead person made me feel so alive. An eternity seemed to have passed before I gathered enough sense to pull away from him. "See you on Sunday night, Chris."

"Have a good night, Jessica!" he called out to me as I started making my way back through the park.

While I drove home, I thought about how the next day was going to be very busy now that I had a lot of stuff to think about. What was I going to do about Hayden? Should I break up with him right away or should I wait until it was official that Chris and I were a couple? It was times like that that I wished I could be in someone else's shoes.

Chapter 2

I had a restless sleep during the night as I wrestled with the idea of breaking up with Hayden. I knew that it was the right thing to do, but it would also be one of the hardest decisions that I'd ever had to make. In the end, I knew that we'd both be better off and when I finally accepted that decision and all of its possible consequences, I found a sort of peace and fell asleep.

I woke up late Saturday morning, had some cereal and tried to put pen to paper on my personal homework assignment. I spent a few hours scribbling down ideas, crossing some out and doing a fair bit of editing. I strained my brain trying to write everything that I could think of, but ended up with not much valid material. I thought that perhaps it might be wise to take a break for a while and see if I could get a hold of Hayden. If things went according to plan, I knew that it was going to be a horrible discussion, but it was going to happen sooner or later and I picked 'sooner'.

I got dressed up in a sexy red dress with spaghetti straps and matching strappy heels so that I could try to feel as good as I could while I tore out Hayden's heart. It was probably a really selfish thing to do, but I figured that I'd be an absolute wreck if

I talked with him while I just wore sweats. There was no need to make an already horrible task even more miserable with my sartorial choices.

"Here goes nothing," I said to myself as I picked up the phone and began to dial Hayden's number. The phone rang a few times and I started thinking that perhaps he wasn't available again, but I held on a little longer. Just as I was about to hang up, someone on the other end picked up the receiver.

"Hello?" the voice called.

"Hayden?"

"Jessica! What's up? How are you? Long time, no see!"

"Yeah, I know. Actually, that's why I'm calling. I really need to talk to you about something."

"Oh, okay," Hayden's voice was suddenly devoid of all the happiness he had been feeling just a moment ago. "When do you want to talk?"

"Right away, if it's possible. It's really urgent," I replied, trying to keep my voice level.

"I had a busy day planned," he said and I rolled my eyes, "but I'll rearrange some things if it really means a lot to you."

"Thanks a lot, Hayden. I'll be here all day, so whenever you can come by my place is fine with me."

"Sure. See you later, baby. I love you," he said as he hung up the phone.

"Fuck! Why did he have to say that? Why couldn't he have just said 'See you later' and left it at that?" I thought to myself. I didn't think I was going to be strong enough to get through it, sexy red dress or not. His words had just poured a little more salt on the wound and I had a feeling that the wound was just going to keep getting bigger and deeper by the time that our meeting was through. Maybe it would end up as big as one of the craters on the moon?

I ate and tried to go back to my writing while I waited for Hayden's arrival. My mind wandered around, coming up with all sorts of possible reactions that he'd have to my news. That wasn't a very good train of thought to follow, so I tried to pour my energy back into my task and thought of my vampire for inspiration. I was so absorbed in my work that I almost jumped out of my skin when there was a knock on the door.

I checked the clock on the kitchen wall and saw that it was already past 3 o'clock. Where did the time go? "Coming!" I shouted as I quickly hid my papers in a barely-used cookbook.

"Hi, Jessi. You look really good!" Hayden exclaimed when I opened the door and invited him in.

"Thanks. So do you." He was wearing one of his designer suits in a dark blue that brought out his green eyes and his shoulder-length blond hair gleamed in the sunlight. Everything about his appearance screamed of his wealth and was just another painful reminder of why I had to do what I was about to do.

"What did you want to talk to me about so badly?"

"You're going to want to sit down for this," I said, trying to put a hint of seriousness into my voice.

"It's that bad, huh?" he asked. I nodded in response and led him into the living room. He sat down on the oversized beige couch and I sat down in the matching armchair across from him.

"I feel like we haven't really had much time to be together for a while and I'm really tired of trying to conduct a relationship through your voicemail." Hayden looked like he was about to interject and defend himself, but I put my hand up and continued on. "I appreciate that you enjoy your job and that you're really good at it, but it's important that we also get to spend time together. I love you very much, but I feel that I'm taking a backseat to your work and I can't go on like this anymore. I'm so sorry."

"I'm sorry, too. I didn't really realize that you felt this way before. I wish you'd told me earlier."

"I wish I had, too, but I didn't know how to get your attention long enough to say anything."

"Well, you've got it now," he said.

"There's more that I have to get off my chest while you're here." I took a deep breath. It was time to lay out the last of the cards on the table. "I've started seeing someone else and I want to break up with you." As soon as I said those words, the tension in the room became so thick that you could cut it with a knife, as the saying goes. I wished that I could read his mind, but I didn't need to because the look on his face pretty much said it all. He was shocked and pissed off all at the same time.

"How could you do this to me? How could you cheat on me?" Hayden asked me, quite obviously hurt by my admission.

"I got tired of waiting around for you to have some time off. I was tired of having to spend night after night alone, because you were at a business meeting or you were out of town seeing a client. There were some times when I really needed to be with someone and you let me down. This isn't how I wanted things to end, but there were extenuating circumstances."

"So everything is *my* fault?" he stood up and shouted. "You didn't seem to mind too much when I'd bring you back gifts of expensive jewelry."

"I know. I'm not a saint in this, either and I never claimed to be. The jewelry was great, I'm not going to deny that, but I'd rather have had more time with you. If I could go back in time and do it over again, I'd give back all of the necklaces and bracelets and demand more of your time instead of just settling for a bunch of pretty trinkets."

"Everything that I did was for *you*. All of the meetings and trips were to make money so that we could build our futures together. I thought that I'd be the breadwinner and you could finally quit that job that you've complained about so much and find something else to enjoy doing. Maybe one day, you could have been a stay-at-home mom to our kids and I'd support everyone and give you a great life where you wouldn't have to worry about money."

I scoffed at the ridiculousness of his words and shook my head. "What the hell are you talking about? You've never had to work a day in your life. Your family has so much money that you practically have it coming out of your ass!" I shot back. "You could just as easily have lived off of the family fortune for the rest of your life and then maybe we wouldn't be in this situation right now. *You* were the one who wanted to prove that you weren't just another spoiled, rich brat mooching off of your parents. *You* were the one who wanted to make a name for himself."

"I...I...uh...," Hayden stammered, at a loss for words. He couldn't say anything else; he knew that I had owned him with that last comment. Seeing that he was backed into a corner, he tried to change the subject. "You said that this isn't how you wanted things to end, so you *did* want things to end?"

"No, that's not what I meant!" I said, throwing up my hands in exasperation and trying desperately to cling onto my dignity. "Dammit! Why would I have wanted to end what we had together? We've been dating for four years and I've loved you all that time, but shit happens. People grow apart and things happen that are hard to control. Did you really expect me to hang around forever like some doll on a shelf waiting to be played with? There's only so much I can take and I've reached my limit.

"The bottom line is this: I'm not happy anymore and I deserve to be treated better. I want to be with someone who would be around when I want and need them—someone reliable and you don't fit the criteria anymore. I hate this so much and you have no idea how much this is hurting me." I felt very close to breaking down and crying, but I had no intentions of letting him see me that way. I figured that he didn't really deserve it after what he'd put me through.

"So who is he and what's he got that I don't? How long has this been going on?"

"You don't know him and I'm not going to tell you who it is anyway, because I don't want you to go after him. I don't want you to get hurt and I just started seeing him this week."

"*Now* you decide that you care about me getting hurt!" he laughed. "You're priceless!"

"As for what he's got, well, let's just say that he's been around a while and knows how to treat a woman."

"And I *don't*? I used to wine and dine you. Remember?"

"Yeah, key word being 'used to.' You haven't taken me out since I don't know when. It's always work, work, and more work. When I'm working, you're not and when I'm not, you are. It's been hard to find any time when both of us have been free for a conversation never mind going out on an actual date," I said.

"Jessi, if you stay with me, I promise that I'll make changes. I'll cut back on my hours and do whatever you ask of me. Just please don't leave me." He got down on his knees and held my hands in his, looking up at me with pleading eyes.

"How can I trust you? I mean, so much damage has been done and I don't think I can go through this again." Hayden got back onto his feet, stormed through the house and slammed the door behind him. I closed my eyes and waited for the tears to begin falling down my face as I stood motionless in the middle of the living room. *"What have I done? Am I making the right decision?"* I thought to myself.

I ran up the stairs to my bedroom, lay down on the bed and began crying my heart out. I felt like I had enough tears coming out of my eyes to fill a river. I cried for a while, stopped for a few moments, replayed the big argument with Hayden in my mind and repeated the whole process over and over until I fell asleep.

When I woke up hours later, I went into the kitchen, took the papers out of the cookbook and ripped them up. I wasn't going to need those lists of pros and cons anymore where I compared Hayden and Chris. I'd made my decision and there was no going back. I fixed myself something to eat and while I ate, I made my list of ground rules for Chris. Within ten minutes, I'd had five points written on paper and I was pretty satisfied with what I'd done.

I phoned up Natalie to tell her the big news. As I was dialing, I looked up at the clock and saw that it was around 10 at night. It occurred to me then that maybe she was out at a club somewhere and I should hang up and try again the next day. She picked up the phone and told me that she was glad I'd phoned, because she'd been sick all day with the flu and needed some cheering up.

I proceeded to give her a play-by-play account of the argument with Hayden and occasionally she chimed in with an "Oh my God!" or an "I can't believe he said that!" It was nice to have someone on my side. "I'm glad that you dumped him. What a douchebag!"

"It's sad that this all happened, but maybe it's for the best, you know?" I said.

"That's a good way of looking at it," she agreed. "Jessi, I'm here for you if you need me, but not right now because I don't want you catching these nasty germs."

"Thanks, Natalie. Get well soon! If you want, I could come by tomorrow and give you a pot of chicken noodle soup. I could just drop it off at your door and ring your doorbell so that you know I've been by."

"I've been chugging that down like there's no tomorrow. I'll be surprised if I don't turn into a damn chicken soon. So, thanks, but no thanks. It was nice of you to offer, anyway."

"Good night, then," I said.

"Good night," she replied and hung up the phone. I paced around the living room, trying to think of something that I could do. I'd already had a long nap and wasn't tired, so sleeping wasn't an option and I hadn't felt like going out anywhere. Thinking of nothing better to do, I ended up plunking myself down on the couch in front of the TV.

I had no idea what was on, so I did some channel surfing and stopped when I came to some vampire movie. While I watched it, I imagined Chris and I doing what the characters on the screen were doing. I imagined him biting me in a seductive way and then making crazy, passionate, vampire love to me. It was probably sad of me to do that, but I didn't care. What was wrong with a little fantasizing?

When the movie came to a really gross part where the main vampire ripped apart another vampire and blood spurted out of the body, I quickly changed the channel and turned on an episode of a favorite comedy. I was definitely in need of some laughter after the day I'd had. I half-watched the show as I got out my laptop computer and went to an online chat room where I was pretending to be a twenty-two year-old stripper from Los Angeles named "Barbi Doll". It was hilarious until a forty year-old guy who called himself "hot4girlz" started sending me some really gross private messages and I logged off.

I put the computer back under the coffee table and went around the house to do some much-needed cleaning with the TV still on as background noise. As much as I tried to keep the house in good shape there were some spots that were like dust magnets.

By the time that I had done as much as I could stand, I'd filled up almost a whole wastebasket, but on the plus side, I had found a few dollars in change that had fallen behind some furniture.

I was so tired from all of the housework that I crashed out on the couch and the sounds of the TV lulled me to sleep. I had no idea what the time was and I didn't really care. When I woke up on Sunday, I felt almost refreshed like I'd had a change of batteries. The whole situation with Chris felt like I was standing on a precipice and I was getting ready to leap into the unknown—exhilarating but scary as hell. I couldn't wait to see him that night and start off on this journey together as cheesy as that sounded.

I was hungry as hell and made myself some waffles. I tried to pass the time by doing anything that I could think of: cleaning places that I didn't get to the night before, catching up on e-mail, the laundry, going to the store to get the newspaper and going to the gym to exercise. I hadn't been there for a while, but I worked up a pretty good sweat and took a well-deserved shower when I came back home.

My new relationship with Chris made me think of what little I really knew about vampires and so I decided to make a trip to the library. Hollingsford had a very small one and I doubted very much that they'd have what I wanted so I would make a trip out to Munroeville where I had a membership to the Hillside Public Library. It was only about ten blocks away from my store, so I frequented it quite often and, thankfully for me, it was open everyday except holidays.

I had plenty of time to go there and back and still get dressed for my date, so I quickly gathered up my handbag, slipped on a light jacket and shoes and was out the door heading for my car. Although the drive to the city went much faster than usual, it still wasn't fast enough for my impatient self.

As soon as I arrived at the library, I made a beeline for the computer that had a catalogue of all of the books available and was greeted by a long list of various titles on my chosen subject. I scrolled through them and used a pen and paper next to the computer to scribble down titles and author names. I was amazed at just how many books were written about vampires and these were probably just a small sampling of everything ever printed. Amongst the listed titles were all sorts of books about vampire myths and legends from around the world and books about vampires in popular culture as well as a myriad of novels.

I narrowed the list down to about a dozen of the most promising contenders and proceeded to hunt them down on the shelves. I didn't know if I'd ever have enough time to read them all, but even if I just skimmed some of the information, I figured that that was better than nothing. I was just as impatient on the way back home as I was getting to the city because I was excited to get started on my reading and somewhat afraid of what I might learn. What could I read about that was any worse than what I'd already been imagining? I didn't know and I wasn't sure if I could handle it, but at the same time, I wanted to know everything that I could so that I was prepared.

I still had a couple of hours to kill before it was time for me to leave for my date, so I chose a few of the books to skim through. I flipped through a book about common myths until a page heading caught my attention regarding vampire feeding habits. The section was accompanied by a very detailed illustration of a male vampire feeding on some poor, unsuspecting female victim.

Although I was scared out of my wits at nearly being in the same situation just days before, the safety of my bedroom removed my fear of the subject matter. I felt like a scientist who was simply doing some necessary research. The more that I read about it, the more fascinated and repulsed I was. In the same way that some people are fans of horror movies, I found it hard to turn away from the violence and gore and, I must admit, I even got a little thrill out of it.

It was around 6 o'clock when I started to get ready for my date with destiny. I figured that I'd dress up a little more fancy than the first time. I wore my sexy red dress again which was newly-washed, the matching heels, white hoop earrings, white plastic bracelets and my black leather coat. To complete the ensemble, I spritzed some of my favorite perfume onto my wrists and neck. I smelled, looked and felt pretty damn good, but I still had this nagging feeling in the back of my mind questioning if I was doing the right thing. If I listened to it too much, well, I didn't want to think about what would happen in that scenario. All I knew in that moment was that I wanted to be with my vampire.

Chapter 3

I got to the city shortly before sundown and parked the car in one of the downtown lots where the money you pay depends on how long the car was parked there. I considered going to wait for Chris in our favorite alley, but thought that maybe it would be wiser to go somewhere else, just in case someone caught on to us. Instead, I walked to the park where we had our first date and waited on a bench underneath one of the lampposts. As I straightened out my outfit and brushed my hair again, I noticed that the light made it shine like spun gold.

"Hi, there," Chris said from behind me. I didn't see or hear him approach me so where did he come from? Maybe this was just one of those vampire things that I'd have to get used to.

"Shit! You scared me!" I exclaimed.

"Sorry about that. Anyway, you look really good."

"Thanks. You're pretty handsome yourself." Chris was wearing tight black jeans, a red dress shirt and the same black dress shoes that he had worn on our first date. "So, where are we going?"

"There's a nightclub in the area," Chris replied.

"I thought you were going to be taking me to see things I'd never dreamed of?" I asked him.

"I will. This isn't your ordinary nightclub."

"Are we walking there? Is it far?"

"It's just down the street, but I thought we'd take my car. I've got it parked nearby," he said.

"Oh, okay." We walked just down the block and sure enough, his car was parked on the main street. "Holy shit!" I exclaimed as I saw it. I didn't know what the make of his car was, but it was bright red, sleek and looked like it was probably imported from Europe and so it would have cost a bundle. Chris said that he had lots of money and here was some proof of that.

"You like that, huh?" he smiled at me. "She's a beauty." We got into the car, buckled up and sped off. We pulled up in front of a warehouse that looked like it hadn't been used in years.

"I thought we were going to a nightclub?" I asked, confused.

"This is it." Chris saw me looking at it dubiously. "It was built in here to dissuade humans from going inside. Only those who need to know about it know that it exists."

"If the warehouse is supposed to be a disguise, then shouldn't you have parked somewhere else? I mean, if someone comes by here, they're going to be wondering what's going on, especially with such a fancy car around."

"This is the first time I've ever come here by car and anyway, no one comes around here this late at night unless they're going to the club. You've probably noticed that this area isn't exactly booming," he said. I looked around and saw that he was right. The surrounding buildings were in various states of disrepair just waiting for the city to demolish them and put them out of their misery. There were a few buildings that were in fairly good condition, but they were boarded up, which was kind of depressing.

When we entered the club, it didn't look that different from any other: stylish red, black and white décor, dance music blasting from huge speakers, a multicolored dance floor and various booths and tables scattered around. Off to the side, there was a large silver bar that stood out from everything else and there were signs behind the bar advertising various brands of alcohol. To the right of the bar, there was a stage for live entertainment. A sign by the entrance proclaimed that a band called The Grateful Undead would be performing.

"The Grateful Undead?" I asked, trying to stifle a giggle.

"They're really good," Chris said. "That's why I wanted to bring you here tonight."

"This place doesn't look that much different from any other nightclub that I've been to." As soon as I said that, I took a good, long look around at the faces of the other patrons and it dawned on me that most of them had the same pale complexion as Chris. This was a vampire nightclub. "Oh." I didn't know how many of them were in the place, but I started to feel really uneasy about being there amongst so many monsters. What if Chris decided to turn against me? I figured that there was no way I would have been able to get out of the club alive.

"Figured it out, have you?" he smiled again.

"I had no idea that vampires did things like this."

"We do a lot more than kill people—we just don't like to advertise that fact."

"What are those humans doing here, then?" I subtly nodded to a group of males and females that were dressed like they didn't belong there.

"Some vampires bring their prey here, kind of like playing with their food before they kill them and some vampires invite special people here just for their own entertainment. I think it's almost a guarantee that you'll be the only human leaving here alive," Chris explained. I couldn't help but shudder at such disgusting ideas but then mentally chided myself against it. If I was serious about being with a vampire, I would have to work on hiding my true feelings about what they did so that I could fit in better.

"I thought you said that any humans who know about vampires only ended up living for a few seconds after they found out?"

"We like to have some fun and make an exception to the rule once in a while."

"And now, ladies and gentlemen," the emcee proclaimed, "for your listening pleasure, here they are—The Grateful Undead!" The club burst into applause as the band came on and introduced the first song of the night—a hit called "You Make Me Wanna Come out of My Coffin". The concept of a band of dead people was weird, but I must admit, the song was actually pretty catchy. I couldn't really relate to the lyrics, but the beat was good. I decided that I'd ask Chris if he owned any of their CDs and if I could borrow them some time.

Chris led me onto the dance floor and I was really reluctant. I had no idea of what was appropriate for a place like this, so I tried to look around at what everyone else was doing and followed their examples. Around the middle of the song, I gave it a try and began to loosen up a bit. I was actually having a lot of fun until I noticed a few other male and female vampires checking me out. I felt like some tantalizing piece of meat on display in a butcher's shop, which, I suppose, I was in a way. It was such a tease to have a human in their midst that would be off-limits to them. Chris never had to speak a word to lay his claim on me—his body movements said it all. He danced so close to me that I could feel his breath on my neck and he tried to guard me with his arms. It would've been more romantic if the circumstances weren't quite so creepy.

I tried to ignore the other vampires and we danced for a few more songs, then Chris led me over to a booth as far away from the stage as possible. "I'm going up to the bar. What do you want to drink, Jessica?" he asked me.

"I'll have a Cosmopolitan if they can do one."

"Coming right up," he said as he headed off to the bar. I looked around at the club, trying to soak in the surroundings and felt really vulnerable without Chris being by my side to be my protector. Thankfully, it wasn't long before he was back with our drinks. Gotta love that super vampire speed.

"Thanks, baby." I took a sip of my Cosmopolitan and was amazed at how good it was while Chris took a swig from his bottle of beer. "The bartender really knows their stuff. I think this is the best one I've ever had, but since when do vampires drink alcohol? I've never heard of that before."

"Stick with me long enough and you'll learn a lot more than that," he smiled. "We don't drink it that often, because it doesn't really do anything for us. We don't get drunk off of it like you humans do, but it just makes us feel good for a little while. It's mainly a social thing."

"Oh, okay." It made a lot of sense to me the way that he explained it. "Chris, I've got those rules made up like I said I'd do."

"Do we have to talk about that right now?"

"No."

"How about you tell me about them in the car?" he suggested.

"Sure, whatever you want," I agreed. We sat in silence for a little while, sipping our drinks, listening to the music and watching the dancers writhing madly around to the beat. Eventually, the band announced that they were going to take a break and it got a little less noisy in the room.

"Tell me the honest truth, Jessica: what do you really think of me?" Chris asked. I hated being put on the spot like this and he grinned, enjoying my discomfort.

"Well, I hated the way that you scared the hell out of me when you tried to attack me the night we met, but you already knew that. Other than that, I find you very attractive and I'm starting to find out that you're actually a really nice guy, I mean, for a vampire. You've also got obviously great taste in fashion and cars."

"And in women," he flashed his pearly whites at me and winked. I chuckled in response and felt my cheeks blushing from the compliment.

"There's that, too."

"Tell me, are you scared of me?"

"A little, yeah," I admitted, not daring to look directly into his eyes.

"That's good. That'll help to keep you alive in case I do something to you," he backtracked off of my horrified look, "not that I intend to do anything anymore. I'm just saying that there's always a possibility of a worst case scenario occurring. No matter how much I like you, nothing can change the fact that I'm a vampire and I will do what comes naturally to my kind."

"Alright, I get it. A tiger can't change its stripes, as the saying goes. Now, it's your turn: what do you really think about me?" I asked him.

"When I met you and smelled your blood for the first time, I wanted so badly to kill you. I wanted to feel your blood trickling down my throat, filling me up with your life and, to be honest, I still want to. I don't think I've ever wanted to drink a human more, but I've also never physically wanted a human more. I'm very attracted to you. I love the way that your hair shines, I love the color of your eyes, your smile and the way that you make me feel. I also love the way that that dress clings to your body." His eyes seductively scanned me and his fangs popped out to show his appreciation.

I flipped back my hair and toyed around with the little paper umbrella in my drink. "Chris, is it wrong that I want to take you into the bathroom right now and have my way with you?" If it was possible for a vampire to blush, I was sure that he would've done so right then and there. Instead, he ran one of his hands up my leg, then up my thigh and I stopped him before he could go any further. I wanted an answer and I had it right there.

"Why'd you do that?" he asked, his fangs retracting. He sounded confused and I honestly couldn't blame him for feeling that way, especially since I wasn't exactly being subtle about my physical desire for him.

"Let's get out of here," I ordered. I wanted him badly, but I didn't want to put on a show in public, especially not with a bunch of vampires around. I had no idea what they would have done or thought about us getting intimate like that and I really didn't want to find out.

"And go where?"

"Would you able to come to my place?" I asked him.

"Yes. It won't be sunrise for at least five more hours. I'll be safe." We left the booth and as we walked across to the exit, I thought that I could feel all eyes on us. Maybe I was just being paranoid, but I didn't bother looking back to see if I was right or not. We got back into his car and sped off again. He drove me to the lot where my car was parked so that I wouldn't have to walk through the park to get there.

"We should talk about the rules now."

"Okay, go ahead. I'm listening," he said.

"#1—You are only permitted to drink my blood during sex, unless I choose to give consent for some other occasion. For example, your birthday or anniversary of your death or whatever you celebrate. #2—You must give me three days to recuperate after drinking my blood; however, we can still have sex during that time. #3—When you drink from me, you must stick to only a few spots so that I can bandage them up easily otherwise someone could get suspicious. It'd be easy to explain away one or two places by saying that I cut myself shaving or I got a paper cut. #4—You must respect me and stop when I tell you to. #5—If you fail to stop when I tell you to, I will be allowed to use whatever means necessary to try to stop you and you can't fight back. Does this sound fair to you?"

Chris thought about it for a minute. "Yes. What if I do everything that you want? That seems like a lot to ask of me."

"I'm quite prepared to make it worth your while," I said with a suggestive smile on my face.

"I like the sound of that," he beamed. When we got to the lot, I exited the car and climbed into my own, then started heading to Hollingsford with Chris following right behind me.

I went a little over the speed limit, but I was just so excited by the prospect of being with him that I wanted to get home as quickly as possible. Thankfully, there were no cops around to pull us over. I guessed that it was my lucky day, in more ways than one.

Chris and I pulled up to my house within seconds of each other and as soon as I had unlocked the front door, he had his hands and lips all over me. "Hold that thought," I said to him as I entered the house. He paused at the threshold and I thought that maybe I'd done something wrong. "What's the matter?"

"I can't come in unless you invite me in."

"Why?"

"It's a vampire rule. You have to verbally give me an invite and once you do that, I'll always be able to get into your house without any problem," Chris explained.

"Oh, okay. Please come in," I gestured for him to enter. Now that the invisible barrier or whatever had been removed, he stepped into the house and I locked the door behind him. He took me to the couch and pushed me down on it, then climbed on top of me and kissed me more passionately. "Let's go somewhere more comfortable," I suggested.

"Where'd you have in mind?" he asked. I glanced upwards at the ceiling and he understood. I led him up to my bedroom, slipped off my shoes and then lay down on the bed, gesturing for him to join me. He kicked off his shoes and socks then climbed on top of me again. "Now, where were we? Ah, yes," he said and then kissed me hard. I could feel the urgency in his cold, dead lips. He really wanted, maybe even needed, to be with me and feel the release that only sex could give you. I felt the same way about him and wondered if he'd gone as long without intimacy as I had. I didn't think I could even remember the last time I'd been with Hayden that way.

Before we got started, I pulled away from him. "Are we going to need this?" I asked as I pulled out an unused condom from my nightstand. I hoped that it was still good to use, because I didn't know when I'd bought them.

"No. One of the many perks of having sex with a vampire is that there's no risk of catching a disease or getting pregnant," he replied and I put the condom back in the nightstand.

Chris got off the bed and began undoing his shirt. "Let me get that," I said and he walked over to where I was. I made short work of the shirt and threw it on the floor, then made my way down to his pants, which ended up right beside it. Now, he was clad in nothing but his form-fitting underwear, which I took my time sliding off just to tease him a bit.

"My turn," he said right before he began to pull my dress over my head. He kissed my neck while he unhooked my bra and then slid off my red lace panties. I lay back down on the bed and his eyes took in my naked form, very pleased with what he saw if you know what I mean.

Chris looked even better without clothes on than I had imagined. His body was well-toned and he had a six-pack of abs that most guys would only have if they spent every day at the gym for a year. I couldn't stand it anymore, and I had to summon up all of my willpower to not scream out, "Fuck me now!" It didn't matter that I didn't say it, because he got on me right at that moment almost as if he knew what I was thinking.

Chris positioned himself, then eased into me and it hurt so much that I let out a little moan. "Am I hurting you, baby?" he muttered, caressing my hair with one hand and supporting himself with the other.

"A little bit."

"Do you want me to stop?"

"No. We haven't even started. I just haven't had sex for a while, that's all. Keep going," I said to him.

"Just let me know when I *do* hurt you too much, 'k?" I just nodded in response and he went to work on me. Thankfully, the pain had already begun to recede so I would be able to enjoy it. The way that he moved his body around like an expert made me wonder just how much experience he'd had. He gripped my hips and we moved together in an almost perfect rhythm.

I arched my back and tried to push myself up to meet him so that he wouldn't have to do everything, but he was going too forcefully for me and I just gave up and lay back down.

I wanted to suck on his nipples, but he was moving too fast to get my mouth on him so instead I ran my hands along his pale, hairless chest. His skin was so smooth and cold beneath my hands, sort of like a block of ice or a slab of marble, only better. I held him close to me, running my fingers through his hair and breathing in his scent. I hadn't noticed it before, but he smelled of an intoxicating mix of musk and sandalwood.

All of a sudden, he started to bite me and thrust harder. I couldn't be sure which hurt more, but I had a feeling that Chris was at his peak. It wasn't long after that that I hit mine and Chris withdrew himself, collapsing on the bed beside me. I was out of breath and my heart was beating like crazy, but it was a great feeling. He looked at me and smiled, glad that I was satisfied with his performance.

I reached up and touched the spot where he bit me while in the throes of passion and my fingers came away coated in blood. "Sorry about that," Chris apologized. "I'll fix that." He licked the blood off of my fingers in a very seductive way and I bit my lip as I watched. When he was done, he went into the bathroom and came back with a bandage that he put on the wound.

"Thanks," I said.

"How do you feel now? I hope that I didn't drink too much."

"I feel fine so far." I tried to stand up to get dressed, but I nearly fell over. Thanks to his lightning-fast vampire reflexes, Chris caught me before I hit the floor.

"Looks like you're not quite as fine as you thought you were," he said.

"Yeah. Looks like."

"If you really want to get dressed, I'll get your things for you. You should probably stay in bed for a while."

"You don't have to tell me twice. Falling on my ass was *not* in my plans for today," I said. Chris laughed and it made him seem almost human. He was gorgeous, but when he laughed or smiled, it seemed like his whole face lit up, although that could have just been the effect that the lighting had on his pale face—I didn't know.

He handed me my clothes and I tried to put them on underneath the sheets. Unfortunately, I couldn't hook up my bra and he saw me struggling with it. "Need a hand?" he offered.

"Yes, please." I sat up, holding the sheet against my chest and he had the hooks fastened in a matter of seconds. "Thanks." I continued to get dressed and Chris began to put on his underwear and pants. I was glad that he stopped there, because I couldn't get enough of looking at his bare chest.

"At the risk of sounding clichéd—was it as good for you as it was for me?" I asked him, a sly grin on my face.

"I thought it was pretty obvious," he grinned back with a twinkle in his eyes.

"I can honestly say that I've never felt anything like that before—I could get used to this. Never in my wildest dreams did I ever think that I'd be having sex with a vampire."

"If you think that was good, you haven't seen anything yet. There's a lot more where that came from."

"I'm looking forward to it." I paused for a moment. "Just for the record, I don't usually have sex with someone on the second date."

"Then why did you do it with me?"

"You're special. I guess you seem to bring out a whole other side of me. I mean, I wouldn't let just anyone else bite me, either." I decided to change the subject. "Tell me a little more about yourself."

"What do you want to know?" he asked.

"I know how you died, but what about your human life? Who were your parents? What did they do for a living?"

"I was born in Memphis on June 1st, 1859 on an exceptionally hot spring day. I lived there until I was about sixteen, when I ran away from home. My parents wanted me to become a missionary with our church and they wouldn't listen to me when I told them that I had no intentions of doing such a thing. I wanted to travel outside of Tennessee, but they said that I could do that if I became a missionary. I tried to tell them that it wasn't the same thing and we got into a big fight about it.

"For the next six years, I traveled around the South doing odd jobs on farms and anywhere else that an extra hand was needed. I didn't make that much money, but I was given free room and board, so that was fine by me. After a while, I made my way up to New York and made better money selling trinkets on the street to tourists."

"What sorts of trinkets?"

"Stuff like books, horseshoes, medicines, candies, jewelry and kids' toys. As for my parents, my dad was a blacksmith and my mom was a Sunday school teacher. It was one of the few jobs that she could do with eight kids to look after at home."

"Is that why she was so insistent on you being a missionary?"

"Pretty much, yeah. Well, that and the fact that she grew up in a very strict religious family. She figured that since she was raised that way and turned out alright, that she'd try to do the same to me. I bet it'd really piss her off that I became a vampire," he grinned, probably relishing the thought of what his mother would think if she could see him now.

"Did you ever see your family again after you left home?" I asked.

"Yeah. When I got tired of traipsing around, I came back to Memphis and my parents welcomed me back with open arms. They were worried that I had died somewhere and forgot all about the fight we had. I was only back a short while before I was shot and turned into a vampire.

"Years later, I visited them to see how they were doing. What I mean by 'visited' is that I hid behind a bush and watched them without them ever knowing that I was there. I just wanted to make sure that they were okay."

"And were they?"

"My mom looked so haggard and frail like she was near death's door and my dad didn't look much better. They'd both seen better days. Watching them made me feel so guilty about having eternal life and never getting to age, even though I knew that it wasn't my fault that this happened to me," Chris said, his voice sounding wistful at the memory.

"Did you ever think of turning them?" I asked him, hoping that my question wasn't offensive.

"Yeah, but it really wouldn't have made much of a difference. They were too far gone for vampirism to really have had a benefit for them. Perhaps their health would've increased by a small fraction, but they would have looked frail and emaciated forever. If their minds were mostly gone, too, they'd also be stuck like that forever. I thought that it'd be much more humane to just let nature take its course. At least they had my brothers and sisters to take care of them, so it's not like I had left them all on their own."

"That's so sad, but I think that you made the right choice. I couldn't imagine killing my parents no matter how much they piss me off, especially if I had to see them live forever as shells of their former selves."

"I've told you about my parents, now I want to hear about yours," Chris said.

"There's not really much to tell. My mom is a dental assistant and my dad is a truck driver. We get along for the most part, but I haven't seen them for a few years. My dad has a pretty bad gambling problem and lost some money. I tried to help them out with paying the bills, but things kept getting worse and I'd finally had enough. The last straw was when their house was about to go into foreclosure because, even with my help, they couldn't keep up with the mortgage."

"How much debt were they in if you don't me asking?"

"I'm not sure of any exact numbers, but I think it was somewhere around $400,000 or maybe even more. I'd bet that it's a lot worse than that now," I said.

"Wow."

"Yeah. I hated leaving them high and dry like that, but if I didn't, they'd have dragged me down and my credit would have been all shot to hell. I've got a little collection of money going for them and I'll send it off eventually. It's nothing major—just a bunch of loose change that I'll cash in at the bank when I have enough."

"Sounds like you're a good daughter," he said, trying to sound sympathetic.

"Thanks."

"Do you have any other brothers or sisters to help out?"

"No, it's just me," I said.

"Oh," he said and then a silence fell over the room.

"Sorry to be such a Debbie Downer, but you asked about them."

"I'm not sure what that means."

"Never mind then. Do we have time to do it again before you have to go into hiding for the day?" I asked Chris and he checked his watch.

"No, sorry. I don't think I can even make it home safely as it is," he replied.

"You can stay here, then. I've got a basement and we can just make some adjustments." We went downstairs and I suggested that he stay in this room that a previous owner had used as an office. It bugged me that it had no windows, but that finally came in handy, so I guessed that I should be somewhat thankful to them.

"We still need to close up the rest of the basement," he said.

"I'll go out to the shed and see what I can find there. Be right back," I called out as I went up the stairs and out the door to the shed in the backyard. I hadn't used it much, so it was a big mess. I rummaged around for a few minutes until I found a couple of hammers, an unopened box of nails and a bunch of pieces of wood. The wood was in different sizes, but big enough that they would be of some use to us.

I walked back a bit more slowly, burdened by so much weight. It would have been almost comical how I dealt with trying to open the door, but I was in a rush and there'd be time to laugh later. Chris had obviously heard the racket I was making with the tools, because he appeared at the top of the stairs to lend me a hand. "Let me take those," he said as he took the wood from my arms.

We proceeded to board all of the windows and checked them multiple times to make sure that there were no cracks. Just to be extra safe, we also made sure that the curtains were drawn close. Once they had all passed inspection, Chris told me to "Have a good day and I'll see you tonight when you get home." In return, I wished him a "Good sleep" and shut the basement door behind me. When I got back upstairs, it dawned on me that I had to go to work later that day and I hadn't slept for what seemed like eons, so as soon as my head hit the pillow, I was out like a light.

Chapter 4

During the night, I had a crazy dream about Chris and I that was inspired by the passage that I'd read from. In it, he was staring at me with bloodthirsty eyes and his fangs were extended all the way, hungry for my taste. He slowly advanced on me like a lion approaches its weaker prey and before I knew it, he had pierced my skin and then I felt the hot rush of blood traveling down my skin. I moaned at the feeling it had evoked in me, pleasure and pain intermingling to overcome all of my senses in equal measure.

I woke up mid-morning on Monday feeling, not exactly refreshed, but like I could at least get through the day. I had a quick bite to eat and then rushed around getting my things together for work and then thought of Chris downstairs in the office room. I knew that he wouldn't be up for a while yet, but maybe I would leave him a note or something to do just in case he got up before I got home. I looked at the shelves in the living room and found a few books that I thought maybe he could read if the mood struck him. I also went though my DVD collection and put a few cases on the coffee table.

While I drove into the city, I popped a few CDs into the player of the car stereo and sang along. I probably looked like a complete dork to the other drivers, but I didn't give a shit. Singing along always put me in a good mood and I needed to be in one that day. It was time for the store's annual evaluation and there would be someone from the company's headquarters coming in for it. I knew exactly who it was that'd be doing the evaluation and they had always been such an asshole to me that I called her The Bitchinator. Thankfully, someone else had done it the year before for a change and they had been really nice. I couldn't remember what her name was, though. Bobbi? Betty? Barbara? It was something that started with a "b" anyway. We chatted and laughed like old friends and I passed with flying colors. I hoped that she would be back to do the evaluation again, but I couldn't help feeling that I wouldn't be that lucky.

Almost as soon as I walked into the employees' lounge, Natalie Johnson pounced on me. "Did you get laid last night?"

"Huh? What?" I said, caught off guard.

"You've got this glow about you today."

"I do not!" I protested and took out my pocket compact to check on myself in the mirror.

"Yeah, you do."

I glared at her. "How did you know I got laid?"

"I didn't until you told me just now. I lied about the glow thing," she beamed. I was busted so there was no sense in lying my way out of it. "So, who was it?"

"Someone that you don't know."

"Ooh! Do tell! When can I meet him?" Natalie's eyes lit up, anxiously awaiting some juicy gossip that I wasn't going to give to her.

"Not until I know for sure what's going on between us," I said nonchalantly.

"Oh, okay," her face fell. "Well, at least you've gotten over Hayden, haven't you?"

"Yeah."

"You're not regretting it, are you?"

"Of course not. I feel better than I've felt in a long time. It's like this weight has been lifted off of my shoulders and I'm seeing the world in a new light," I proclaimed, hoping that I didn't sound like some new-age hippie-type.

"That's good. You deserve someone who treats you right and this new guy does, doesn't he?" she asked.

"Yeah, in more ways than I can count." I didn't want to continue on down this road, so I changed topics. "Are you ready for the evaluation, Nat?"

"As ready as I ever am. Do you think The Bitchinator will go easy on you this time?"

"She never has before so why start now? I still have no idea what she has against me. Do you know if she's heard some nasty rumors about me?"

"Not that I can think of. Unless . . ." Natalie trailed off.

"Unless what?" I asked, taking a pause from putting on my makeup.

"You know Ashley Rogers in Housewares?"

"Yeah, what about her?"

"I've heard it through the grapevine that she's always had her eye on Hayden. I think that maybe it's *her* who's been talking shit about you to The Bitchinator. If she couldn't have your man, she was going to try to screw you out of your job. I could be completely wrong about this, but so far she's the only suspect."

"At least that's a starting point," I conceded.

"You know I've got your back. If I hear anything else, I'll let you know, 'k?"

"Great. Thanks."

"What'll you do if it *is* her?" Natalie asked me.

"Killing her with kindness is always a good way to go. I can also tell her that she's welcome to have Hayden's ass now. Maybe if she has him, all of this childish nonsense can stop. I just won't tell her about the crap that he pulled with me. I'll let her find out on her own and then she'll see that the grass isn't always greener on the other side," I replied.

"Maybe she'll beg you to take him back?"

"She can beg all she wants, but that doesn't mean that I'll give a damn."

"You're so catty! I like it!" Natalie exclaimed. "You should be that way more often." I mimicked a cat clawing at something invisible and we both laughed.

Throughout the day, I thought about this whole Ashley Rogers situation. I had never really had anything to do with her, come to think of it, I didn't remember ever actually talking to her other than an occasional "Hi" just to be friendly. She'd never let on that she was a jealous bitch, but I guessed that she was one of those people who fakes being nice to everyone. Well, two could play at that game.

I kept my eyes and ears open as much as I could, but nothing important came of it. The only things I learned about were how big a gossip someone's next-door neighbor was—Pot. Kettle. Black—you do the math—and how another customer's teenage son was currently in jail for the fourth time this year. I hoped that Natalie was having better luck, but even if she wasn't, there was always another day. I hoped that maybe someday soon someone would slip up and give us the info that we were looking for.

When I was done with my last customer of the day, I went to the employees' bathroom to wash my hands where Natalie caught up with me. I looked around the room to make sure that no one was listening in. "Any luck?"

"Not yet, sorry. Did you hear anything?"

"No."

"Maybe I should say something to her and kind of lead her into a trap," Natalie suggested.

"Like what?" I asked, curious about her plan.

"I'll ask her if there are any guys that she has her eye on or if she's already seeing someone. I could do it under the pretense of trying to fix her up with someone."

"That might work."

"For your sake, I really hope so," Natalie smiled.

"Do you have a mini voice recorder or an MP3 player with a mike on it?" I asked her.

"Yeah."

"Then bring that tomorrow and record her so that we'll have proof."

"Alright. See you tomorrow," Natalie said, giving me a quick, friendly hug.

"Bye!" I called out as she left the bathroom. I re-applied my lipstick, spritzed on some perfume, took one last look in the mirror, grabbed my bag and headed for home. Despite not having gotten the confession, I felt pretty good because I would be seeing Chris soon. On the drive home, I cranked up the stereo and sang at the top of my lungs so I was pretty happy when I walked into the house.

I put my things away in my room and tried to step as quietly as I could just in case the noise would have woken him up, despite the fact that there was still some light out. I ate my supper in front of the TV while I watched the news. All of the big stories were about some sort of tragedy: a mass shooting at a Memphis high school, earthquake in Los Angeles and a big car accident in New Orleans, which had backed up traffic on a freeway for miles around.

I was washing the dishes and putting them away when I felt a little shiver and I looked up to see Chris entering the kitchen. "Hi, Jessica," he greeted me before taking me into his arms for a kiss. "Did you miss me?"

"Of course, I did."

"How was work?"

"Same as usual; however, I did find out something interesting," I said.

"Like what?" he asked and I proceeded to tell him the whole story right up to the plan that Natalie and I had just concocted. "Good luck with that. I wish that I could go and help you out."

"Yeah, but then there's the whole trying-not-to-burst-into-flames-from-the-sun issue. We'll be fine, but thanks, anyway. Are you hungry? I know that vampires don't eat human food, but if you wanted some blood . . ."

"No, I'm good. If I hadn't taken from you last night, then I'd probably be starving now. I might have to feed again in another day or two, though."

"Oh, okay. I just wasn't keen on being around a hungry vampire. I mean, I don't know what you'd be like if you really needed to eat and I don't think I'm in a hurry to find out," I said.

"Do you want to have sex again?" he asked, perhaps a little too eagerly.

"I'm still spent from last night, to be honest. I could give you a little treat, though," I smiled, slyly.

"What kind of treat?" I took him by the hand and headed upstairs to my bedroom. When we got there, I sat him down on the bed and straddled him then I lifted up his shirt and began playing around with his nipples. At first, I licked them with my tongue and then gently pulled on them with my teeth. If it had hurt at all, Chris sure didn't show it. He closed his eyes, gritted his teeth and moaned quietly, but I wasn't done yet. Next, I slid my right hand down his pants, past his underwear and gripped his package. I gently massaged it, moving my hand back and forth along its length as far as his pants would allow me to go. Just as he was about to get hard, I let go of it and took my hand out of his pants. I knew that it was such a tease, but he certainly seemed to enjoy it—I even heard him panting like a dog.

"You liked that, eh?" I teased him.

When he finally caught his breath, he replied, "Yeah. I just wish we could've gone further."

"Maybe if you're a good little boy, I will next time."

"I'll hold you to that, you know."

"How about you hold me now?" I asked Chris, extending my arms towards him. When Chris had calmed down, he took me in his arms and we lay down together with my body leaning against his. My head rested on his chest like a pillow, although it wasn't nearly as comfortable as one. "I like this," I murmured.

"I do, too," he said, glancing down into my eyes and softly stroking my hair.

"Chris, what is it like being a vampire? It's probably a stupid thing to ask, I know, but I'm really curious."

"That's a huge question. That's like being asked 'What's it like to be human?'"

"Okay, fair enough, but you can't really blame me for trying," I smiled and paused for a beat. "This is going to sound really weird, I know, but can I feel your fangs?"

"What do you mean?" he asked.

"I want to see how sharp they are. Can I touch them with my fingers or with my tongue?"

"I'm not so sure that that's a good idea."

"Please? I just want to try to learn everything about what it's like to be you. I'm like a scientist and you're my research subject—you fascinate me. It's not everyday someone like me gets to meet a vampire."

"Alright, but just be careful. If I break a fang, it won't grow back for a while and it'll hurt a lot," he gave in.

"I'll be as gentle as possible, I promise." My right hand trembled ever so slightly as it neared Chris' face and, with one finger, I reached out and touched a fang. I let the finger trace the shape of the tooth, which felt just like his skin. I thought that it was so weird and cool all at the same time to be touching such a famous part of a vampire's anatomy. It had occurred to me in the moment that there was a very real possibility of being the only person in history who'd ever been allowed to have such close contact with an intimate part of a vampire like that.

As my finger traveled downwards, I pricked it on the razor-sharp point and Chris licked at the blood that had burbled up from the wound. The bit of bloodlust that he was experiencing quickly turned into regular lust as he looked up into my eyes again and kissed me hard, fangs still out. I let my tongue flick out and caress one of them, tasting him and the little bit of my blood that still lingered on it.

"What do you like about being a vampire?" I asked as I pulled away from him and we both tried to calm down again.

"Having super strength, speed, hearing and healing abilities is pretty sweet."

"That's kind of obvious, though. I mean, there must be more about it that you like."

"I guess I've never really thought about it before," he admitted. "I've been a vampire for so long, that it's pretty normal for me. I can't really remember what it was like to be human." There was a long pause before he spoke again. "Why do you want to know? Is this still part of your curiosity or do you want to become a vampire?"

"If I said 'yes', would you turn me into one?"

"That's not usually how it works, but I might be willing to make an exception for you if you really wanted it. I'd miss having sex with you, though."

"What do you mean? We could still do it if I was a vampire, couldn't we?" I asked, a little confused by his words.

"Yeah, but sex with a human is so much better, especially when you get to drink from them. Vampires tend to have a 'been there, done that' kind of attitude because they've been around the block a hundred times or more, whereas humans are more easily impressed and I don't mean that as a bad thing, by the way."

"How many humans have you ever had sex with?" As soon as I spoke the words, I wished I could take them back. Maybe I really didn't want to know the answer, but at the same time, I just couldn't help myself.

"Including you, about twelve, I think," he replied.

"How many vampires have you been with?"

"Less than that. I only hooked up with others when I was young and didn't really know better."

"Oh, I see," was all I could reply and then we lay there in silence until I fell asleep.

Hours later, I woke up to find a note lying on the bed next to me from Chris which said:

> *I had a nice night together, Jessica.*
> *If you're reading this, you'll know that*
> *I've left your house. I'm sorry that I*
> *didn't wake you up to say goodbye,*
> *but you looked so peaceful and I*
> *didn't want to disturb you. Call me later, 'k?*
> *My number is: 555-0818*
> *Much love,*
> *Chris S.*

"Much love"? What did *that* mean? Was he already in love with me? Was he just saying that to be polite? Was there some other hidden meaning? No! I decided right there and then that I wouldn't be one of those women who over-analyzed things to death. I didn't know what Chris meant by what he'd said, but I would just wait until he clarified himself or else ask him directly. Playing games and reading too much into things never got you anywhere good in my experience.

The next day passed by in a blur. The store had a big promotion on and I was practically run off of my feet. For most of the day, I had a massive line-up of women and even a few men, who I assumed were drag queens, waiting for me to work on them. I'd never seen the cosmetics counter so busy before, but I guess when you could get 50% off of anything in the store for only one day, people come out of the woodwork to take advantage.

During my brief, but well-deserved lunch break, I walked around the store and saw that all of the other departments were just as swamped as mine. I wondered if Natalie would still be able to do her detective work. She wasn't by herself in the Women's Wear department, so I figured that she could take a break from time to time as long as someone else was there to cover for her. Perhaps all of the chaos and confusion going on would even help her out when she finally got to confront Ashley or maybe that was just wishful thinking.

By the end of my shift, I was so tired that I had to splash my face with cold water in the bathroom just to stay awake for the drive home. When I arrived at the house in one piece, I crashed out on the couch, waking up a few hours later because I thought that I'd heard a creepy noise outside. I got up to push back the curtains and look out the kitchen window, but all I saw was a blurry silhouette and a flash of what I thought might have been brown hair.

I dialed Natalie's number and we chatted for a bit about the crazy day at work and she informed me that she hadn't been able to talk with Ashley yet. Damn. I didn't tell her about the mysterious noise and the retreating figure that I'd seen, because I wasn't even sure myself what or whom I'd seen or if I'd just been imagining the whole thing.

After I hung up on her, I thought about phoning Chris. It was dark enough now that he should be up. I didn't have the number memorized yet, so I went upstairs to retrieve the letter he had left me. I punched in the numbers, waited for the phone to connect and was pleased that he'd answered it after only one ring. "Hello?" he asked. "Who is this?" I wondered why he asked who was calling, but then it had occurred to me that perhaps he didn't recognize my phone number.

"Hi, Chris," I said. After such a hectic day, I was glad to hear his voice.

"Jessica? I see you read my note."

"Yeah."

"I'm still sorry that I didn't wake you up to say goodbye."

"That's alright," I tried to reassure him.

"What's up?" he asked.

"I just wanted to see how you were doing."

"I'm fine, thanks, but now isn't the best time to talk. I'm going out in a bit."

"Oh," I said, slightly crestfallen. Although I had been pretty tired, it would've been nice to get to spend at least an hour with my new boyfriend.

"It's just some vampire business."

"What for? On second thought, I probably shouldn't pry. You don't have to tell me if you don't want to."

"I will tell you, just not yet," he said.

"Then when?"

"Are you busy tomorrow night?"

"No," I replied.

"I'll come by your place around eight, is that alright?"

"Sure."

"I've got to go now, Jessica, but I'm glad that you called. I'll talk to you again soon."

"Bye, Chris." I hung up the phone, slowly made my way up the stairs and collapsed into my warm bed. "*What can't he tell me yet?*" I thought to myself. "*Is he in trouble? Am I in trouble?*" I couldn't help wondering if he was plotting to kill me after all and he was going to gather up a bunch of his vampire buddies to help. He could have been the world's greatest actor and faked his feelings for me, for all I knew. I hated that he was keeping this secret even though I would eventually find out whatever it was, but until he told me about it, I would end up making myself sick with worry.

Wednesday started off with a lot of promise. Natalie and I had planned to double our efforts in tripping up Ashley by having each of us bring in something to record her confessions. Instead of going to the deli for lunch, I decided to brown bag it and see if I could score the big opportunity in the break room. I was also pretty well-rested, which would come in handy. Dating a vampire doesn't exactly make for a good sleep schedule, so not being able to see him the night before had been a blessing in disguise.

By the time that I arrived at work, Natalie was waiting for me in the employees' lounge with a huge smile on her face. "What's up?" I asked her.

"Oh my gosh! I've got great news!" she exclaimed as I was putting away my bag and coat in my locker.

"You *didn't!*"

"I did!"

"*How?*"

"I bumped into her doing that accidentally-on-purpose thing, then I apologized to her and said that I hadn't talked to her for a while and wanted to catch up. One thing led to another and I got her on tape. Listen." Natalie played the recording for me and my mouth fell open in shock.

"We've got her right where we want her. Thanks a bunch, Nat," I said, a mischievous grin on my face. I had the temptation to rub my hands together like a villain does when they have a great idea for an evil plot, but then thought that would be too cheesy.

"What are you going to do now?" she asked me with the wide smile still pasted on her face.

"I'll confront her at lunch. May I borrow your recorder? I'd love to see the expression on her face when the audio plays back."

"Yeah, but just be careful with it, okay?" Natalie said as she handed the device over to me and I put it in my locker underneath my coat.

"Of course."

"I'll see if I can get a break in a few hours. I don't want to miss this."

"See you later," I called out to her as I headed into the store.

I was just as nervous about the upcoming event as I was about my first date with Chris, if you could believe it. I tried to put it out of my mind and focus on the woman in front of me who came in decked out in clown makeup. She wasn't literally dressed up like a clown, but her face looked so caked on that she may as well have had big, floppy shoes and a red ball for a nose to complete the ensemble. Did she even own a mirror? It would be one hell of a mess to clean up, but I was thankful to have something to occupy my mind for the time being.

After the clown woman had left, I had a bit of downtime before the next customer came to the counter. It was looking like the day was going to be a lot slower than the previous one had been, which was fine by me. I thought that the more energy I could conserve, the better, because I had no idea how this thing with Ashley would turn out. Would we fight or would it just be a shouting match? I had no desire to get physical with anyone except for Chris, so hopefully it would be the latter option.

Thinking of Chris, I wondered again what his secret was although he sounded so vague about it. Should I prepare for the worst? I didn't really have anything to go on and so my mind came up with all sorts of horrible possibilities. Perhaps someone would order him to kill me once and for all or maybe Chris himself would be condemned to death and he'll tell me that we would be spending our last nights together.

At 1 o'clock, I left for my lunch break. I headed to my locker to get my food first and slipped the recorder in my pocket without anyone noticing, then went into the break room. To my dismay and relief, Ashley wasn't there, but Natalie was. "Is she coming?" I whispered to her.

"Yeah. Are you ready?"

"Not really."

"You'll be fine, and like I've said before, I've got your back," she said and I unwrapped my egg salad sandwich. I had eaten half of it when Ashley burst through the door, followed by a few other women that I wasn't very familiar with. "Let's get ready to rumble!" Natalie whispered to me and I gulped. I had hoped to finish my food before we got started, but at the same time, I just wanted it all to be finally over with.

"Hey, Jessica. What are you doing eating *here*?" Ashley asked me in a snooty tone of voice that reminded me of those stereotypical sorority sister characters in movies.

"Actually, I've got some business to sort out with you."

"What sort of business?"

"This," I said as I took out the recorder and then pressed the playback button. All of a sudden, the room was silent as the recording of Ashley's voice was heard. *"No, I'm not seeing anyone right now, but yeah, I do have my eye on someone. It's no secret that I like Hayden van Austen nor is it a secret that I think that Jessica doesn't deserve him. A man like that needs to be with someone who's got class and style and someone who's his equal—like me. Besides, we'd look better together."* I clicked off the recorder and tossed it to Natalie, who caught it with a smug look on her face.

Ashley's eyes flared red with anger. "How dare you record me without my knowledge!" she shouted.

"How dare I? *How dare I?*" I snarled. "You're the one who just admitted that you wanted my boyfriend. You didn't say it, but you practically implied that you'd steal him, too. You bitch!"

"Don't call me a bitch, you slut!" she shot back. I can take being called all sorts of things, but when she yelled out the "s word" that really set me off. I swung at her head with my right fist, but I missed and my hand connected with the wall. It stung like a mother, but I didn't care. The rage that I felt gave me a huge rush of adrenaline and almost nothing would stop me until I got my revenge on Ashley. She laughed at my missed shot, but I vowed that I wouldn't make the same mistake again.

I hit her again with my left fist and it connected with her jaw. I couldn't be sure, but I thought I'd heard the sound of a bone breaking and I hoped that it was on her end. She rubbed the spot with both of her hands and glared at me with pure hatred in her eyes. In retaliation, she grabbed my hair by the roots and pulled so hard that I thought she was going to rip it out, then she kicked me in the groin and I nearly doubled over in pain. It hurt more than when Chris bit me and sucked my blood, but at least I could take comfort in the fact that Ashley nearly broke her heel in the effort.

After a few more punches were thrown by each of us, I was dragged away from Ashley by Natalie. She tried with all of her might to restrain me from doing any further damage and I could see that Ashley was also being restrained by one of the women that I didn't know. I had no idea what I looked like, but I was sure that I was in better shape than Ashley. She had the beginning of a bruise on her jaw, a few more fresh bruises elsewhere on her face and blood was trickling out of her nose.

"That's enough!" Nikki Stevens called out. I didn't really know anything about her except that she worked in Children's Wear and she associated herself with Ashley, which didn't exactly put her in my good books.

"Yeah, Jessica!" Ashley snarled. "You better cover up the mess you made on my face, *Miss Makeup Expert.*"

"Why? Your mom was the one that made it in the first place when she gave birth to you! Go and ask *her* for help!" I shouted. Everyone in the room gasped and let out a chorus of "ooh"s when I said that. Natalie did one better and cried out an "Oh snap!" while giving me a high-five.

"I demand you apologize to me right now!" Ashley exclaimed.

"Why should I?" I asked her.

"Well, there's the fact that you just beat the crap out of me for no good reason."

"I thought I had a pretty damn good reason. You were going to try to steal Hayden from me."

"No, I wasn't. *She* was." Ashley pointed to Nikki who was standing near the door to the break room.

"Why should I believe you? I've just heard your recorded confession."

"I'm not going to lie, yeah, it makes me sound guilty, but I'll show you some proof." Ashley walked over to the locker that she shared with Nikki, opened it and rifled through a bunch of books before handing me a plastic folder. Inside of it, there were pages of notations and photographs of Hayden by himself and some of him with me, except that my head had been cut out of the picture. I scanned through the information quickly and my jaw dropped. I couldn't believe what I was seeing. Among the notations were various plans to try to break us up and ruin my life like some sort of real-life version of *Mean Girls*.

"I can't believe I'm saying this, but I'm sorry, Ashley," I said, pouring as much sincerity as I could into my words. "I feel terrible now."

"You should be and I hope that you're going to kick her ass, too."

"I think that I've done enough of that for one day. I probably wouldn't have the strength to do it, anyway, but Natalie's welcome to give it a try on my behalf if she wants," I said, turning towards my best friend.

"Thanks for the offer, Jessi, but you know I'm not really the fighting type." Without warning, Natalie grabbed Nikki by the shoulders and asked me, "What are you going to do with *her*?"

"Follow me," I said, still clutching the folder of evidence. Natalie trailed along behind me, dragging Nikki as best as she could. I went to the main office of the store to confront The Bitchinator and forced Nikki to confess to what she did to me. The Bitchinator listened intently at the whole story, then reprimanded Nikki for her deplorable behavior and apologized to me for everything that I'd gone through over the years. Hallelujah, the nightmare was finally over and the good guy had won! For the rest of the day, gossip spread around the store as everyone discussed what had unfolded in the break room and even some of the customers came up to me to ask for my account of the story.

When my shift was over, I was incredibly relieved and I felt like I'd been to hell and back, but I'd survived and come out victorious. I had covered up the bruises on my face with foundation and a bit of blush right after the scene in the office and I touched it up again before I left to go home. It wasn't a perfect job, but if you didn't look too closely, you couldn't really tell what had happened. On my way home, I picked up a burger and fries from a drive-thru, because I was in the mood to treat myself instead of cooking at home.

After supper, I went online to check on my e-mails and then I read some of this romance novel that I had started a few days before. It was one of those cheesy Harlequin books featuring some handsome guy on the cover with an equally gorgeous woman who looked like they were about to rip each other's clothes off. Normally, I didn't read this sort of books, but I picked some up at a library book sale for fifty cents each, so I thought *"What the hell? Why not?"* I was always up for a laugh and in case you were wondering, the book was about this guy who posed as a soldier in order to sleep with a bunch of women. He'd tell them lies about being shipped out the next day and not knowing if he was going to come back alive so that they'd feel pity for him. It worked until he found this woman that made him want to change the error of his ways because she was the love of his life. It was complete bullshit, but it was entertaining bullshit.

Promptly at eight, Chris knocked on my back door. "Come on in!" I called out and he entered the house.

"Jessi! How are you?" He hugged me and I gladly returned the gesture.

"Better, now that you're here."

"How was work?" he asked.

"It was a crazy day. You know that situation that I told you about before?"

"With that co-worker?"

"Yeah. My friend recorded her admitting stuff about how she wanted my ex and thought that I didn't deserve him, so it seemed obvious that she was the one who was talking trash about me, right?" Chris nodded in agreement and I continued on with the story. "Well, we got into this big fight in the break room and she tells me that she's innocent. As it turns out, this other woman at the store was the one who was talking behind my back. She had a bunch of papers in her locker with all of these plans and ideas written down and I showed them to The Bitchinator. I guess that I should probably stop calling her that now," I chuckled to myself.

"Why did she leave evidence in her locker? That was a really amateur move," he said.

"Honestly, I don't know and I don't really care. Maybe she never thought she'd be ratted out or maybe she's just plain stupid and careless. Either way, she got what she deserved and all I give a damn about is that this whole ordeal is over and done with."

"You actually got into a fight?"

"Yeah. Is that so hard to believe?"

"I don't know. You just don't really seem to me like the type to do that sort of thing," Chris replied, subtly sizing me up.

"This was the first time," I admitted.

"What did you do?"

"It didn't start off very well. I aimed at her head and missed so my fist hit a wall."

"Ouch!"

"Yeah. She pulled my hair and kicked me, but I got in some pretty good punches."

"That's my girl!" he smiled.

"She was pretty bruised up and I think I may have broken her jaw. I shouldn't be pleased with myself for doing what I did, but I kind of am. I was actually pretty bad-ass if I do say so myself."

"How badly were you hurt?"

"I'm sore around my stomach, but my face took the most beating," I replied.

"It doesn't look bad to me," he said.

"That's because I slathered on a bunch of foundation to cover it up. If you really want to see the damage, I'll wipe it off."

"Yes, please." I went to the bathroom and came back momentarily, in all my glory. "You're beautiful," he whispered.

"Even with all of the purple and blue marks?" I asked dubiously.

"Yes."

"Are you just saying that so that I'll keep sleeping with you and giving you my blood?"

"No. Well, okay, maybe a little," Chris grinned. "I get that you have to wear makeup to go to work, but when you're with me you don't need all of that. I like you just the way you are—bruises and all. Besides, those are like your badges of honor and you should show them off. This face," he gripped it gently, "says '*I'm a bad-ass and you shouldn't mess with me.*' I'm really proud of you, Jessi."

"Hey!"

"What?"

"I just realized that tonight is the first time that you've called me Jessi."

"Is it?" he thought for a bit. "Yeah, I guess you're right."

"Remember how I said that only my friends call me that? Do you consider us friends now or are we more than that?" I asked him.

"Well, do you have sex with all of your friends?"

"No," I chuckled.

"Then there's your answer."

"So," I wrapped my arms around his muscular chest, "can I officially call you my boyfriend now?"

"If it makes you happy, then yeah."

"Will you call me your girlfriend?"

"Of course," he replied.

"Then let's celebrate."

"Alright, but first, I have something for you." Chris reached into a pocket of his jacket and took out a small box from some jewelry store. He handed it to me, gently placing it in my right hand and I opened it to find a gorgeous, diamond tennis bracelet.

"It's beautiful," I said, awestruck by the extravagant gift.

"Not as beautiful as you."

"What's this for?"

"I saw it in a store and thought of you," he said, shrugging.

"How sweet are *you*?" I asked, my face beaming at the sight of my new bauble.

"I also thought that it might help cushion the blow that I'm about to deliver."

"Just lay it on me. I'm a big girl, I can take it," I said, placing the bracelet back in its box.

"Alright, here goes. Do you remember the nightclub I took you to on our second date?" he asked me.

"How could I forget?" My mind briefly flashed back to the image of the club filled with vampires and a select group of their human toys who probably ended up tossed somewhere like trash when the novelty of their company had finally worn off. The club itself was nice on the inside, but being in the midst of so many monsters was completely unnerving.

"Well, last night I found out that some vamps who were there have reported us to the Council and now we're in deep shit."

"What are you talking about? What's *the Council*?"

"The Council of the Night is like this vampire court. They punish vamps that do things they shouldn't and now they're after us because I haven't killed you yet. We never should have gone to that club. I knew that we were taking a big risk, well, that *I* was taking a big risk, but I just wanted to show you a good time. Do you remember seeing any vamps checking you out?"

"Yeah. I thought that was just a normal thing, though, like an animal sizing up its prey," I admitted.

"Most of them were probably doing that, but some of them took it upon themselves to use their observations to tattle on me. I wish I knew who did it." Chris bit his lower lip and I watched a few spots of blood appear. His tongue flicked out and he licked at them.

"Did you eat recently?"

"Yeah, I went hunting last night. Why?"

"Looking at the blood on your lip just made me wonder. You said the other day that you were going to feed," I said.

"I'm fine for a few more days."

"Good." I paused for a few moments. "What's going to happen now?"

"I'll understand it if you don't want to be with me anymore."

I put my hands on his shoulders and looked deeply into his eyes, trying to reassure him. "Chris, I think that I love you. Whatever happens, we'll get through it together even if it ends up being the two of us against the world."

"The Council is going to send assassins to kill you. We won't know when, where or how many, but they'll keep sending them until the job is done." Despite the matter-of-fact way that he spoke, it pained me to see the look of despair written on his face. "I wish that I could turn back time, Jessi. I would never have taken you to the club if I'd known that this was going to be the result," he said, gently placing his arms around me in an awkward embrace.

"I don't want to die like this," I whispered against his chest. "What happened wasn't my fault and I don't deserve to be punished for it." Without warning, a few silent tears escaped from my eyes and Chris lightly touched my cheeks to wipe them away. "*Could this really be happening to me?*" I thought to myself. "*Why am I being punished for something that I had no control over? What did I ever do to deserve this? How am I going to be killed and will Chris be forced to watch it? I don't think I could bear watching the pain on his face if I die first.*"

"I know, Jessi. I know that you don't deserve it. *I'm* the one who messed up and *I'm* the only one they should be going after."

I gathered up as much courage as I could and tore myself from his arms to look up into his face. "What will happen to you?" I asked him in a voice so soft that I almost couldn't hear myself speak.

"I've heard of vamps that have had their fangs ripped off, so that's a possibility. I've also heard of some that have been kept chained up in cages and gotten badly burned by the sun."

"Did they die?" I asked, horrified. I didn't want to picture Chris meeting this sort of fate, but the unbidden images managed to squeeze their way into my consciousness and I felt more tears forming. When I saw the final image of Chris becoming nothing but a pile of ash, the dam broke and I was awash in a sea of them. He held me close until I'd calmed down enough to listen to him answer my question.

"No. They'd have been burned until their skin bubbled and began to melt, then they'd have been protected and start to heal. The next day, they'd have been burned and made to heal again and it would go on for several days or whenever the Council would get bored of it. At that point, the vampire would most likely meet their final death and probably even be glad for it."

"What does it feel like to burn in the sun?"

"I've never had it happen to me, thankfully. From what I've heard, though, it's sheer torture if you burn long enough. You feel like you'd claw off your own skin just to get away from the pain of it."

"Oh my god!" I clapped my hand to my mouth in horror.

"Vampires can heal quickly, but not even our powers can completely cure that sort of treatment. Vamps who are tortured that way often have horrible scarring on their bodies and faces, especially their faces."

"How can I protect myself from these assassins? You can't always be around to be my bodyguard."

"Well, you seem to be able to hold your own in a fight," he replied.

"Yeah, but there's a huge difference between fighting a human who's almost your equal and fighting a vampire. I couldn't fight you off when you tried to attack me. I mean, I tried, but you were much too strong for me."

"That's true. We'll figure something out, baby. For now, though, can we please just make love?"

"That's a plan that I can definitely get behind," I said with a half-smile on my face.

Chapter 5

A few hours later, I was incredibly sore, but very satisfied. This second attempt at vampire/human sex was much better, because not only did I know what to expect, but Chris also had more energy thanks to his very recent meal. As I lay in my bed with Chris nuzzling into my side, I thought that a performance like that deserved to be followed up by a relaxing cigarette although I didn't smoke. Maybe something else would suffice?

This time around, Chris' hands found their way into certain parts of my body that had never been touched that way before and I certainly let him know how much I loved the way that he was making me feel and that was just his warm up! For the big show, he writhed around on top of me and kept thrusting so hard that I thought the bed would collapse from under us. I kept commanding him to go faster and deeper and he never hesitated to obey me. There were times when our bodies were so entangled that I wasn't sure where I ended and he began. I was wrong about the drive-thru food—*this* was my real treat and I enjoyed every last second of it.

The both of us sweated up a storm and by the end of it, I felt all of my troubles melt away. I didn't remember anything about the work week; I just knew about the pleasure that my body and mind had experienced. Vampire sex was everything that Chris had said it would be and more. I was secretly glad that he'd had so much practice over the years, because I'd been the one to reap all of the benefits.

"Oh my god, that was spectacular!" I exclaimed as I ran my fingers through Chris' tousled hair.

"Better than the first time?"

"Definitely. I mean, that was pretty good, but this was phenomenal."

"I know I didn't bring my A-game the first time, so I figured that I'd make it up to you now," he grinned.

"And you certainly did." A moment passed while I thought of what to say next. "Chris?"

"Yeah?"

"What if you lived here?"

"What do you mean?" he asked, turning over on his side to face me.

"If we're going to be serious with each other, maybe we should live together so that you don't have to travel back and forth from the city to Hollingsford to visit me. If that's too big a decision to make, maybe we could just live together part-time. You could live here from Friday to Monday and live at your place the rest of the time or something."

"I'll think about it," he said and I had the distinct feeling that he was already considering my offer.

"If you don't want to do it, I won't be offended. I just thought it'd be a bit easier for you. At least this way, you don't have to rush off to get home before dawn and we can make the office downstairs more comfy for you if you want," I reasoned.

"I suppose that I could start bottling up some blood to keep in your refrigerator so that I don't always have to run off to eat. You wouldn't mind, would you?"

"Do what you gotta do, Chris, but just don't ever tell me how you got it, 'k?"

"It's a deal." He smiled back at me, fangs bared and we shook hands. The closest that I'd ever come to living with Hayden was when I stayed over at his place after a party and I was too wasted to drive, but I was absolutely head-over-heels for Chris. Everything in my body was screaming that this was a great idea—although that could just have been the after effects of the great sex we'd just had. In any case, he made me feel things that I'd never felt before and I knew deep down in my gut that he was the one for me and that I'd do just about anything for him. Being away from him for more than a day made my heart ache badly, so to have him in my house would be just what the doctor ordered.

For the rest of the week, whenever I didn't have any customers, I spent my free time thinking of my offer to Chris. What would it be like to live with a vampire? Would I have to change the way I live during the day so that I wouldn't bother him while he slept? Would he ever invite his vampire friends over to hang out? I also thought about how we could decorate his new room. On my lunch breaks, I did a little browsing around to try to get some ideas and scribbled a few things down on a notepad to show him later. I also noticed that Ashley and her group of friends were somewhat more hostile towards me. It wasn't to the point of making threats, but rather they would look down on me as if I was the dog poop on the bottom of their shoes.

On Friday night, I called up Chris and told him about the ideas that I'd been gathering. "Wow! You're working pretty fast, aren't you?"

"I'm excited about you living with me, so sue me!" I joked. "When are you coming over?"

"I can be there in about twenty minutes."

"Great. See you then, baby."

"Jessi?" he asked.

"What?"

"I love you."

"I love you, too, Chris," I said and then hung up the phone and sighed. If someone had told me a year or even a few months before that I'd be falling in love with a vampire, I'd have asked them what kind of drugs they were on. It was funny how life took you in directions that you'd never expected, but I wouldn't have traded being with Chris for anything else in the world. Ever since he'd come into my life, it'd gotten a hell of a lot more interesting, that's for sure.

Chris scooped me up in his muscular arms and kissed me with a fervor when he entered the house a while later. He was such a good kisser that I sometimes forgot he wasn't human and that was definitely one of those times. His lips were surprisingly soft and smooth and he used them to great effect. He put me back down onto the floor and my heart beat uncontrollably. "That was some entrance!" I exclaimed.

"I aim to please," he smiled.

"You'll get no arguments from me."

"Can I ask you for a favor?"

"Sure. What do you need?" I asked.

"I've got a lot of stuff to bring over and it can't all fit in my car. Would you be able to go into the city tomorrow and pick some of it up? I've already taken the liberty of putting it in the living room so you'll know what to take," Chris replied.

"How much is there?"

"About five boxes and a few other things."

"I'll see what I can do. Between the backseat and the trunk, it should work out nicely," I said. "If it doesn't, I guess I'll be making two trips."

"Thanks a lot."

"I was going to go into the city anyway to see about buying some fabric and stuff for your room."

"About that . . ." he trailed off.

"What?"

"I came up with some ideas of my own," he said.

"I'm listening," I said.

"Maybe we could do the room in colors like: black, red, white, blue and green. I definitely don't want anything girly either like flowers and hearts."

I took my notepad out of my pocket and wrote that down. "Oh darn! And I found the cutest fabric, too! It had daisies and rainbows on it!" I joked.

"If you got me that, I'd have to bite you," Chris mock-threatened.

"I already let you bite me, so that's not really much of a threat," I laughed.

"I guess not," he agreed.

"It's kind of weird how we're rushing into things. I mean, it was only a few weeks ago that we met and now you're going to move in."

"Is this too fast for you? We don't have to do this."

"Oh, I know. I'm just thinking about how quickly everything's changing and I like it. I also think it's pretty weird to be decorating and planning a life with a vampire," I chuckled to myself and hung my head as I reflected on my strange predicament.

"You just bring out a different side of me, the way that I do to you. I like feeling human the way that I do when I'm with you even though I never thought I would," he said.

"But it goes without saying that you still like being a vampire."

"Of course, but I feel like I have the best of both worlds now."

"Alright, I think that's enough lovey-dovey crap for today," I proclaimed.

"You should work for Hallmark with an attitude like that," Chris joked and I playfully shoved him in the ribs.

"Ha ha, very funny."

"I thought so."

"Getting back to the fabric—obviously I wouldn't buy something with flowers on it for you. You don't exactly strike me as that kind of guy. I don't think I'd even buy that for myself."

"So what *would* you buy for me?" he asked, enjoying putting me on the spot.

I looked Chris up and down and thought for a few moments. "Solid colors are a pretty safe bet, but maybe I'd also go with stripes or some other masculine design—nothing too bold or busy."

"That sounds good."

"What would you buy for *me* if you had to?" I challenged him.

"Something very feminine like pink or purple or maybe a nice, sexy red. For a design, maybe something with hearts, stars or cats."

"Nice choices," I said, impressed by his good taste. "Although I'm not sure how you figured out that I'm a cat fan. You must be a really good guesser."

"I'm just good at studying humans, well, that and I've done some snooping around in your room when you weren't looking," he grinned, looking like a cheeky little boy. I playfully swatted him on the arm to scold him, but it only made him laugh harder. "I've also noticed that you seem to have a fondness for red: the tank top you wore on our first date and then the dress and shoes from our second," Chris remarked when he had calmed down.

"Yeah. I'm not saying that it's my *favorite*, but it's nice to wear sometimes. It's such a fiery color and it makes me feel really attractive."

"It mostly reminds me of blood," he said.

"Yeah, I guess it would." A silence fell over the room as we let that idea sink in. "Chris, I love you so much, but I'm not really comfortable with blood talk. It kind of creeps me out a bit."

"I'm sorry."

"It's not really your fault. It's just going to take a while to get used to everything. I shouldn't stop you from behaving in a way that's natural to you," I tried to reassure him.

"If it really gets to be too much for you, don't hesitate to let me know."

"Thanks, I will."

"I don't want to make you feel uncomfortable in your own home," he said.

"You can think of it as *our* home now, you know."

"Now *that* will take a while for me to get used to."

"Speaking of our home, let's take a look at what we can change to make it something that you can be comfortable with," I suggested. We toured the house, pointing out various pieces of furniture that would need to be re-upholstered, rooms that needed to be re-painted and items that could go in storage and replaced with Chris' belongings. Afterwards, we parked ourselves on the living room couch and watched a few romantic comedies while I snuggled up to him.

I woke up on Saturday morning alone on the couch with a slightly sore back, which I hoped would ease up before I left to go to Munroeville. If it didn't get better, I knew that I would have a hell of a time helping to move Chris' stuff. Just then, I remembered that he hadn't actually told me where his apartment was or given me a key to get in. "*Oh great, just great,*" I thought to myself. I looked around the living room to see if he'd left something there, but no such luck. I went into the kitchen and there, on the dining table, was the info and key that I needed, hand-written on one of the scrap pieces of paper that I kept by the phone in case I had to quickly jot down a number. Although Chris' writing was so beautiful, it took me a little while to decipher it.

I threw on an old pair of blue jeans, a plain black t-shirt and black sneakers and then made myself some toast with a glass of milk. After I'd finished eating, I shoved my keys, Chris' key, his note, my wallet and the list of things to buy for the house into my handbag. When I got into my car, I turned the key in the ignition and it made a weird wheezing sort of noise. It wouldn't turn over properly and so I started freaking out. "This can't happen today!" I muttered to myself. "I've got errands to run, dammit!" Summoning up all of my power, I took a deep breath and counted to twenty, then turned the key again. This time, the engine roared to life and I cheered, and then put the car into gear before it could change its mind.

Over half an hour and a few wrong turns later, I found Chris' apartment building. It looked kind of derelict from the outside and was located in a pretty bad area of town, but then that wasn't much of a problem for Chris. He didn't really have to worry about being attacked by human thugs, but if by some small chance he ever did find himself in a bad situation like that, he could easily take care of himself. I, on the other hand, tried to be extremely wary of my surroundings, especially since the area looked like prime ground for the assassins who were supposed to have been after me. The dark alleys were darker than usual and there was way too much space on the sidewalks that was shrouded in shadows. The assassins could have hidden themselves well and there would be no way to know that they were there until it was too late.

I took another deep breath, put the anti-theft device on the steering wheel, locked the car and hauled ass into the apartment building as fast as I could. The suite was just a couple of floors up, so I hoped that it wouldn't take very long for me to get the boxes loaded into the car. The best way to describe the place was a "hole in the wall". It was big enough for just one occupant and not much else. Light layers of dust coated the wood floors, the rug in the middle of the living room was threadbare and small holes punctuated the walls.

I grabbed the top three boxes on the pile that Chris had made and steadily went down the stairs to the car, putting the first batch into the trunk. When I ran back upstairs to fetch the rest of the boxes, I briefly considered doing a little snooping around, but thought better of it. I didn't really want to spend any more time here than was absolutely necessary; also, I thought that perhaps he would have been able to smell his things and tell that I'd been looking through them without his permission. Instead, I picked up the remaining boxes, locked the door behind me, went back down the stairs and fit the packages into the backseat. When I started up the car and left the area behind, I relaxed a bit. I would have bet anything that Chris wasn't sorry to leave this place behind to come and live with me.

I spent the next few hours browsing around a few stores, trying to find some new furniture, bolts of fabric and wallpaper. After searching through countless designs, I found a few that would be perfect for what I had in mind. Since I couldn't bring home the furniture that I'd picked out, I arranged to have it delivered to the house. Satisfied with my purchases, I headed over to STARS to use my employee discount on some new lingerie and perfume and have a chat with Natalie since I was going to have a few days off early in the week and wouldn't be seeing her for a little while.

By the time that I had left the store, it was already past four in the afternoon and I was pretty hungry from doing so much shopping. I went to a drive-thru to pick up some greasy junk food and then parked in the lot of a nearby gas station to eat. I was in the middle of eating my burger when another car pulled up several feet away and the driver looked over at me. I was kind of embarrassed to be caught eating like that, but I gave a friendly smile and wave to sort of apologize. Although I wasn't done yet, I took off as fast as I could before I attracted other spectators and decided to try to eat on the way home while I drove.

I pulled into my driveway and wished that Chris was up so that he could help me take the boxes and bags in, but he wouldn't have been awake for at least another few hours. The sun was still pretty high overhead and blazing against my skin. I was glad that I had worn a light tank-top and shorts and slathered on some sunscreen before I left the house, although I was sure that the lotion had worn off during the afternoon.

It took a few trips, but I eventually got everything inside the house. I carefully placed the boxes on the living room floor, put the wallpaper and fabric on one of the armchairs and took

Jennifer Green

my other goodies up to my bedroom. I couldn't wait to see the look on Chris' face when he saw me in my new duds. I probably spent more than I should have, but I knew that it would be worth it in the end.

I decided to read my romance novel until he arose and was so absorbed in it that I didn't even notice him come into my bedroom. "Gah!" I screamed and dropped my book on the floor.

Chris picked it up and handed it to me. "I'm sorry, Jessi. I didn't mean to startle you."

"That's okay. Just give me a moment to let my heart fall back out of my throat and into its proper place."

"Is it a good book?" he nodded, indicating the novel.

"It's alright."

"It must be better than just 'alright'. You seemed pretty into it."

"How long were you standing in the doorway?" I asked him, sounding a little accusatory.

"About a minute or so."

"Oh."

"Did you have a good day?"

"It was fine."

"It looks like you did a fair bit of shopping," he glanced at the bags on the bed behind me and I quickly shoved them under. I hadn't wanted him to see my new purchases just yet. I intended to put them away before he got up, but I didn't notice how much time had passed while I was reading.

"Yeah," I replied.

"What was *that* about?"

"Just a surprise for you."

"Will I like it?"

"I can guarantee that you will," I grinned. "I bought some other stuff that I left down in the living room." I led Chris down the stairs and showed him the rest of my purchases. He glanced at it all with an expression that I couldn't quite decode. I think it might have been a mixture of wonderment, curiosity and pleasure, but then again, I could have misinterpreted it.

"Wow."

"And that's not all. I ordered a bedroom set that'll be delivered tomorrow. It's black with silver trim and comes with a bed, dresser and night table."

"Thank you very much. How much do I owe you?" Chris asked as he reached into his pants pocket and got out his checkbook and a pen. He waited for me to answer, the pen in his right hand poised and ready to write down a figure.

"$500," I replied. "I got a really great deal on it."

"Alright." He scribbled it down, ripped off the check and handed it to me.

"Thanks." I looked down at it and thought of how he had written it out without hesitation and of the incredibly expensive car that he drove. "If you don't mind me asking, how did you get to be so rich?"

"I did my fair share of stealing from victims and a few other unsavory activities, but I made most of my money legally by investing."

"In what?"

"Stocks, bonds, T-bills, you name it. Over the years, I've dipped my fingers into a lot of pies. I made some investments that others considered to be pretty risky and I even got laughed at for making them, but that didn't stop me and look who's laughing now!" he exclaimed, giving a chuckle for emphasis.

"So, how much money are you worth?" I asked, curiosity getting the better of me.

"Why? Are you planning on killing me for my fortune?" he half-joked.

I laughed, "Of course not! I just want to know how much money I can look forward to spending on our wedding!"

"*Wedding*?" Chris looked stricken at the mere mention of the word.

"I'm kidding, baby."

"Oh," he said, visibly relaxing.

"Seriously, though, how much are we talking about here?"

"Around $7 million."

"Wow!" I exclaimed.

"How much was your ex worth?"

"Several times more than that, but I didn't care. Money isn't the be-all and end-all. I've learned that the hard way."

"Were you ever going to marry him?" Chris asked, curiosity finally striking him.

"He hadn't asked, but I thought about it. Anyway, just forget about him. The only thing that matters is that I'm with *you* now. Besides, there are two things that Hayden doesn't have: me and a vampire that treats him like a queen."

"You think that I treat you like a queen?"

"Most definitely," I smiled, looking up into Chris' eyes. All of a sudden, he bent down to kiss me and I gave in to the moment, feeling a surge of desire as our lips pressed tightly together.

"What about that surprise for me?" he asked when we had finally parted lips.

"I'm saving it for tomorrow when your new bed arrives. We'll christen it in style."

"I can't wait."

"What are we going to do with all of this stuff?" I asked. "I wouldn't know where to begin."

Chris looked at the collection and I could tell that he was deep in thought. If he had been a cartoon character, I would've been able to see the gears grinding inside his head. "I've got a few ideas."

He scooped up some wallpaper and ordered me to go out to the shed for supplies, and then when I returned, we went downstairs and began to work. I offered the occasional advice, but Chris mostly ran the show. We worked as a great team, although there had been a few mishaps. By the time I was ready to retire for the night, we had moved most of the furniture out of the room and put up wallpaper on two walls.

In the morning, I crept downstairs as quiet as a mouse to inspect what Chris had done after I left. Judging by the noise I'd heard during the night, I figured that he was probably finished with the office-turned-bedroom, but obviously, I would be unable to go into the room to check it out while he was resting.

I had never done much with the basement because it was pretty cold down there, but his presence started to change that. The bare wooden walls were now partially covered in a beautiful Mediterranean blue, which I had originally envisioned for his room. I hadn't felt that I was in the right to argue with him when he was helping to foot the bill, plus it was his room so it was ultimately his choice. When I saw the blue on the walls, I admitted to myself that maybe he was on to something here. A new carpet to cover the cement floor would be the thing to complete the look.

Now that we were working on the basement, I began to think of working some magic on the exterior of the house. The white paint was faded and had been peeling from years of rough weather. I'd never had it painted in the four years that I'd been living there and it looked like the previous owners hadn't had it done, either. Aside from the state of the paintjob, it was a decently-sized multi-story house dating back to the early 1950s with more than enough room for myself.

The delivery people were scheduled to come between 1 and 4 o'clock, so I ate breakfast, got dressed and then puttered around making room in the basement for the new furniture. When the very muscular men came, I declined their offer to put the items in the room and they looked at me as if I were crazy, but shrugged their shoulders as if to say "Suit yourself, lady". After they left, I sat down on the new bed and it was incredibly comfortable, like sitting on a giant marshmallow. I knew that I would have a lot of fun on it with Chris later that night.

I went up to my bedroom to try on my new lingerie and thought that every outfit would blow Chris' mind. I smiled to myself as I tried to picture his reaction and how I would revel in the real thing. Sometimes it was good to be me. I changed back into my regular clothes and went to sleep for a few hours to rest up for the big night knowing that I would need all that I could get for what I had planned. Romance, thy name is Jessica. On second thought, Lust, was probably more accurate.

"Jessi, honey, wake up," Chris gently shook me. "I'm ready for my surprise now."

"What?" I asked groggily.

"That surprise you said you had for me. I'm ready for it now."

"Give me a few minutes, okay?"

"Sure. I'll be waiting in my bedroom."

"Did you put your new bed in it yet?"

"You'll just have to come down and see, won't you?" he said, flashing me a cheeky grin. When he was gone, I put my new black lace teddy back on and sprayed some of my new perfume on every visible area of skin, including my cleavage. I usually didn't put any there, but I had a feeling that it would get some action that night. I threw on the longest coat that I had, slipped on a pair of red heels and made my way to my lover.

I stopped in the doorway of his room and Chris looked up at me eagerly. "This is my surprise?"

"No, this is," I said as I sashayed into the room and undid the coat to reveal my sexy little number. His face lit up and I knew that I had clearly made the right choice of what to wear. Chris stood up and grabbed me, then gently tossed me onto the bed and straddled me. He was just about to rip off my clothes, but I held up my hands and stopped him in time. "Hey! I wanted to get a lot more use out of this than just tonight!"

"Sorry, I was just getting caught up in the moment." He proceeded to slip the undergarment off of my body and tossed it onto his new dresser. Chris slid down my body, past my waistline and inserted his fingers into my private area. I sucked in my breath at the cool touch, but the movement that he did more than made up for it. I could feel him moving his fingers all around, touching my most intimate places and it elicited a low moan from me.

When he removed his fingers, I was both relieved, because I didn't think that I could take anymore, and disappointed. Just when I had let down my guard and was trying to come back down, Chris began to lick and suck hungrily down there. All that I could see from my position lying down was his head bobbing up and down while he worked. I supposed that he just did the thing with his fingers before to make sure that I would be receptive to some action in the area and I was glad that he did. It felt amazing—like a piece of paradise and I wished that he would go on forever.

When he had finished, Chris went upstairs, which confused me as we were just getting started. Within moments, he reappeared with a towel that he placed underneath me. "Just in case," he said. He took off his clothes, got on top of me and continued to pleasure me. I gripped onto the bed frame as hard as I could to keep myself steady but I did allow myself to let out an almost blood-curdling scream of ecstasy. Not surprisingly, that turned Chris on and he got himself all worked up to the point where he had the urge to bite me.

He removed the bandage and then sank his fangs into the spot that he chose the first time he had drunk from me. So much for *that* healing! I turned my head slightly and watched a few drops of blood hit the snow-white towel. My whole body rocked as Chris pounded into me harder than ever before, spurred on by my taste. I don't know how long he kept at it, but when he had finally hit his peak, I was glad to have a break.

He removed himself from me, lay down by my side on the bed and wrapped his arms around me. He licked the newly-opened wound on my neck and I instantly felt it start to heal again. Next, his tongue trailed along to my cleavage and then further to my left breast, which he toyed around with. He licked the nipple, the touch enough to make me quiver with delight, and then he bit the skin just enough to break it. "Ow!" I cried out and pushed Chris away.

"Sorry," he apologized and licked the spot to heal it. "How do you feel?"

"Great, but tired. I mean, I want to go again, but I need to cool off for a while and get a second wind."

"Okay. I understand, but I'm always ready."

"Oh, I know you are," I grinned. "I'm not ready yet for you to fuck me some more, but that doesn't mean we can't still do something."

"What do you have in mind?"

"This," I said as I moved to the foot of the bed and grabbed Chris' manhood, then massaged it in my hands and sucked on it like a lollipop. I quickly discovered that I didn't like this act, but I could feel that Chris did, so I did it anyway. When we'd both had enough and I was feeling refreshed, he got back on top of me and for the next few hours until I fell asleep, we kept taking turns pleasuring each other. Chris did all sorts of things to me that I wouldn't know how to describe, but they had made me feel wonderful and pretty sore all at the same time.

Late the next morning, I found myself back in my bedroom alone. I had slept pretty soundly and I guessed that Chris did too, if he actually slept at all. I still wasn't sure about that part of vampire life and decided to consult my books about it later. When I got up, it was already incredibly warm out so I put on my brown shorts, form-fitting blue T-shirt and white sneakers. After I ate, I headed out towards Munroeville to see about buying some carpet for the basement.

I had a weird feeling while I drove, but I pushed it out of my mind. I hated to dwell on the negative and I didn't want to jinx myself in case the feeling came true. Ever since Chris had told me about the assassins coming after me, I'd been experiencing the occasional pangs of paranoia when he wasn't around. Every shadow and back alley instantly became possible locations for an ambush and I would even grow suspicious of strangers that I saw on the street.

It took a long time for me to find a carpet that I was happy with, but it was worth the wait. It was steel gray and very plush, which would complement the blue walls nicely and feel so soft on my feet. The basement would definitely be cozy when it was completed.

As I walked to the parking lot pleased with my new purchase, I completely forgot to take heed of my surroundings and was passing by an alley when someone grabbed me. I didn't see the hand until it was too late and I couldn't scream for help because the stranger had clapped their hand over my mouth. The scenario was a lot like the first time that I had met Chris, but I felt that there was no way that this would have as happy an ending.

I dropped the roll of carpet and looked around for something to use as a weapon. I hadn't wanted to use the carpet and get it wrecked, but it was too heavy to swing at someone, anyway. I was scared when Chris had attacked me, but that was nothing compared to what I was feeling this time. I was almost certain that I was about to die for sure, because I assumed that this guy was one of the assassins sent to kill me. No matter how careful I thought that I'd been, it wasn't enough and somehow someone had caught up with me.

I began crying as I feared for my life and thought about how I'd never see Chris or Natalie or even my parents ever again. "Shut up, *bitch!*" the guy shouted at me, which only made me cry more. I could tell that I would have yet another horrible headache later. He slapped me in the face and it stung like hell. I hoped that I would be lucky to get out of it with just a slap, but that was really wishful thinking. Although the guy wasn't a vampire, he could certainly have done a lot of damage to me if I didn't play my cards right. I briefly caught a glimpse of a knife sticking out of his pocket, which solidified my feeling.

My eyes went back to glancing around the alley and I found a few planks of wood and a garbage can, but there was no way to reach them. *"Dammit!"* I thought to myself. The situation looked really bleak and to make matters worse, the guy tightened his grip on me. I bit him to try to stall for time and in a vain attempt at getting him to loosen up on me, but it was futile. He kept a hold on me like I was something to cling onto for dear life.

I tried to kick at the pocket where the knife was, thinking that either I could cause it to jam in his leg or that the blade would cut a decent hole through the material and tumble to the ground where he wouldn't have such easy access to it. I managed to get in a few good, hard kicks before he back-handed me, but they did very little if any damage. To my disappointment, the knife was still secured in the pocket and there were no visible signs of blood.

I concentrated on a box a few yards away and just then, out of the corner of my eye, it stirred. I thought that maybe some wind or a rodent had touched it, but when I focused on what looked to be a heavy wooden crate, it also moved. There was no way that *that* could have been budged by the wind or a rodent, so I got to thinking—could *I* have been doing that somehow? It seemed a bit too coincidental that these two objects had the same reactions to me just looking at them.

I squinted my eyes and focused on a small nearby Dumpster, then waited several seconds for something to happen. When nothing did, I began to doubt my theory. As I continued to stare at it, the attacker followed my line of sight. "Why are you staring at a Dumpster?" Just then, as if on cue, the Dumpster zoomed across the alley and hit the guy square on, narrowly missing me by inches. "*Holy shit! What's going on here?*" I thought to myself, thoroughly freaked out and amazed by this turn of events.

Now that I was free again, I picked up the carpet and tried to get as far away from the alley as possible. I burst out of it and was stopped by a few passers-by who saw me crying and looking distraught. I tried to shrug them off politely and told them that I just wanted to go home. Maybe it was silly, but I wanted so badly to have Chris comfort me and hold me in his big, strong arms, telling me that everything would be alright.

I was so shaken by the event in the alley that I considered calling for a cab or for Nat to drive me home. I deliberated with myself for several minutes and decided to drive with the proviso that if it got to be too much, I'd ask for help. I calmed down long enough to buy something to eat from my favorite deli, hoping that I'd feel better with some food in my stomach. I pulled into a rest area on the way home and had my egg salad sandwich and bottle of water. It was a very small comfort, but I hoped that it would tide me over for a while until I could get home.

When I pulled into my driveway, I took out the carpet, opened the front door of the house and just tossed it onto the floor haphazardly. I ran to my room, flopped onto the bed and cried myself to sleep. "Wake up!" Chris said as he gently shook me. "What's wrong?"

"I was attacked in the city this afternoon," I managed to sputter out after what seemed like an eternity of trying to gather my thoughts.

"Oh, Jessi!" he exclaimed and enveloped me in his arms. "Everything's alright now. They won't get you here." I looked up into his eyes and they seemed to tell a different story. "Maybe I should leave you alone."

"No, please don't go. I want the company. I want you to hold me and make me feel safe."

"I think that you've misunderstood me. I should leave your life. I've put you in danger and I couldn't live anymore if you got killed because you were associated with me."

"Ever since we met, as long as I'm alive, my life will always be in danger. At least with you around me, I stand a better chance of survival. Besides, you've made my life better and I know that I've made yours better, too. In my opinion, what we give to each other is worth the risk. Please don't leave me, Chris. I need you," I pleaded. "I love you so much."

"Alright, if you're really sure," he said, sitting down beside me on the bed.

"I've never been surer of anything in my life," I smiled, although it was tainted by the pain in my face.

"You look like you're hurt badly. Do you want me to get you something?"

"Some Tylenol or Advil and a glass of water wouldn't go amiss."

"Coming right up." A few moments later, Chris returned with some pills and water, all of which I gulped down hastily. *"This shit better act fast,"* I thought to myself and relaxed back onto the pillows. "Do you feel up to telling me what happened?" I subtly shook my head as much as I could manage. "I didn't really think so. If there's anything else you need, let me know."

"On second thought, there *is* one thing that I want to talk about. I'm confused about something," I said.

"Alright, what is it?" he asked me.

"You know how you said back at the club that sometimes vampires keep people around for a little while as entertainment before they kill them?"

"Yeah, what about it?"

"The man that attacked me wasn't a vampire; he was a human. How is this possible?" I asked.

"It's such a rare thing that I forgot it could happen. I've heard rumors of vampires hiring humans, but I'd never personally known anyone who'd done such a thing. I've never even heard of the Council doing it before, because they harbor such a hatred of humans that they wouldn't want to associate with them for any reason. I guess that I just pushed them over the edge."

"Funnily enough, that doesn't really comfort me at all."

"Then maybe this will," he said, getting into the bed with me. I carefully scooted over and Chris put his arms around me. I nuzzled up close to him and buried my face in his chest, shutting out the outside world and all of its horrors. God bless my vampire boyfriend. We just lay there in silence, with him stroking my hair and me breathing in his scent, in the aftermath of one of the worst days of my life.

Chapter 6

I awoke the next morning feeling like death had warmed over in my head. Well, alright, I was better than that, but not by much. The pills I had taken the day before helped a bit, but I wasn't out of the woods yet. I knew that I would definitely have to take it easy for the rest of the day in order to kick the pain completely.

Chris was back in his room until nightfall so I had to entertain and fend for myself in the meantime, which was easier said than done in my current state. I managed to eat two pieces of toast and a glass of milk and brought up some DVD box sets to watch on the TV in my room. I didn't actually watch much, because the sound on low volume lulled me back to sleep.

The shrill sound of the phone ringing abruptly ended my sweet bliss and I groaned in protest. I looked over at the clock on my nightstand and the digital readout said that it was only 3 o'clock in the afternoon. Who was phoning me on a weekday? "Hello?" I called out weakly.

"Jessica?" the voice on the other end asked. It was Natalie, of course.

"Yeah."

"You sound like hell."

"Well, I feel like it, too, so it's nice to know that I match," I replied. Nat laughed, but it was more like one of those laughs that you do when you're just trying to be polite to someone rather than because you truly found something funny.

"Are you okay?" she asked, sounding deeply concerned.

"I just have a nasty headache." Technically, that wasn't entirely the truth, but I hadn't wanted her to worry about me too much.

"Oh," she breathed a sigh of relief. "I heard a rumor that you'd gotten beaten up by your new boyfriend and that's why you took a few days off." I was beaten up by someone, alright, but they sure as hell weren't my boyfriend.

"Nope. I just needed some time off to relax and do some errands."

"That's good. I'm sorry, but I've got to go now. I used a break to phone you."

"Thanks for your concern, Nat," I said.

"It's no problem. Want me to drop off some soup?"

"No, that's alright, but thanks, anyway."

"Is your new boy toy playing nurse with you?" she asked, teasing me.

"Yeah."

"Good. If he wasn't, I'd have to kick his ass." I laughed because there was no way that she would have been able to take Chris on even if he wasn't a vampire. Natalie was tall and slender whereas he was built like a tank—not exactly an even fight. "See you soon, Jessi. Take care."

"You, too," I replied and hung up the phone. It took a long time, but I eventually went back to sleep. I came to when I heard Chris making noise in the kitchen. I supposed that he was either trying to make something for me to eat or else he was doing some cleaning to help me out—either one was fine by me.

"How are you feeling tonight?" he asked me from my doorway before entering my room.

"Better. I woke up feeling pretty crappy, but it's slowly going away now. I'll probably be fine tomorrow, but until then, I'm not going to be able to do anything crazy."

"I had plans to go into the city to get the rest of my stuff, but I can wait for a few days until you're back on your feet. I'd hate to leave you behind when you're not well."

"Just go and get it over with."

"Really?"

"Yeah. Go before I change my mind," I replied.

"I can't until you give me back my key," he said.

"Oh, right. It's on the key ring in my purse." Chris picked up the bag, dug around in it and then extracted the key from the rest before tossing the bag back onto the floor.

"I won't be gone long, okay?"

I nodded. "What if they found out where I live? What if they're lying in wait for you to leave the house so they can get me alone again?" I think that maybe I watched too much TV and too many movies to have such paranoid ideas in my head. I decided that it would be comedies and love stories only for me from then on or for at least a little while.

"Did anyone follow you home yesterday?" he asked.

"I didn't see anyone; then again, I was too upset to have noticed much."

"If anyone is out there, I'll take them out when I go. They won't be a match for me. If it'll make you feel better, you can stay in my room and hide. I'll leave you a weapon just in case." Off of my worried look, he backtracked, "You won't need it, but maybe it'll give you some peace of mind." He kissed me on the forehead. "I love you, Jessi. I wouldn't leave if you wouldn't be safe."

"Be as quick as you can."

"I will," he said and then got up to go.

I watched him through my bedroom window as he exited the house and walked out to his car. He was about to unlock the driver's side door when he paused and made like he was listening intently for something. A fear crept up inside me. What if I was right? What if I really *had* been followed? I doubted that my attacker would try again so soon; the Dumpster made sure of that. He probably wasn't dead, but he would be out of commission for a while. More than likely, the Council would have an army of killers in their employ—both human and vampire. Now that it was dark, there would be twice as many out there to track me down. There was also a chance that the noise could have simply been an animal of some sort. I hoped that it was the latter. Either way, Chris could handle himself just fine.

Just as I silently decided that I was getting all worked up over nothing, Chris got punched in the face. I couldn't see who or what had done it, but Chris sure could. He threw punch after punch with the expertise of a pro boxer. Every time that he took a hit, I could see that he was growing more and more pissed off and it wasn't long before his fangs came out.

The intruder aimed his fist again, this time hoping to knock out Chris' fangs in a disturbingly gutsy move. Did he have a death wish? I wondered as I watched the scene play out below. If he had succeeded, Chris would have been in such intense pain that he would have been vulnerable to being staked and the man would have had no more barriers standing in his way to get to me.

Fortunately for us, Chris overpowered the assassin and I watched in horror and morbid fascination as my vampire lover sank his fangs into his opponent's neck. They must have been human, because I didn't think that one vamp would drink from another like that. When he was done, Chris glanced up at the window and looked ashamed that I'd seen what he had done.

I tore myself away from the window and walked quickly to the basement. I felt sick as I replayed the scene in my head. It was one thing to watch him take my blood when we had sex, because we both got something out of that. It was quite another to watch Chris take someone else's and see him take some sick pleasure in it. True, he did it with good intentions—after all, the person wanted to hurt me—but that was of little comfort in the moment. There was no way to deny that my boyfriend was a monster by nature, now that I'd seen him in action firsthand. I would still love him, of course, but man, I must have been crazy.

I went into Chris' room as instructed, locked the door securely and searched his shelves for a book or magazine to peruse while I waited for his return. He had loads of classics like *War and Peace, David Copperfield, The Jungle Book* and *The Catcher in the Rye* just to name a few. He also had historical books, biographies and novels written in foreign languages that I couldn't understand. Where he was a very well-read guy, I seemed pretty shallow by comparison with all of my romance novels and teen fiction. In my opinion, a good book was a good book no matter what section of a store it's found in.

I flipped through some magazines, not actually stopping to read any articles. My mind was elsewhere until an ad caught my attention and jerked me out of my reverie. Hayden was promoting his services as an investment banker proclaiming himself to be "one of the best in the business." I felt a pang in my heart when I saw his picture. I guessed that I still had some feelings for him, but then I thought of what happened between us and the pang died down. Before I could go any further down memory lane, I promptly shut the magazine, threw it back onto the stack and moved onto a different one.

I was relieved when Chris got back, although I wasn't sure if the scene that I'd witnessed earlier would complicate things between us. "We need to talk," he said as he opened his bedroom door.

"We *do*?" I thought it was pretty obvious what went on and the less said, the better as far as I was concerned.

"Yeah."

"Let's not do this," I begged.

"I'm not going to apologize for what I did to protect you, but I *am* sorry that you saw it."

"That makes two of us. I can accept what you are and what you do, but that doesn't mean that I have to like it."

"I never said that you did," Chris said. A heavy silence fell over the room and I felt the weight of our words crushing me. It was a very uncomfortable feeling and I felt somewhat conflicting emotions regarding what I'd recently witnessed in my yard.

"Do you still want to know about what happened yesterday?" I asked, breaking the tension moments later.

"Yes."

I couldn't look him in the eyes as I spoke, "I went to the city to buy a new carpet for the basement and I was feeling really good about it. I was walking to get back to my car on a buyer's high and then someone grabbed me. I never got a good look at the guy's face, but I know that he was definitely human. He had a firm grip on me and his hands were huge. I couldn't scream, but I *did* try to bite him."

"Did he let you go then?"

"No. I thought I was a goner, but then something weird happened."

"Weird how?" he asked.

"I was looking around for some kind of weapon to use against him and I made this Dumpster move. I didn't physically touch it because it was too far away, but somehow it moved and hit this guy really hard and that's how I escaped," I recounted.

"Wow."

"You don't believe me, do you?" I asked.

"No, I do. I'm just stunned."

"A *vampire* is stunned? I wouldn't have thought that was possible after all the things you must have seen and done. This must be big."

"It is. You seem to have the power of telekinesis," he proclaimed.

"Wait a minute. You're telling me that I have the ability to move things with my *mind*?" I asked, not sure if I'd heard him correctly.

"You can believe in vampires, but not in *this*?" he asked me incredulously with his eyebrows raised.

"I suppose that you have a point there," I conceded, "although I never believed in vampires either before *you* came along. This is nuts."

"Think a bit: has this ever happened to you before? Maybe something happened in your past that you couldn't explain?"

I closed my eyes to concentrate, but nothing came to mind. "Never."

"Maybe it only chose to appear at a time when you needed it the most. Your life was in mortal danger because of me and so perhaps your subconscious mind acted on instinct to protect you," Chris reasoned. I chewed on my lower lip as I pondered this idea. "There isn't an exact science to supernatural things like this. There could be all sorts of other possible reasons. At least now I know that there's nothing wrong with me."

"But then why hadn't I been to make you move like I did with the Dumpster? You stayed right with me the whole time."

"As I said, there's no exact science to this. Maybe on some level you knew that I wasn't really going to hurt you or maybe telekinesis doesn't affect vampires the way that it affects humans. I think that for now, at least, all we can do is guess."

"Alright," I replied, somewhat mollified by his answers, even though they seemed to raise even more questions. I changed the subject before thinking about it any further made me insane. "Now what do we do? Should we go to the Council?"

"No. I mean, we will, just not yet. We have to see if there's a third attack before we go to such extreme measures."

"*What*? *Why*?" I choked out, unable to believe what I was hearing.

"We need more to back up our claims. I hate this, too, but this is just following protocol."

"To hell with protocol, this is my *life* on the line we're talking about here!"

"Don't you think I *know* that?" Chris raised his voice at me for the time since I met him. "If there was another way, I'd take it," he said, gripping my head and turning it to face him. "You *have* to believe me."

I looked away again and tried to fight against the stream of tears that threatened to fall from my eyes. "I do," I whispered.

"Say it louder if you really mean it."

"I do."

"Louder still."

"I *fucking* believe you! Is that what you wanted to hear? Are you happy now?" I shouted.

"Yes," he smiled.

"Good!" I exclaimed, adrenaline causing my heartbeat to pulse like a jackhammer. He pulled me into his arms and kissed me passionately, wanting to make up and I stopped before things got too physical. I wasn't in the mood and I still felt a twinge of pain in my head, which wasn't helped by all of the yelling. "When we *do* go to the Council with our problem, what'll happen?"

"I'll tell them to call off the attacks."

"And if they don't comply?" I asked, not sure if I really wanted to hear the answer.

"I'll threaten them. I'll make them see to reason or die trying."

"It's the dying part that I have problems with."

"I don't want to lose you," Chris said in a low voice, rubbing his face against my hair.

"Well, I don't want to lose you, either," I said. Another silence fell over us.

"I'll move Heaven and Earth if I have to in order to make sure that doesn't happen," Chris replied.

Just then, I was overcome with emotion and kissed him passionately. "My hero. Would you really do that for me?"

"Absolutely."

"Would I be able to go with you to see the Council?"

"I don't think that's a good idea. No human would be welcome there unless they're dinner," he said.

"I understand, but I still want to come. Maybe between the two of us we can convince them to change their minds. Maybe we could show them how good we are together and what we mean to each other," I reasoned.

"Trust me when I say that it won't work. The Council doesn't care about human concepts like love, compassion and respect. They only care about things like violence, vengeance, blood and torture."

"I don't care. Until we get this settled and over with, my life is at risk no matter what happens. I want to go into the belly of the beast and stand up for my life and I won't let you talk me out of it."

Chris paused for a moment and sighed. "If you're really sure."

"I am."

"No offense, but you're crazy."

"I already knew that," I smiled. "I'd have to be to date a vampire, especially one that's tried to kill me."

"Are you *ever* going to let me live that down?"

"Nope!" I said, still smiling.

"Then come here and I'll attack you again," Chris said. I moved closer to him, and then he straddled me and smothered me with kisses.

I went to work the next day feeling much better. The twinge of pain in my head had dwindled down to an occasional pang just to remind me to take care if I didn't want it to flare up again. Almost as soon as I walked into the employees' lounge, Nat carefully pounced on me. "How are you today?"

"I'm better, thanks. What about yourself?"

"I'm good. What did you do on your time off besides the headache?"

"My new boyfriend moved in with me. We've been getting his stuff over to the house and fixing it up a bit," I replied.

"You never told me *that* when I called you the other day!" Nat exclaimed as she playfully slapped me on the arm.

"Sorry. I guess it slipped my mind."

"You two must be getting pretty serious to be moving in together already."

"Yeah," I said and thought to myself that she didn't know the half of it.

"How long have you been dating? Just a few weeks?" she asked and I nodded. "Boy must work fast to get you to agree to this so soon. I mean, you were with Hayden for four years and never got this far. So, how is he in bed?"

"Who? Hayden?"

"No—the new guy, of course."

"I'm not telling *you!*" I laughed.

"That bad, huh?" she asked, a hint of pity in her voice.

"Nat, if he was bad, why would I want to be with him? I don't want a sexless relationship. It might work for some people, but not for me. I've been there and done that and I don't want to do it again."

"Good point. So, when do I get to meet him? You said I could when you knew what was going on between you."

"How about Friday night?" I suggested.

"Sounds good."

"I'll have to check with Chris to make sure. I'll let you know, okay?"

"Sure. See you later," Natalie said as she went back into the store. What had I gotten myself into? I wondered to myself. I knew it was inevitable that Nat would meet Chris, but I hadn't anticipated it so soon. We were already dealing with so many things on our plate that we hadn't needed to add one more thing. Then again, maybe that was exactly why we needed the brief respite.

I figured that a night of fun with another human could have been good for the both of us and maybe even inspire him for the meeting in front of the Council. I also hoped that he would behave like a human while he was in Nat's presence. I doubted that she would have been as open-minded to the idea of a vampire in our midst as I was, never mind that one was living in the same house as me. We would just have to take extra precautions and hope for the best.

Later on Wednesday night, I was lying on the couch watching TV when Chris got up. "What's on?" he asked from the doorway.

"*Friends.*"

"Can I join you?"

"Of course," I replied and sat up so that he could take a seat. When he sat down, he pulled me close to him and I lay across his lap. To the outside world, we would have looked like an average couple and for all intents and purposes we sort of were, unless you counted the coital blood-drinking. "Would it be alright if a friend of mine came over on Friday night? She really wants to meet you."

"Technically, it's your house so you can invite anyone you want," he replied.

"I know. I just wanted to make sure that things were okay with you before another human came over. It wouldn't do any good if your cover is blown. Natalie is a good person, but I have no idea what she'd do if she found out what you really were. It's best not to take chances."

"You don't need to worry about me, baby. I know how to behave myself. I haven't survived this long without learning a few tricks."

"So I'll tell her that we're on for Friday?"

"Yeah."

"It'd be nice if we had the carpet laid down before she comes over," I said.

"Want to do it now?" Chris asked me.

"After the show is over." We watched the TV, laughing in the appropriate spots and then I switched if off when the program had finished.

Two hours later, the basement was finally complete and it looked very modern and stylish. I sat down on the old couch that Chris must have re-upholstered one night and the carpet was so soft under my bare feet, like freshly-mown grass. "This. Is. The. Life. I've got my man and I've got my house pimped out looking new and improved. What could be better than this?" I asked no one in particular.

"Oh, I can think of a few things," Chris said, a devilish gleam in his eyes.

"You're so naughty, but can we do something else first?"

"What did you have in mind?"

"Putting out some of your belongings. All of your stuff is down here. It just seems strange that we're living together, but no one would know it unless they went into your room. I wouldn't mind, but if we're going to have someone visiting, we should keep up appearances so that we don't tip them off, you know? If you want to, we could put everything back afterwards." Chris looked like he was about to say something and then closed his mouth again. "Are you okay with this plan?"

A moment passed before he spoke, "Yeah, but we may as well just keep everything out instead of moving it all back and forth whenever one of your friends comes over. That doesn't make much sense to me."

"I guess you're right. So, what can we use?" I asked him and he brought out a box labeled *Miscellaneous*, which was filled with all sorts of things that he'd collected over the years. There were ceremonial masks from a few Indian tribes, paintings, photographs, vases and assorted trinkets. I suspected that the paintings were the original copies rather than mass-produced prints, but I didn't have the nerve to ask so I put them in my safe just in case.

The photos, on the other hand, went wherever we could find suitable spots. Some ended up displayed on the shelves in the living room, some were hung on the kitchen walls and some went in my bedroom. It didn't take long before almost every room bore some token of Chris' life and a reminder that more than one person lived there. "Voilà!" I exclaimed when the last trinket was put on the shelf. "Done! You are officially living here." Off of his quizzical look, I said, "You know what I mean."

"Yeah, but its funny when you get all flustered because you're not sure how to refer to me. For the record, it doesn't really matter what you want to call me. Just go with whatever you feel most comfortable with."

"Hardy har har," I said, sarcastically. "I'm glad that I amuse you."

"The pleasure's all mine and speaking of pleasure, can we have sex now?"

I smiled at Chris. "Who's my horny little vampire tonight?" I giggled as he scooped me up and we went into my bedroom where he ravaged my body in a good way.

As soon as I saw Natalie the next day, I talked to her about our little get-together. "He said that tomorrow night is fine."

"Great. Should I bring anything?"

"That's not necessary, but if you wanted to bring over some wine coolers, I wouldn't object to that!" I grinned.

"I'll think about it."

"Alright," I said and patted her gently on the back. I had a really slow day at work; in fact it was so slow that I was assigned to work in the customer service department. I developed a new respect for the customer service people for dealing with so many assholes day in and day out.

I got bitched out by a woman who wanted to return an item that broke, even though she had bought it over a year before. I knew that that wasn't store policy and I pointed that out to her over and over again, but she wouldn't stop arguing with me. I ended up calling a manager over to deal with the situation. Geez, the nerve of some people! I couldn't wait to get home that night and unwind after being yelled at most of the day by people who needed to lash out at someone to cover up for their own stupidity.

I popped into the local Stop-n-Shop on the way home and picked up a chef's salad, which I ate while watching a rerun of *Buffy the Vampire Slayer*. It was the episode where Buffy and Cordelia were running for Homecoming Queen and got hunted down by a group of bad guys in a contest of another kind. The episode was somewhat scary, while being light-hearted and funny at the same time. By the time Chris joined me in the kitchen, I was cleaning up and the show was over.

"How was your day?" he asked as he wrapped his arms around my waist and kissed the top of my head.

"I don't think that it could have been much worse. I was sent to another department just for today and customers yelled and berated me. I swear that I was ready to clock someone in the head. I never want to go through that again."

"How about I give you a massage?"

"Do you really know how to do one or is this just a way to get me into bed?" I teased.

"You know as well as I do that I don't need to work very hard to get you into bed," he winked and I blushed bright red. "No, I really *can* do them. What kind do you want? Swedish? Shiatsu? Something else?"

"Surprise me." I had no idea about the different styles there were; I just wanted something to ease the tension in my body. Chris led me back into the living room, motioning for me to sit on the couch, and then he settled down on it, facing my back. He started with my shoulders, rubbing them sensually and I closed my eyes to concentrate on what he was doing. Several minutes later, Chris made me lie down on my stomach so that he could rub my back. He started from the top, near my neck and slowly made his way down by my butt. I moaned over and over again in pleasure as his hands worked their magic and I felt myself loosening up. He worked on my feet next and I thought that he might comment on their sorry state, but either he was too nice to say anything or it just didn't bother him.

When he was done, I felt like a million bucks. "Thanks, Chris. That was great. I don't think that I've ever felt more relaxed."

"Any time."

"I'll hold you to that," I smiled.

"Can you show me how you do telekinesis?"

"I don't know if I can. I still haven't quite wrapped my head around it yet."

"I mean, just do what you did and I'll watch. I've never seen anyone do this before," he said. "*Oh, great, I'm like a freak show now*," I thought and then mentally chided myself for thinking something so stupid and mean-spirited about Chris. I couldn't fault him for being interested in my newfound ability—hell, I would have been, too. We made quite the pair: a member of the undead and a freak who can move things with her mind.

"What do you want me to try with?" I asked him.

Chris glanced around and suggested, "How about a book?"

"Okay." I focused on the object for several seconds, imagining it floating over our heads and then it replicated the action exactly as I had pictured it in my mind. It was very weird, but also very cool.

"Impressive," he said.

"Thanks. I just pictured in my head what I wanted it to do and that's what happened—no biggie."

"It looks like you've got the hang of it already."

"I don't know. I just tried a theory to see if it would work and it did, but it might not work all the time. I mean, what if I'm unable to concentrate properly?" I asked him.

"Get as much practice as possible. How about we go outside? That way we have more room," Chris suggested.

"Sure." We headed out into the backyard and I picked up a piece of wood to weigh it and judge whether it'd be suitable to use for practicing, because I had no idea of how heavy an object I could do. I figured that I should do this in baby steps and start off with something fairly light. I put it back down on the ground and focused on it, then made it levitate in mid-air and float a few feet away from where I stood.

I made it slowly float back again, but then I thought I heard a suspicious noise and lost my concentration. The wood hit Chris in the head and he yelped in pain. "Sorry!" I cried out frantically. "Are you alright?"

He shook his head to check himself out. "Yeah. Luckily, my kind doesn't get hurt very easily, although that *did* sting a bit. If you can ever do that on purpose to someone who is trying to kill you, they shouldn't be much of a match."

"That's good to know, especially coming from a vampire," I said. Chris beamed in response and flashed his fangs at me. He found some twigs and other bits and pieces scattered around the yard and I "threw" them elsewhere while he fetched them like a faithful dog. Things were going fine until I heard yet another sound that broke my focus, and then Chris let out a noise that I could only describe as being animalistic in nature.

I instantly turned around and my jaw dropped when I saw a sharp twig protruding from his right side and blood seeping out from the wound. "Oh my god!" My eyes were wide in shock, but I did manage to notice that I didn't come close to hitting his heart so I knew that he'd be okay eventually. I reached out to him to remove the stick, but he snarled at me and flashed his fangs in a menacing way that said, *"Back the fuck up!"* I jumped backwards and nearly stumbled over my own feet in an effort to get out of his way as quickly as possible. "Let me help you," I pleaded. In response, he snarled again and I was seriously afraid of him for the first time since we'd met.

I went back inside the house and lay down on the couch to watch TV while Chris cooled off or whatever he was going to do. After some time, I heard both the back door and the door to his bedroom slam shut and I never saw him again that night.

Chapter 7

On Friday, Chris woke up and acted like nothing had happened the night before. I asked Natalie if she could come over at 8 o'clock so that I could talk things over with him before she arrived. "How are you?" he asked me, as pleasant as a vampire could ever get.

"I'm wondering what was up with you last night. You were all touchy-feely while you were giving me that massage and then you lashed out at me when you got struck by that stick."

"I'm really sorry. Did I hurt you?"

"Not unless you count my feelings. You scared me so badly."

"That was kind of the point. I wanted you to go away so that I wouldn't do something that I'd regret later."

"Couldn't you have done it in a nicer way or something so that I knew what the hell was going on?" I accused him.

"I was getting hungry and wasn't thinking straight. I fed late last night so I'm fine now," he said.

"Just try not to let it happen again, okay? I hate being so scared of you."

"It's not always fun being me, either. I told you before that you wouldn't want to be around a hungry vampire. I guess that I was worse off than I thought. I was all caught up in helping you out, but I'll make sure to feed more often from here on."

"So are we cool now and can we put this little episode behind us?" I asked him.

"Yes. Again, I'm very sorry."

"That's alright. I suppose that I get kind of cranky myself when I need to eat, except that I don't have the ability to rip someone's throat out." A few moments of heavy silence passed before I spoke again, "Is your wound all healed yet?"

Chris lifted up his shirt to check it out and it was still in pretty rough shape, even with his enhanced healing abilities. "No, not quite."

"It heals my wounds quickly when you lick me, so would I be able to reciprocate?" I wondered aloud.

"I don't know. Try it and see," he replied. I moved closer to him, then got down on my knees and touched the area with my tongue. I couldn't believe that I was actually doing it, but stranger things had been happening in my life as of late. I closed my eyes and tried not to think about what the wound looked like; I just thought about helping out my boyfriend to get better and let my tongue roam around. Moments later, I opened my eyes again and the wound was nowhere to be found. Had it really worked? It looked like it unless I had mistakenly ended up licking in the wrong spot.

"Well, I tried," I said as I got back to my feet.

"Thanks, Jessi. It's gone now, well, almost. I can still see some light scarring," Chris said as he inspected himself.

"No problem. Just glad I can help, although, to be honest, I'd rather not have to do that again."

"Yeah."

"So, now that the gross part of the evening's program is over with, let's get on with the rest of the show. I just want tonight to be over with already."

"Why do you say that? I thought this was your friend? Do you not want me to meet her?" Chris asked in an accusing tone.

"No, I'm just nervous about this, plus, it's not exactly my ideal way to spend a night. Speaking of friends, now that you live here, feel free to invite whomever you want. All I ask is that you make sure they know that I'm off-limits to them," I admitted.

"I don't really have friends, except for you. Vampires don't tend to get along with others of our own kind, because of our competitive instincts. It's rare for us to be friendly in the way that humans are with each other. I suppose you could say that I *do* have some acquaintances that I'm fairly close to, though. We've gone out hunting on many occasions and fought alongside each other."

"Would I like any of your acquaintances?"

"I honestly don't know, but I doubt that they'd like you much, except for as a snack. I suppose that stranger things have happened, though," Chris replied.

"Oh," was all I could think to say. Just then, there was a knock at the door and I straightened up my black dress pants and royal blue sleeveless top before I went to the door. I glanced around the kitchen and everything looked great. I had three place settings put out and a floral centerpiece that had lilies, daisies and some purple flowers whose name I wasn't aware of.

I opened the door and Natalie hugged me before I could say "Hi". Her long brown hair flowed down her back, held in place by a crimson-colored hair band, and gray eye shadow accentuated her green eyes. She wore a bright purple party dress with a matching belt around her slender waist and beige sandals that made me feel a little under-dressed. "I brought those wine coolers like you said—hope you like cranberry—and a little housewarming present."

"I was sort of kidding about the wine coolers, but thanks, anyway. You really didn't have to bring a gift, too." Natalie handed the drinks to Chris, which he put in the refrigerator while she gave me the gift.

"Open it," Nat commanded me, eager to see my reaction as she slid off her sandals at the door.

"I should introduce you first." I turned to each of them in turn, "Chris, this is my best friend at work, Natalie Johnson. Nat, this is my boyfriend, Chris Sinclair." Natalie held out her hand to shake his and there was a momentary pause as Chris debated whether or not it was a good idea to touch her for fear that she might feel his cold hand and be freaked out. He shook hands and she didn't seem to notice anything out of the ordinary, or if she did, she made no mention of it. I silently let go of a breath that I didn't realize I had been holding in.

They exchanged pleasantries—"Nice to meet you"—and then directed their eyes towards me. I carefully unwrapped the paper to find a box, which held a giant purple candle inside. "Thanks."

"It's scented like wild berries," she remarked. I sniffed the candle to see for myself and found it to be subtle, but pleasant. I placed it back in the box for the time being and put it on the coffee table. I wasn't a fan of candles, but I guessed that it was the thought that counted. "Why don't you light it now?"

"I don't have any matches or a lighter. Looks like I'll have to run out and get some soon."

"Oh, okay."

"I don't usually have any need for them, but I guess I do now," I chuckled nervously.

"I just thought that it would be kind of romantic," Nat explained.

"I see that, yeah, and it'll last a long time, which is great," I tried to feign excitement, but I had a feeling that she could see through my ruse even though she never said anything about it.

She looked around at my set-up on the dining table in the kitchen and clasped her hands together. "What are we having for supper?"

"I rushed home from work to go to the grocery store and made some Caesar salad and chicken burgers. I also bought a cheese and fruit plate for appetizers."

"Sounds good, but you didn't have to go all-out just for me."

"It's not really much trouble, Nat. Besides, anything that's leftover will be meals for tomorrow so I don't have to cook again," I laughed and she and Chris joined in. "Before we eat, we should show you the newly-finished basement. It was just done the other day, in fact." The three of us went downstairs and immediately, Nat was astonished by what she saw.

"Oh my gosh! The last time I was here, it looked like a dungeon. It's like a whole new place. You can actually spend some time down here now! All you still need is a nice big widescreen TV and a home theater."

"Yeah, but first we need the money to buy all of that," I replied.

"Oh, yeah," she said, a little embarrassed by her over-excitement. Natalie looked around again and spotted Chris' locked bedroom door. "What's in there?" she nodded towards it.

"That's Chris' room."

"You guys sleep in separate rooms?"

"Don't be silly!" I chuckled. "Why would we do *that*? No, it's just for when he wants to be alone. If we were always together, we'd probably drive each other crazy," I half-lied.

"Can I see it?" Nat asked with a child's eagerness.

Chris and I exchanged glances. He had some pretty creepy things in there and some pretty mundane things that, upon closer inspection, would tip someone off as to his true age and there was no way that we could allow her to see them. "I'm sorry, but no. I like to keep my privacy," he replied.

"Oh, okay, I understand."

"Thanks. Perhaps I could bring out a few things to show you another time instead."

"I'd like that," she smiled and he returned the sentiment. Now that our guest had been placated, we headed back upstairs to the kitchen. As Chris and Natalie sat down, I raced around gathering up the food and placing it on the table next to the centerpiece, which I pushed aside.

"Would you like a wine cooler?" I asked Natalie. "They should be nice and ice cold now."

"Yes, please." I retrieved a couple of bottles from the fridge and handed one to her. She popped the top off of it and took a swig. "Glad to see that you didn't burn anything this time!" Nat exclaimed. "Your cooking skills must have improved."

"What are you talking about?" Chris asked, genuinely curious to hear a bit of gossip.

I sat down and groaned in embarrassment, "Don't tell him!" I also popped the top off of my bottle and sipped some of it, which was really refreshing.

"Why not? It's not like you have anything to hide from him now that you're living together." Nat turned to Chris and said, "A little while after I met her, we were over at my place having a girls' night in kind of thing—you know like watching chick flicks, eating popcorn and that sort of thing—and we were going to do a homemade pizza. Well, Jessi here burned the hell out of the crust, because she left it in the oven a bit too long. Not only that, but the stove started to catch on fire. To this day, I still don't know how the hell she managed to pull *that* one off! The smoke alarm in my apartment was blaring and the fire department was called in to see what was going on. There we were in our nighties trying to explain to these hot firefighters that we were just making dinner. Talk about embarrassing!"

Chris laughed so hard that he nearly choked on some air. "Oh my god! I'm glad that you guys were alright, at least."

"Yeah, but I can't say the same thing about the poor pizza," Nat lamented.

"So what did you guys end up eating?"

"We obviously had to throw out the burnt pizza so we ordered out for Chinese instead."

"That's the only time I've ever burned anything and she keeps throwing it in my face!" I interjected, laughing along with everyone.

"You should have seen her *face* that night! I thought that she was going to die right there on the spot!" Natalie and Chris continued laughing and I could feel my face going bright red at the memory.

"Let's dig in!" I exclaimed to change the subject and everyone began helping themselves to the food. Although Chris didn't need to eat, he had a bit to keep up the charade of being human. A few moments of silence passed as we ate and savored the meal.

"This is really good, Jessi," Nat said. "My compliments to the chef."

I did a mock bow in my seat, "Thank you, thank you."

"Tell me a bit about yourself," Chris said to Natalie, making polite conversation.

"Well, I'm originally from Montgomery, Alabama. My parents split up when I was a kid and I moved to Nashville with my dad, which is where I stayed until I turned 21. I married a record producer shortly before I left there."

"Would I know anything he's done?"

"No, it was just some local stuff. To even call it music is a bit of a stretch. I remember going with him one night to a club to see this band that called themselves Blood Larvae. I can stand listening to some heavy metal music that most people would find obnoxious, but even *I* couldn't stand this. It was sort of like someone had thrown a bunch of metal objects into a trash compactor and they were all scraping together. Let me tell you, I needed a few stiff drinks to endure that mess," Nat said, taking a sip of her wine cooler.

"I didn't know that you were married," I said.

"It's not something that I like to talk about much. It brings up too many horrible memories, but it gets a bit easier to do now that so many years have passed since then."

"Do you mind telling us what happened?"

"He went to some record industry convention in Vegas and hooked up with this skank that worked for his label. She figured that she'd seduce him while I wasn't around, but Karma got her pretty good for that one. My ex dumped her for another young piece of ass after having four kids with her and she eventually had to quit her job with the label. The last that I'd heard of her, she became a hooker to support the kids and her drug habit. Not that I'm bitter or anything."

"Wow, that's awful. I'm really sorry about all of that. How long were you guys married? It sounds like maybe the two of you were too young and rushed into things too quickly. No offense," Chris remarked.

Natalie scowled a little at the accusation for a brief moment and then let it pass rather than allowing it to spoil the night. "Just six months, but I made damn sure that I took him to the cleaners and went after some pretty pennies. So, how did you guys meet?" Natalie asked, trying to turn the conversation to a much happier topic.

I exchanged brief glances with Chris and wondered what to say, but Nat was waiting for a response so I thought quickly. "We met in the city one night after I got off work."

Chris saw what I was trying to do with my vague statement so he took up the thread, and then ran with it. "I hid in an alley waiting for some friends to come by so that I could play a joke on them. Instead, I ended up startling an innocent stranger," he looked down and gave my shoulder a squeeze as he said this, "and I apologized to her profusely, then things went from there."

"I guess that's something to tell your kids when they get older or are you not thinking that far yet?" Nat asked, looking from Chris' face to mine and back again.

"We haven't even been going out for a month, so we're nowhere near close to crossing *that* bridge," I said. I looked at Chris again and we both thought the same thing; we'd never be able to have kids together, but we'd pretend that we'd give it some serious thought just to keep up the pretense for Natalie.

"I'm sorry, I've made you uncomfortable. I shouldn't have said anything like that. It's none of my business. I should have learned a long time ago not to interfere with other people's lives like that."

"It's okay, Nat, really," I tried to reassure her and squeezed her shoulder as gently as I could. "Besides, if you didn't interfere the way that you do, then you wouldn't be you and I like you just the way you are." She smiled at me. "That was cheesy as hell, wasn't it? I've got to stop watching *Bridget Jones's Diary* so much." Natalie and I laughed together and we continued eating.

"That's a great movie," she said. "I haven't seen it in a long time, though."

While I still had my mind on the subject of life with a vampire, I decided to dip my toes and test the waters. "I have a random question, Nat."

"Alright, shoot."

"Do you believe in vampires?" I asked her, carefully watching her reaction. Chris glanced at me and I shot him a look that said *"Don't worry; I know what I'm doing."*

"Like *actual* vampires that kill people and drink blood?"

"Yeah."

Natalie laughed at such a silly notion and Chris fought to keep his facial reaction in check. "No, that's just ridiculous. I mean, if vampires were real, you'd think that there would've been something on the news about it. It'd be a pretty big story. I think that they're just something made up for movies and TV shows to scare the daylights out of people for entertainment just like ghosts, goblins and other things that go bump in the night," she shrugged, dismissing the idea as complete nonsense.

"Don't you ever wonder whether there are more things out there than we're aware of right now? Things that we're just not ready to accept yet?"

"Now you're getting all philosophical on me, Jessi. The only beings that I believe in are God and Jesus and that's all fine by me. I don't need to believe in anything else."

"Okay, that's cool. Let's just say for the sake of argument that vampires *did* exist: what would you think?" I asked, hoping that I wasn't cluing her in to what was really going on with my new relationship.

"Well, gosh, I don't know," she paused. "Where's this all coming from? Do you know something that I don't?"

"No. You know me—I just think of all sorts of weird random things from time to time to amuse myself with."

"Yeah. I guess I just never really thought about it before. I honestly don't know what to think—it's kind of a weird idea to begin with." There was a moment of silence before Nat changed the subject. "What do you do for a living, Chris?" Knowing the truth of the matter, I was pretty interested to hear what kind of answer he would give, while trying to look like I already knew what he'd say. I just concentrated on trying not to let my forkful of salad fall onto my lap.

"I'm an entrepreneur," he replied.

"Doing what?" Nat asked, curious.

"I dabble in a lot of things. I don't mean that to sound shady or anything—I'm not doing anything illegal. I just try to fill the place of whatever's in demand. If someone needs to hire a service of some sort, I'll find someone to do the work for them or do it myself if it's within my capabilities, such as painting a house. I try to connect the buyer of a good or service with a seller, kind of like Craigslist or eBay."

I was very impressed at Chris' little story and his ability to lie on the spot. I almost thought that he'd backed himself into a corner, but he passed with flying colors. In fact, he was so convincing that I nearly believed him myself. "Is that your car outside? The bright red one?"

"Yeah."

"You must be doing pretty well for yourself, then."

"I'm doing alright, yeah," Chris said, trying to be modest.

"What sort of horsepower does it have and how fast can it go?" Nat asked, intrigued.

"450 hp and 250 mph, respectively."

"Wow."

"I haven't had it for very long so I've never gotten to take it that high yet. I'd have to do it on some highway in the middle of nowhere," Chris admitted.

"Of course. No sense in taking a car like that to the limit unless you've got an uninterrupted road where you can really let it loose. I'll bet it purrs like a big ol' cat," she said.

"Are you a car fan?"

"Not really—I've just dated a lot of guys with cars. Unfortunately, all they had were crappy little beaters, sort of like the guys themselves. They'd often talk about cars that they wished they could afford like Porsches, Lamborghinis and Maseratis. Only in their dreams could they ever hope to get wheels like that," she scoffed. "I do know enough to know that whatever car you have is exotic and really pricey. I hope that you have some good anti-theft devices on it, because it'd be a damn shame if something happened to it. I'd like to go for a ride sometime, if you wouldn't mind."

"I've got the latest in security for it, but thanks for your concern. I could easily buy another one if I had to, although I'd rather not go through all of the hassle and inconvenience of doing so. Perhaps we will make a date for that ride some time. We could all go out somewhere for a road trip and make a day of it." Chris turned to me and asked, "What do you think, baby?"

"Yeah, that'd be cool. We should go sometime soon while it's still warm out. Maybe to the beach?" I obviously had no intention of letting her know that a beach trip

would be out of the question unless either Nat and I went by ourselves or we waited until nightfall so that Chris could join us. *"Would Chris lend me his car?"* I briefly thought to myself and then pushed the idea aside until the time for the trip came.

"If we do go there, can you give me some warning? I need to go shopping for a new bathing suit and there's no telling how long it'll take for me to find something that fits," Nat replied.

I laughed, "Sure thing."

"Did Jessi tell you about the trouble at work recently?" Natalie asked Chris.

"With that woman who tried to ruin her reputation?"

"Yeah. You really should have seen her fight against Ashley—the one who we thought was behind it all. She really whaled on her like a prize fighter. You would have been so proud of her. I'm sure Hayden wouldn't have felt the same way, though. He really doesn't like violence of any kind. He considers it to be barbaric and thinks of himself to be above all of that," she said as she rolled her eyes.

The mention of my ex brought with it an uneasy silence. Natalie realized her error and turned red with embarrassment. She looked at her watch and remarked, "Look at the time! It's nearly midnight and I've still got to travel back to Munroeville. I should be going now."

"You could stay here overnight rather than traveling in the dark," I offered. "I could put you up in my room while I sleep on the couch."

"Thanks, but I don't want to impose on you."

"It's no trouble at all."

"Just the same, I should get going. I have to be up early to go to work, anyway. Thanks again for supper and for having me over. We should do this again some time."

"Sure," I smiled.

"It was nice to meet you, Chris," Nat said and shook his hand again.

"It was nice to meet you, too," he replied, returning the gesture. "Thanks for coming, for the gift and for helping out Jessi with that work situation. She was really troubled by it, as I'm sure you already knew."

"That's what friends are for, aren't they? Speaking of which, Jessi, are you ever going to tell me the real reason why you asked me about the vampires? I mean, I know what you said, but you seemed to be pushing the subject pretty hard."

"I just thought that it'd make for an interesting conversation topic," I said, trying to sound as innocent as possible.

"Oh, well, okay. Good night, you guys!"

"Have a good night!" I called out at the door as Natalie was leaving. "Drive safe!" She waved back at us, got into her car and pulled out of the driveway. When her taillights had faded away, we went back into the house and breathed a sigh of relief that it was finally over. I collected the dishes and put them in a pile on the counter, deciding that I would get around to them some time the next day.

"What'd you think of her?" I asked Chris.

"She seems very nice. She's quite talkative, though."

"Yeah. She can really talk your ear off sometimes. You'd be scared to see my phone bill, especially after she's had a bad date or broken up with a guy. She can go on for hours and hours talking about how horrible the guy was and all of the things he did wrong."

"No offense, but she also seems to be a bit scatterbrained."

"Well, she was diagnosed with ADD when she was a kid, but I think that she's just one of those people that get a bit too excited sometimes and rush from one thing to another. I do it myself sometimes and I've never been diagnosed with anything. In any case, she lives a normal life and as long as it doesn't interfere with how she does her job, then who really cares?"

"I guess you're right."

"I'm glad that you got along with my friend. It really means a lot to me," I said, grasping Chris' hands and looking up into his eyes.

"I'd do just about anything for you, Jessi."

"Oh, baby," I purred, kissing him on the lips. He kissed me back, but I was getting incredibly exhausted and I gently pushed him away after a few moments. "I really need to go to sleep."

"I thought that maybe we could clean up in here first. I'll put on a pot of coffee if it'll help you stay awake a little longer," he offered.

I hesitated, "Okay. Make it really strong, though." Chris did as he was told and I started to put some things away like the fruit and cheese plate that was barely touched. *"Oh well, that will be my breakfast in the morning,"* I thought to myself.

"Here you go," he said as he handed me the steaming cup. I sipped it carefully and the hot beverage spread through me like a wildfire. I felt like I was getting temporarily re-energized, but for how long, I had no idea as I rarely drank coffee. When I needed energy, I preferred to do things the old-fashioned way and get some sleep or do a little exercise.

"Thanks a lot. I really needed that. How about I wash the dishes and you dry? That way, if I crash out, I'll be done first," I suggested.

"Alright," Chris said and he sat down while he waited for me to get the sink ready. I poured a generous dollop of dishwashing liquid in, then turned on the hot water tap and within a few minutes, the sink was filled with suds. I threw in the cutlery first and he turned on the radio in the kitchen so that we could listen to music and make the time pass more quickly. As we worked, I sang along with the radio. "You have a beautiful voice."

I blushed bright red at his compliment. "You really think so?"

"Yeah. You could be a famous singer."

"I don't know about that. I just do it for fun in the car when I'm alone."

"You've told me how you wanted to do something more with your life and your voice could be your ticket to fame and fortune. I know that it'd be a long shot, but I think that you should go for it," he said.

I chuckled, "I wouldn't even know where to begin."

"Try asking Natalie and see if she's got any ideas. She was married to a producer so there's a chance that she might still have some information and see about getting you in touch with the right people."

"I'd have to think about this a while."

"Well, if you do go through with it and you get famous, just don't forget about me," he smiled.

"How could I *ever* forget you?" I flashed Chris a grin and then he scooped me up in a big bear hug and took me downstairs to his room.

Chapter 8

Over the course of the next two weeks, Chris and I had settled into a routine. I'd get up and go to work at 10 o'clock, and then come home in the early evening to eat and watch TV until Chris woke up. After that, we'd spend the rest of the night hanging out until 3AM so that I could try to get some sleep before repeating the whole process the next day. Some nights, we would have marathon sex sessions and on other nights when we needed a break, we'd just stay up talking and watching movies like a regular couple would. As boring as it sounded, it was also quite nice and I especially enjoyed the absence of attacks by the Council's assassins.

I had a few theories about it that I'd voiced to Chris. Perhaps the Council was trying to lull us into a false hope that'd they finally relented or else they were trying to regroup and come up with a new strategy since they'd failed thus far. The both sounded pretty plausible to us, and Chris suggested that I remain vigilant no matter what. "It's always better to be safe than sorry," were his exact words. Yeah, that's really easy to say when you've got fangs and all sorts of super powers at your disposal to use to protect yourself. Even so, he was absolutely right and I tried my best to abide by that advice.

Early one Saturday morning in mid-July, I walked over to the local Stop-n-Shop to pick up a few things for the weekend. I walked around the store for a while, getting my items, checking out the sale deals and thinking if there was anything else that I wanted. *"Do I feel like having spaghetti marinara and meatballs for supper?"* I thought to myself.

After I made my purchases, I walked out of the store again and was only about a block away before I was struck from behind by a solid object. Baseball bat? Hockey stick? Whatever it was, it had hurt like hell. My bags flew out of my hands and onto the ground. I was grateful that everything was over-packaged so that nothing was damaged and I wouldn't have to waste more money to replace it all. It was one time that I thought the environment-loving tree huggers could kiss my ass. Clearly, the assassins were coming back in style.

I looked at my surroundings, trying to gather myself together as best as I could. "You'll pay for that!" I shouted. I couldn't see the face of the man who had attacked me as it was covered in one of those black ski masks with holes cut out for their eyes and mouth that thieves usually wore. What I could do though, was feel one of the man's hands pulling on my hair and the other hand holding onto my wrist so tight that I thought my veins might pop out.

"What are you going to do," the stranger shot back, "hit me with a loaf of bread?"

"No, I thought that I might do this," I calmly replied as I swung my leg around and delivered a high kick. It sent the assassin stumbling around on the sidewalk, trying to regain his footing while I got ready for the next move. I put up my fists in a fighting stance that I'd seen in movies and sent him a few quick punches that collided with various parts of his face.

"You *really* shouldn't have done that," he growled. Before I could begin another round, he pulled on my hair in an even tighter grip that I thought might rip my scalp off. Out of the corner of my eye, I spotted a garbage can. It wasn't full from what I could see, but I figured that I'd be able to move it fairly easily and still have it be able to do enough damage to let me get away.

I focused on it for a few seconds, summoning up every ounce of concentration that I had and then it sailed through the air at a high speed leaving no time for the attacker to duck and take cover. When the can collided with the guy's face, there was a loud crunch, and as I quickly collected my belongings, I glimpsed blood streaming down his face while he clutched at it. It served the bastard right.

I ran home as fast as my legs could carry me. When I got there, I locked the back door behind me, ran to the front door to double-check that it was also secured, and then made sure that all of the windows were shut tight, including the blinds. I hadn't noticed anyone following me and I hated being a prisoner in my own home, but I figured it was best to not take any chances of being seen for the time being. When I was satisfied and had put my groceries away, I went into the bathroom to take an Aspirin to stave off the headache that was threatening to erupt and then went to my bedroom to lie down and go to sleep.

Hours later, I awoke to the sound of Chris banging around in the kitchen and I checked the clock on the nightstand next to my bed. To my surprise, it was already past 7 o'clock. It didn't feel like I'd been sleeping for eight hours straight. I hadn't eaten since the early morning, so my stomach was growling fairly loudly. "Are you okay?" Chris asked me as I entered the kitchen. "You look like hell."

I looked at my reflection in the large window by the sink. My hair was all rumpled, I had bags under my eyes, my makeup was smeared and my eyes were puffy. "I feel like it, too." I sat down at the dining table and Chris handed me a glass of iced tea. "I was attacked again today."

His face became creased with worry and then darkened in anger. "Tell me all about it." I went into as much detail as I could remember and the expression on Chris' face kept getting graver by the second. "That does it! We're going to the Council as soon as possible."

"And how soon is *that*?"

"They'll be meeting in two days. Until that time, I don't want you going out anywhere without me," he said, his tone of voice suggesting that he wouldn't negotiate on a compromise.

"What about work?" I asked. Although I couldn't afford to lose a day, I reasoned that I also couldn't afford to lose my life. Money wasn't worth much compared to my safety.

"Call in a sick day or something."

"Fine, I'll come up with an excuse. Where is this meeting taking place, anyway?" I sipped the drink and it quenched my thirst.

"There's an abandoned warehouse outside of town," he replied. *"What is it with vampires and abandoned warehouses?"* I thought to myself. *"Why not something with style like a nice mansion or a penthouse condo?"*

"I wish that this was all over now," I said, a slight feeling of melancholy in my voice.

"It will be soon, my love," Chris said, gently lifting my head and making me meet his eyes. There was a hint of hope in them, but it hadn't been enough to erase my mood.

"Not soon enough. I can't relax and I should be happy spending time with you."

"You're not happy with me?"

I chuckled and tried to explain myself, "Of course I'm happy with you. You're the best thing in my life, Chris, but I've been on my guard ever since you told me about the assassins coming after me. There's this constant nagging in the back of my mind warning me to be careful and I'm so paranoid wondering if someone is going to jump out from behind a door and ambush me. I hate being afraid for my life like this."

"I know you do and I hate seeing what it's doing to you. If I could go back in time, I would, and then we'd never have gone to that stupid club so that none of this would have ever happened."

"If wishes were horses . . ."

"Huh?"

"I think it's from some quote. I don't know where I got it from, though. I just thought it kind of fit the moment," I replied.

"You have some pretty random thoughts," he said.

"I've been told that," I half-smiled at Chris. "I guess I should phone work tomorrow afternoon and tell them that I won't be coming in on Monday. It's too late to call tonight."

"Have you figured out an excuse yet?"

"I think I'll just say that I need a personal day, that way they probably won't ask me any questions that I can't answer. If they insist on a response, I'll just say something vague like 'Something came up at the last minute.'"

Chris nodded his head in approval. "Alright, then. I hope we'll have everything covered."

"Yeah." I fell silent and let my mind wander around, a fact which didn't escape his notice.

"What are you thinking about now?"

"That getting involved with you was both the best and the worst thing that's ever happened to me," I admitted.

"I see," he said, crestfallen. I looked at his face and, judging by his expression, I'd hurt his feelings unintentionally.

"If I have to do this all again just to be with you, I will, it just sucks while it's happening, you know? There isn't much I wouldn't do for you, Chris. You are my heart and soul and there is no 'me' without you. You complete me." I paused for a moment and chuckled, "Oh great, now I sound like a fucking Hallmark card. How cheesy was *that*?"

Chris leaned over to press his lips to mine, and then his hands made their way under my shirt, searching for the back of my bra. I pulled away from him and a look of confusion colored his face. "Chris, I don't want to make love until I can completely relax and enjoy it again. Please say that you understand."

He thought for a few seconds and then replied, "I do."

"I love when we get intimate, but I don't want that tainted by this fear that I have."

"And I want you to enjoy yourself with me, so if I have to wait for that, then that's what I'll do. I don't want to wait forever, though."

"Neither do I. I think that I'd kill myself if it ever came to that. I need your love like a fish needs water." There was a brief pause while I thought about that last statement and then I burst into laughter. "I'm just full of hokey sayings tonight."

"Yeah, but I appreciate the sentiment, anyway," he said.

"Thanks."

"If you killed yourself and I turned you, then our problems would all be over."

"You're not seriously suggesting that I off myself, *are you*?" I asked, not sure if he was being sarcastic or not.

Chris was taken aback. "No, of course not! I was talking shit like I know you were when you mentioned killing yourself."

"I was just being dramatic, but would you have agreed to turn me if I really was serious?" I asked.

He thought for a second and then replied, "Yeah, in a heartbeat."

"Maybe one day it'll happen."

"You've thought about it?"

"A little," I admitted. "I'm scared to hell of dying, but the idea of being with you forever makes it a little less terrifying. Everyone dies some time, so isn't it better to choose when it's your time to go and have a loved one turn you into a vampire rather than risk getting shot in the street like a dog by some criminal and left to rot or slowly fade away to a shell of your former self because of some horrible debilitating disease?"

"Won't you miss being human and your friends and family?" he asked.

"Of course. It all just gets to be a drag sometimes. When my human life ends, I'll have a new life with all sorts of new experiences and we can hunt together. We'll be on the same schedule and I won't have to live an exhausting double life."

"That sounds like you've been thinking of this more than just a little."

"Yeah, well . . ." I trailed off, not knowing how to end that thought. "Dating a vampire is making me think of things that I've never thought of before and making me see other things in a different light."

"Is that good?"

"I like to think so. Another thing that I'm thinking of is that I've got the best boyfriend in the world."

"You *do*? Who is he? Where is he?" Chris asked, pretending to look around for my imaginary paramour.

"Right in front of me," I beamed, wrapping my arms around him.

"I knew that," he said, grinning. "Part of my job of being the best boyfriend in the world is to take care of you and I won't disappoint." He turned around and picked up something that I couldn't see, but I sure could smell it. "Close your eyes," he commanded me and I obeyed, eagerly awaiting my surprise. "You can open them now." I did as I was told and found myself facing a plate full of fruit, pancakes and breakfast sausages that had been arranged in a meticulous and artful way.

"It's beautiful," I remarked.

I looked down at the food and thought of what a shame it would be to ruin the arrangement. "Go on and eat," he encouraged me. I hesitated briefly, and then dug my knife and fork in to cut off a piece of sausage. I tasted it and it was cooked to perfection. Chris watched me savor the meal for a while and then got up from his seat.

"Where are you going?"

"Watching you eat is making me hungry. I'm going out to feed for a while." "Okay," I said and continued to eat. By the time that he came back, I'd finished the meal and washed the few dishes that were out.

"How do you feel now?" Chris asked when he entered the kitchen.

"Better, thanks. That was really good cooking for a vampire."

"I guess it comes from having such a heightened sense of smell."

"How was *your* meal?" I asked him.

"You don't really want to know, do you?"

"No, I was just trying to be polite. Anyway, I'm glad that you're feeling better, too."

"Yeah, thanks," he said. A moment of silence passed as Chris and I stood staring at each other. "Do you think that I'm a monster? Be honest with me and I promise that I won't be offended."

I gave my words careful consideration before I spoke. "Yes, I do. You're sweet to me, but at the end of the day, you drink blood from people and you've killed in the past. I don't know if you kill anyone now aside from that guy who was outside the house a few weeks ago, and I really don't want to know, either. If that doesn't qualify you as a monster, then I don't know what does."

"Alright. Thanks for not pulling any punches. I wanted to know what you really thought and I got it."

"If it helps, I think that you're the sexiest monster I've ever seen. Then again, there really isn't that much competition."

"Not really, but thanks for trying, anyway," he smiled and came to stand next to me.

"Any time," I smiled back. "While we're doing this honesty thing, can I ask *you* a question?"

"Of course. Go ahead." Chris leaned back on the counter and turned his head to face me.

"Do you think it's stupid of me to try to ignore what you do? I mean, I know what you do when you feed, but I'd rather not know the whole truth and try to pretend that you're a normal guy. I've been doing some reading about vampires, but when I read, none of it seems real so it doesn't bother me as much as the reality of it does. Does that make any sense to you?"

"It's not stupid of you to ignore it. In fact, I don't blame you for doing it. It's an ugly truth and it takes a strong person to not only face it, but to look past it and see to the heart of the person that the vampire used to be. You can never forget what I really am and what I do, but you also shouldn't bury your head in the sand and deny it all. You saw me in a moment of my true nature, yet you're still here by my side so that must count for something. You're special, Jessi—one of a kind."

I gazed up into Chris' eyes and saw the love displayed there for all to see and then I rested my head on his chest. After a few seconds, he picked me up and took me into the living room to lie down on the couch and I held my position. "That's a bit better," he said.

"How can a monster be so sweet and romantic? How can a monster love me and how can I love one back? It doesn't make sense to me, which is why I think that you still have some sense of humanity in you, no matter how small it may be."

"Love doesn't always make sense nor does it have to—that's the beauty of it. You just have to follow your heart and do what feels right."

"Did you ever think that this would happen to you? Falling in love with a human?" I asked him, slowly running my hand down his chest.

"Never. I've slaughtered many in my time, but I'd never entertained any feelings for one until you came along. The closest that I came were the few times when I'd thought that I would've fancied them if I were still human, but then the bloodlust would quickly overtake me and I'd lose myself in the frenzy."

"Am I weird for loving a vampire?"

"Well, since I'm the vampire in question, I'm going to have to say 'no.'" Chris smiled and I chuckled.

"Do you think of yourself as a monster?"

Chris contemplated his answer, "Yes and no. Yes, because like you said, I drink blood from people and I have killed countless humans. No, because I view myself differently than a human would. What I do is all a part of my nature and I've been doing it for so long that I don't really remember any other way of life. I need food to survive just like anyone else, but my version of food just happens to be human blood. If there was any other way to feed myself, perhaps I'd use that instead if it tasted right to me. As it stands, human blood is the only thing that serves this purpose."

"What about when Nat was over and I saw you eating?" I asked, curious.

"I thought you would have figured out that I only did it so as not to arouse her suspicions."

"I did."

"Vampires rarely eat human food, but when they do it's mainly either to combat boredom or to try to fit in with the population if they're looking for potential prey."

"Speaking of the other night, remember how Nat asked us about having kids?" I asked Chris and he nodded his head. "Did you ever want to have any when you were alive?"

"No. My life was a bit of a mess back then as I'd told you. Why do you ask? You know we can never mate together. Are you reconsidering being with me because I can't give you children?" he asked, taken aback by the possibility.

"No! I was just wondering about your thoughts on the subject. When I was with Hayden, I thought about kids and being a mother, but now that I'm with you, I'd rather just have you all to myself. Besides, I don't think that raising a child with a vampire is the best of ideas, especially when I'm already risking my own life. I couldn't do that to an innocent child, too."

"I'm sorry for overreacting like that. I guess I'm just afraid that one day you'll change your mind and leave me for someone who can give you what I can't."

"Not everything in life is something I want to experience. Don't beat yourself up about it, Chris. I'm the only one to blame for missing out on something, because it was *my* choice to miss out on it," I said, trying to reassure him.

"I understand," he said, giving a slight nod.

"Good."

"But it's hard to get rid of that guilt."

"I hope, no, I *think* that you can do it," I said, squeezing his hand.

"So do I." A moment of silence fell over us as we thought about what our future had in store for us. "So, read any good books lately?" Chris asked to break the ice.

"A little. I took out some books on vampires from one of the libraries in the city."

"Why? I could tell you anything that you wanted to know."

"I don't want to waste all of our time together by talking about it. I don't mind doing my own research," I replied. "It gives me something to do during my breaks at work."

"May I see them?" he asked.

"Be my guest." Chris carried me up the stairs to my bedroom where we spent the rest of the night poring over the mythology texts and he pointed out some of the inaccuracies in them like how vampires preferred to sleep in coffins filled with dirt and how they could turn themselves into animals.

As a child, anything supernatural-related used to scare the daylights out of me and that hadn't really changed until just recently. I mean, I could tolerate some of the lighter shows and movies, but that was about it. I knew about some of the vampire basics before I had met Chris, but he would really be giving me a crash course in the realities of the darker side of life.

The next day, I woke up pretty late in the morning since I hadn't gotten to sleep until the early hours. I fixed myself something to eat, then went on the computer to check on some e-mails while I waited until just after the store opened. I figured that I'd let everyone open up and get settled in before I called to tell them the bad news.

"STARS department store—Kathy speaking. How may I help you?" a voice on the other end answered.

"This is Jessica Winters from Cosmetics. I'm just calling in to say that I won't be able to come in to work tomorrow."

"Oh, okay. May I ask why?" Kathy asked, sounding quite uninterested.

"I've got a personal issue that's come up recently."

"And how long will you be out for?"

"Hopefully just tomorrow," I replied.

"If you need more time, you'll have to confirm it with your supervisor."

"I know."

"And there's a possibility that you'll have to use up a sick day," she informed me.

"I know."

"Alright then, thanks for calling." Kathy hung up and I placed the receiver of the phone back in its cradle on the wall. I wondered what I could do now that I had so much time to kill. Chris had told me not to go anywhere without him until this was all over, but how did he really expect me to abide by that? Didn't he realize that I might go crazy if I had to stay cooped up for very long? I guessed that I'd just have to try my best; after all, Chris couldn't exactly help me during the day if I were to get myself into a sticky situation. It would only be for a couple of days and if I kept busy, they'd fly by.

I went around the house to do some light cleaning and then I went through a bunch of papers and other odds and ends to see what I could get rid of. I lit the candle that Natalie had brought over, letting the pleasant wild berry smell of it waft all over the house while I worked.

When I was done my organizing, I put on my red and black bikini and my cheap $20 Wal-Mart sunglasses before going outside into the backyard to lie back on my lounge chair and catch a little sun. I knew what Chris had told me, but I didn't think that I was breaking any rule. I went into the shed and took out a crowbar for some protection and peace of mind. I only stayed out long enough to top up my tan a bit. The fresh air felt good to breathe in and the sun on my skin was just glorious.

I went back inside the house after a while and changed back into my regular clothes, then set about making some salad. I turned the radio on at a low volume so that I could have some background music as I chopped up the vegetables and pretended that I was some famous celebrity chef like Emeril Lagasse or Rachel Ray.

When I was done with my creation, I settled down onto the couch in the living room with my dinner to watch TV. I flipped through the channels and found nothing on that I was interested in seeing thanks to the usual crappy Sunday night programming, so I popped in a DVD and sat back down to watch the movie *Clueless*. I hadn't seen it in a long time and it was a good way to end the day. About half-way through the movie, Chris poked his head around the wall between the kitchen and living room. "What are you watching?"

"*Clueless.*"

"Never heard of it. Is it good?"

"Yeah, but I don't know if you'd like it. It's kind of a girly movie," I replied.

"What else did you do today?" he asked, sitting down beside me.

"I called the store and told them that I'd need some time off."

"How did that go?"

"I didn't have any trouble, thank goodness. I just said that I had a personal issue that came up recently and the person I talked to just told me stuff about store protocol—no biggie. I was so afraid that she'd want me to elaborate and get specific on what the problem was, but she just let it drop. I don't think she wanted to listen to me any more than I wanted to talk to her."

"Good," Chris said.

"I also did some cleaning, some organizing and went outside to tan."

"You went outside? I told you not to go anywhere without me."

"Technically, I didn't. I was only out in the backyard and I had a weapon with me just in case," I reasoned.

"It doesn't matter. You were still out of the house and therefore, you were susceptible to being attacked again," he said as calmly as possible. I could tell that he was trying really hard not to raise his voice, knowing that it would get him nowhere.

"But I *wasn't* attacked. Nothing happened except a bit of tanning fun. Besides, if someone really wanted to get me, wouldn't they be able to find their way into the house somehow? They could break down a door or bust a window or worse yet, burn the place down."

"Yeah, but . . ."

I held up my hand and cut him off. "Nothing happened. I just needed to get out of the house for a while, that's all and I don't regret what I did."

"What if something *had* happened and you weren't able to use your power?" he asked me, trying to make me see how reckless I'd been.

"Well, if worst came to worst, I guess I'd have to kick the guy in the crotch and bite him until he let me go or something. Maybe I'd also throw in some head butting for good measure."

"Never *ever* disobey me again."

"*What the fuck*? You don't own me!" I shot back, my blood beginning to boil. I wasn't anyone's property and I would not allow anyone to assume that I was.

"I'm just trying to protect you, goddammit!" Chris shouted at me.

"You don't have to yell, Chris, I'm *not* deaf!"

"I'm sorry for swearing, but I'm frustrated that you're not doing what I tell you to. It was a very simple request for your own protection."

"You're not the only one who's frustrated here. You have to understand that I'm not used to being caged up like an animal at the zoo."

"Please promise me that you won't do it again, okay? It's just until tomorrow night."

I sighed, then nodded and replied, "I promise, but what if I really need something or there's an emergency?"

"Couldn't you call someone for help like a neighbor?" he asked in a much more calm voice.

"I suppose so, but I'm not particularly close to any of them. I don't know how much help they'd be if push came to shove."

"Well then, just cross your fingers that you won't need to find out for sure."

"What's the plan for tonight?" I asked, my voice sounding almost lifeless.

"If there's anything you need for the next few days, we'll go out and do some shopping," he replied.

I paused for a moment to think about that and said, "Give me a few minutes to make a list."

Ten minutes later, we were out the door and on our way to the Stop-n-Shop near the site of the third attack. It gave me the willies to go back to the scene of the crime as so to speak, but in this town, choices were pretty limited, especially if you were trying to shop at night. Although the convenience store was open around the clock, what little they offered cost a bundle. I knew that I'd have to come back to the Stop-n-Shop sooner or later, so it looked like I would be doing it sooner.

The two of us wandered down aisle after aisle scouring the shelves for the items on my list and anything else of interest that perhaps I'd forgotten about or had an impulse to buy. It was kind of surreal to do something so ordinary and mundane with a vampire, but at the same time, he came in handy when I couldn't reach something that was too high on the shelf.

At the checkout counter, while I had been in the process of taking some money out of my wallet, Chris slapped down his credit card. "That'll be $59.55," said the clerk as he swiped the card and then handed it back.

"You really didn't have to do that," I said as we left the store.

"It's no big deal. I thought that I'd just help out a bit, that's all."

"Well, thanks. We should get these groceries home and then we can come back out if you want to go somewhere else."

"Or you could wait here while I take them home," he offered.

"Wouldn't that be violating your rule about not going somewhere without you?" I asked.

"Yeah, but I'd only be gone for about a minute at the most; I can run really fast."

"So there's no danger of anyone seeing you?"

"If they do, I'll be like a blur to them," Chris assured me. "I just need your house key."

"Be careful, baby," I said, passing it to him.

"Same to you," he said and took off like a rocket into the night. I stood leaning against the side of the building for a few seconds and then thought the better of it. Instead, I began to walk towards the main area of town and only got about a block away from the store before Chris caught up with me.

"Hi, again," I greeted him.

"I told you I wouldn't be gone long. Now, where to?"

"How about *you* pick?"

"Alright," he replied. Chris led us into a bar called Hank's Place and steered me over to a table near the back. I looked around at the place that I'd passed by hundreds of times, but had never been in before and now I knew why. From the outside it looked fairly dirty and the inside was even worse. It was decked out in hillbilly chic complete with severed animal heads mounted on the walls like hunters trophies, replicas of rifles and shotguns—or maybe they were real ones—and road signs, which, I assumed were stolen. Why Chris wanted to come in here, I had no idea, but I hoped that no one I knew had seen me come in.

A waiter took our drink orders—a Budweiser for Chris and a chocolate martini for me—and delivered them a few minutes later. Just then, Hayden entered the bar and spotted me. "*What is* he *doing in here of all people*?" I thought to myself. With all of the money he had, I never figured him for slumming it in a place like that. Of all the bars in the world, he had to end up in mine. Maybe I should have ordered a stiffer drink?

While I wondered what was going on and sipped my martini, he began to walk over to our table. "Oh no!" I groaned.

"What's wrong?"

"My ex just came in and he's heading this way."

"So, I get to finally meet the guy whose heart you broke," Chris said, smirking like he was getting ready to gloat.

"I'd rather that we left now," I muttered.

"I don't want to be rude," he said in a sarcastic tone, which suggested that he just wanted to stay to check out the idiot who lost the best thing he ever had.

"And *I* don't want anyone to make a scene."

"I owe some thanks to him."

"For *what*?" I asked, although I was afraid I already knew the answer.

"For screwing up what he had with you." Yep, it was just as I had thought. We couldn't argue any further now that Hayden was only a few feet away and so we just sat, waiting for the inevitable to take place.

Hayden sauntered up to the table, dressed to the nines in one of his usual custom-made designer Italian suits—this one was navy blue—that he wore with a matching tie. "Jessi, what a pleasant surprise! What are you doing here?" he said with mock sincerity, glancing down at the drink in my hand and making a point to ignore Chris. It was just as well that my ex hadn't been paying attention to Chris as he was silently eyeing him and giving me a subtle look that said "*I can't believe you were with him.*"

"What are *you* doing here? I hadn't pegged you as the type to set foot in a joint that wasn't rated in the Zagat's guide," I asked Hayden.

"I just needed to use the bathroom and ask for directions. Anyway, how have you been?"

"Good, thanks. And yourself?"

"I could be better," he admitted.

"If you'll excuse me, I'm on a date." When Hayden finally turned to notice Chris for the first time, they sized each other up to check out the competition. Chris slid his arm around me and pulled me closer to him like he was an animal marking its territory. It couldn't have been any more obvious than if he had peed on me, which was a pretty "ew" kind of thought. "Hayden, this is my new boyfriend, Chris Sinclair. Chris, this is my ex, Hayden van Austen."

As the two men stared each other down, I felt an excessive amount of tension and testosterone in the air. I knew that if I didn't try to defuse the situation, there was no telling what could happen. "Now boys, let's all play nice," I said in a faux-motherly tone like I was speaking to a couple of little kids.

"Alright," Chris said reluctantly.

"How come I haven't seen you around town before?" Hayden asked him.

"He just moved here recently," I replied before Chris could.

"Where are you living?"

"With me." As soon as I said those words, Hayden's head quickly snapped towards me.

"*What?*"

"You heard me. We're living together," I said, putting on a confident façade that I didn't really feel.

"How long have you known each other?" he demanded to know, trying to struggle to keep his voice calm.

"About a month or so."

"*A month?*" Hayden chuckled uncomfortably. "I gave you *four years* and asked you to move in with me numerous times, but you kept turning me down. You meet *him*," Hayden nodded his head towards Chris, "and all of a sudden you can't wait to live with someone else. Well, isn't *that* just perfect!"

"Maybe you should go and do what you came to do, Hayden, and we'll mind our own business," I suggested.

"Yeah, sure," Hayden still stared Chris down with a burning hatred and finally tore his eyes away from him a few moments later. He walked back in the other direction, occasionally looking over his shoulder at us and talked to the bartender.

"What did you ever see in him?" Chris asked me.

"You don't know him the way that I do."

"Thank goodness for that. I won't insult him for your sake, but there's something about him that I don't like or trust."

"Like what?" I asked, curious and mildly irritated at Chris' insinuations.

"It's just a feeling that I was getting from him. I don't think that he's over you yet and I don't think that he ever will be. Seeing you again just poured more fuel on the fire."

"I don't really care what he thinks anymore."

"Is that so?" Chris asked, sounding a little dubious.

"Yeah, but I also don't think that there's anything wrong with still being on friendly terms with him."

"I'm not asking you to stop being friends with him, but I think that you should definitely watch yourself if you continue to associate with him. There's no way to predict what someone will do when they're still so in love with you. People in love are capable of doing all sorts of messed up shit as you well know and some will stop at nothing to get what they want. I'd hate to see you become another statistic."

"Thanks for your concern, Chris, but I think that you're making a bigger deal out of it than what it is," I said, trying to play down his fears, but not feeling as confident as I sounded.

"I really hope that you're right, Jessi. Anyway, let's forget all about him and just enjoy being here," Chris said, glancing around at our surroundings and taking it all in for the first time, "if we can."

Chapter 9

On Monday morning, I sat up in bed for a while thinking of what I could do to pass the time before the big meeting that night. It felt really weird to be playing hooky from work. I hadn't done that since I was in the eighth grade, but desperate times called for desperate measures. After I ate, I decided that it would do me some good to do some reading and lose myself in a fantasy world.

I ended up spending the next few hours reading and got so caught up in the story that when I finally stopped, I'd finished the best part of 80 pages. I'd moved on from reading that Harlequin book about the guy posing as a soldier and was now reading one about a man and a woman who were stranded on a deserted island. They had been passengers on a cruise ship that hit a rough storm and then they were tossed overboard with nothing but the clothes on their backs. It was one of those stories where the people hated each other's guts and then found themselves fucking each other's brains out.

I made myself a chicken burger for lunch and then spent the rest of the afternoon doing some baking. I found a bunch of old boxes of mixes that I'd never gotten around to using and within a few hours I'd made enough chocolate-chip cookies, chocolate muffins, brownies and cakes to almost feed an army.

After supper, I fretted about what to wear to the night's big soirée. Chris hadn't exactly told me in great detail about what was going to happen, so I had no clue of what to expect. *"Should I dress casual? Should I dress up?"* I thought to myself. It's not like there were articles in *Vogue* or *Cosmo* that addressed this sort of thing, but if I needed to learn *"60 Ways to Please Your Man in Bed"* or *"How to Achieve Orgasm Before Your Man Does"*, then I had the goods.

"You look good," Chris commented on my eventual choice of a pair of skinny black jeans, form-fitting blue t-shirt with a scoop neck and black and white Sketchers sneakers.

"Thanks. I wasn't sure what to wear, so I just went with something casual, but still nice enough to be sort of dressy and that I can run in easily if need be," I replied.

"I wish that I could rip off your clothes right now and have my way with you, you look so enticing." He gently grabbed me and pulled me close to his body.

I giggled like a school girl. "Your time will come later, until then, keep it in your pants, alright?"

"I'll try," he flashed his fangs in a sly grin. As we left the house, I grabbed a black cropped jacket off of its hanger in the hall closet and closed up all of the windows and doors. We drove in Chris' car and got to the site with time to spare before the meeting began.

From the outside, the warehouse looked like the twin of the one that housed the vampire nightclub, but I supposed that that shouldn't have come as a shock. If you've seen one derelict warehouse, you've pretty much seen them all. I still couldn't help feeling a bit of apprehension about the whole ordeal and I tried to shake it off. Negative vibes wouldn't help me get through it and I'd need all the help that I could get.

We entered the dank building, which was sparsely lit against the dark gray cement walls. It wouldn't be hard for a vampire to see though the dark, but I'd have to try to position myself near the few lights if at all possible. While I thought that it wouldn't have been quite so bad to be kept in the dark, if you'll pardon the pun, I'd rather have been able to see who was going to be deciding my fate.

"Alfonso, my man!" Chris called out to a dark-skinned vampire across the room. The stranger quickly strode over to us followed by a red-haired woman who was holding his hand. "How are you? Long time, no see!"

"I'm good, thanks. And yourself?"

"I've never been better."

"Who is *this* delectable dish?" Alfonso asked Chris, licking his fangs in pleasure at the sight of me. The woman caught him doing that and punched him hard in the arm, displeased that he was ogling me. He snarled at her and then turned back to look at me, as if he hadn't been interrupted.

"This is my girlfriend, Jessica."

"Girlfriend?" Alfonso sniffed the air around me. "She's *human*. Why haven't you killed her yet? Have you forgotten that you're a vampire? Are you a human lover now?" he sneered with derision at such an idea.

"Don't revoke my membership card yet," Chris shot back. "I love her and that's why we're here. *Someone* ratted us out to the Council and they've been sending out assassins to kill her ever since. We want to make a plea to spare her life."

"Oh, isn't that sweet and touching," Alfonso said, his voice dripping with sarcasm. "Pass me a bucket, because I think I'm going to puke." I rolled my eyes at his sentiment. "Look, Chris, you know I like you and as such, I've got to advise you that you're making a huge mistake here. Our kind is not meant to live with humans. We are the predators and they are the prey."

"The two of us seem to be doing alright so far," Chris gave my shoulder a squeeze.

"Well, I guess that every group has to have a freak in it." Alfonso turned to his companion and they laughed in unison.

Chris leaned in close to him, fangs bared and barked, "Say that again right to my face!"

"You're a *freak*!" Alfonso snarled and then stalked away with the redhead.

"Go fuck yourself."

"That was intense," I remarked. "Is that one of the vampires that you're acquaintances with?"

"He was, but not anymore. I won't tolerate anyone speaking ill of you."

"But wouldn't pretty much everyone here be doing that, too?" I swept my hands to gesture around the room. "It wouldn't really be wise to make enemies with all of the other vampires, especially if we're trying to get them to do something for us."

"Alfonso has no weight to pull with the Council, plus, I don't take kindly to being insulted no matter the circumstances. Perhaps one day I may find it in my unbeating heart to forgive him or perhaps one day he will come around to see my point of view. Until such time, I don't give a flying shit what he thinks. He can kiss daylight for all I care."

"Wow." I had never heard Chris talk like that before, so I was pretty speechless. To try to fill the uncomfortable silence, I looked around the room and my eyes fell upon a group of people shrouded in shadow. I squinted to see if I could make the figures out better, but to no avail. Although I couldn't see them well, I couldn't tear my eyes away from them for some unknown reason. After a few moments, they stepped towards one of the lights and I was amazed at what I saw.

"What are they?" I nodded my head towards the group.

"Zombies," he replied quite simply.

"Get the *fuck* out of here!" I whispered. "*Really*?"

"Really."

"Well, I'll be damned." The zombies didn't look anything like what zombies in TV shows and movies were portrayed to be as far as I knew. These ones had the hair colors that they must have had while they were alive (black, brown, blonde, red and some colors that were not so natural). Their clothes were stylish yet ragged from years of wear and tear and their translucent skin accentuated their veins and pitch-black eyes that contrasted with the smiles on their faces.

Usually, zombies in the movies had angry or hungry sorts of expressions on their faces, but I found the permanent smiles to be even more unsettling. I shuddered as I pictured one of them bearing down on me in pursuit of my flesh and smiling as they ripped me limb from limb. Gross me out.

"What do you think?" Chris asked me.

"They're kind of pretty in a really creepy sort of way, but what do they do? What do they eat?"

"They do whatever their master tells them to. They could carry out all sorts of tasks from brutally killing someone right on down to sweeping the steps. They have a limited brain capacity, of course, so anything that they're told to do has to be a fairly simple task. They're essentially treated like slaves so that their master can avoid getting his or her hands dirty if at all possible.

"I don't have much experience with zombies, but from what I *do* know, they enjoy eating human brains, but only the live ones. If they're not fresh, they could be harmful to them. They will also eat human flesh, both live and from corpses, but it doesn't satisfy them as much as the brains do," Chris explained.

"They really take flesh from dead bodies?" I asked, shuddering as I fought back the bile that was rising up in my throat.

"Yeah. I've never witnessed it myself, but that is my understanding. Even *I* find it to be pretty gruesome, so that's saying something. That's why there are the occasional stories in the news about graves being dug up."

"I always thought that those were about some dumbass punk teenagers just wanting to be destructive and disrespectful."

Chris shook his head. "Sometimes they are. Usually it's because the masters dig up the graves, open up the coffins and then let the zombies feast upon them like a buffet."

"I wish I didn't know about that."

"Well, you *did* ask," he replied.

"I know and now I'm really wishing that I didn't." Chris chuckled at me and at that moment, a hush fell over the room. "What's going on?" I whispered.

"The meeting's about to start," he muttered. The barely lit warehouse felt even darker as the members of the Council took center stage on a dais that was situated near the back wall. The space instantly buzzed and crackled with a sense of power. I could already tell that they were people that you didn't want to mess with. The lights that were currently on in the room switched off and there was another flicker before they came back on, but now they were on near the dais so that only the members of the Council were bathed in light. Clearly, these guys liked to be in the spotlight.

"I call to order this meeting of The Council of the Night," a tall, male vampire bellowed. With my limited human eyesight I had to squint to see him better, but he looked to be quite thin with gray hair and elegant features. I wondered if perhaps he was from the time of the Renaissance, because he had a classic facial structure that I thought I'd recognized from my high school history texts. Then again, maybe he had just been blessed with a good plastic surgeon. In any case, he looked quite intimidating and it was no wonder to me how he came to be the head of the Council.

"The first order of business is Ares and his zombies." A vampire who must have been Ares walked up to the dais, stopping several feet away. The head vampire turned to face the newcomer and said, "There have been complaints that your army of zombies have been getting out of control."

"I know, sir, but you see . . ."

"I don't have time for nor am I interested in your excuses."

"Yes, sir," Ares bowed his head in deference.

"See to it that you get your army back under your control or else there will be consequences."

Another council member, a short, stocky, blond man, interjected, "Failure to comply will result in either the total destruction of your zombies or your own death. In the event that you die, the zombies will become property of the Council and their ultimate fate will be up to our discretion."

"Do you understand and accept the terms of the situation?" the head of the Council asked.

"Yes, sir."

"Then you may be dismissed." He waved off Ares who then began walking backwards away from the dais, his head bowed again in respect until he blended back in with the crowd. "Who's next?"

"Councilman Louis, Cameron has been having a problem with his nest," the short, blond man informed him.

"What sort of problem?" he asked as Cameron was beckoned up to the dais.

"Sir, I'm the head of a rather large nest. There are fourteen of us in total now, but there used to be more. Fighting within the nest has caused our number to dwindle down from twenty."

"This sounds like something that you should be handling yourself. What do you want *me* to do about it?"

"I've tried everything that I could think of to control my vampires."

The Councilman leaned in closer to Cameron and snarled, "Then try *harder.*"

"But sir . . ."

Louis sighed in exasperation, "Very well then. I command you to divide up the nest into three smaller groups. Choose those vampires that you deem to be the strongest and use them to form a new nest. The remainders will be forced to fend for themselves."

"Thank you, sir," Cameron bowed.

"And if you ever come to the Council for such matters again, you won't find me to be so charitable."

"Yes, sir. I won't bother you with such a problem ever again."

"Why bother being a leader if you can't control those under your watch? Get out of my sight now!" Louis commanded him.

Cameron walked backwards as quickly as he could and nearly stumbled over a bump in the floor. "Who's next?"

"That's all for tonight," the blond vampire replied.

"Not exactly," Chris chimed in and he started walking towards the dais with me right behind him. He held my hand and I could feel all eyes on me, even though I couldn't actually see them. It reminded me of that night in the vampire nightclub when all of the trouble started.

"I've never seen you here before, Christopher Sinclair. To what do we owe this pleasure?"

"We're here to ask the Council to call off the attacks on my girlfriend, Jessica," he replied, his voice steady as a rock. The Councilman looked me over and I was creeped out by the way that he was checking me out, but I made sure not to show it as Chris and I would have to be on our best behavior until the matter was resolved. As we stood in front of the large gathering of vampires, I felt even more fearful than I had been before, but I resolved to stay strong and make it through the night in one piece.

Louis sniffed the air. "She's a *human*. Why should we give help to such a lower being?"

"I love her." A raucous laughter rang out from every member of the Council and from most of the crowd. Chris looked back at the mass of vampires and scowled at them, then turned back to face the dais. I was too frightened to look around at everyone else's reactions; however I did put on my own expression of displeasure and annoyance at such a crude display of behavior. I gently clasped Chris' hand to give him the strength, support and inspiration that he needed to persuade these monsters that I was worth saving.

"The only loves that vampires know of are the love of killing and the love of drinking blood. Any other kind of love is a human feeling which is beneath us. When we died and became vampires, we left all such feelings behind and were liberated. Why would you want to go back to being a slave to your emotions? Why would you want to go back to being a lower life form?"

"I don't believe that I *am* a lower life form," Chris replied and some vampires in the crowd scoffed, but he ignored them this time.

"Then what *are* you?" the head vampire asked him, leaning forward with a strange curiosity.

"I'm a vampire who's better than you because I was given the chance to re-connect with my humanity and I took the risk of opening up my heart to someone outside of my own kind," Chris snarled, getting in Louis' face.

"You think you're better than me because of this?"

"Yeah."

"Well, I think that you've lost your mind," Louis snapped at him.

Chris slapped the sides of the dais so hard that it began to crack and then continued talking, ignoring Louis' look of anger. "Maybe I have, but I don't care. All I give a damn about is that Jessica has made me feel things that I haven't felt in over a century and given me the greatest pleasures that I've ever known. Think whatever you want of me for saying this, but I would die a thousand times over if it meant that her life would be spared. We love each other and nothing that anyone else can do or say will ever change that. If we can't stay together in this life, then perhaps we will meet again one day in the next and be reunited forever there."

I'm not ashamed to say that as I listened to Chris speak, a few tears began to escape my eyes. His words were so full of power, sincerity and love. I didn't see how anyone could deny us anything after he said that, unless they were absolutely devoid of any spark of humanity. I never felt more proud of Chris than I had in that moment and I reached out to touch his arm to show that I appreciated his little speech.

"Oh, how touching," Louis said sarcastically, making a mocking gesture with his frail-looking pale hands. "I still don't see why we should call off the attacks. In my opinion, the more humans that die, the better, just as long as we drain them first. Human beings are a stain on the fabric of society and I long to see the day when all that remains on earth are our kind." He turned to the blond vampire, giving the impression that the case was closed, and then muttered something unintelligible to my ears.

"Look!" I exclaimed, trying to get his attention back. His head immediately snapped towards me, irritation etched on his face. "I know that you hate all humans and you don't care about their feelings, but Chris and I want to be together for the rest of our lives. I don't see what harm it can do to just leave us alone in peace. I love him more than I've ever loved anybody before. He means the world to me and I know that he feels the same way so please call off the attacks right now," I pleaded, tears streaming down my cheeks.

"I love it when humans beg for their life," Louis said to a tall, black-haired female vampire. "They're so pathetic and it really puts them in their place." The woman chuckled in agreement. "Alright, I'll be generous just this once and grant you your request. I do have one condition, though: if either of you make one wrong move, you will die, *human*. If such an occasion should arise and Chris interferes, he will be punished severely. I assume that he has knowledge of what sort of possible fates will await him?"

"Yes, sir," Chris replied.

"Good. Hopefully, these threats will be more than enough to keep you in line." I began to cry in earnest at the news, which only made the head of the Council shake his head in disgust. "Why not let us put you out of your misery right now and get it all over with?" he asked with his voice full of contempt. The crowd cheered the idea on and that just made me cry even harder. "You cry when you think you're facing certain death and you still cry when I spare your life. Disgusting."

Chris turned to face the onlookers and yelled, "Shut the fuck up!" It seemed that the plan for making nice with the

Council had gone right out the window. I hoped that the outburst wouldn't be counted in our little deal.

"*Excuse me*?" Louis said, taken aback.

"Can't you see how much everything has been hurting her? She doesn't want to die and definitely not by your hand or fang."

"Loving a human has made you soft, Christopher, and she wouldn't be dying by my hand. I wouldn't want to touch a human and risk being tainted the way that this one has tainted you. Perhaps I'll get Ares' army of zombies to do the trick. How will you love your human when her flesh and brain are all torn away?"

"Don't you fucking *dare* touch her!" Chris' fangs popped out in anger.

"My, my! Perhaps I was wrong about you being so soft. It seems that you've got as much rage and anger as ever, but it's such a shame that some of it has been misdirected. You are a vampire, and as such, you belong with your undead brethren and not the human population. You cannot truly live as a human," Louis said.

"I seem to be doing well so far."

"Very well, then. I guess that there is nothing more to say on the subject if you remain unwilling to change your mind. I have no more to say to you right now. Please get out of my sight," the head of the Council commanded, his voice dripping with disdain. He turned to the black-haired woman and said, "How can someone go so wrong? Dating a human? That's just vile." I could see the woman's lips open to respond, but before long Chris and I were walking out of earshot so I couldn't tell what she had said. I was certain that Chris had heard it, though. I didn't want to ask him about it, because I was sure that whatever was said, it would just piss me off even more and I'd had more than enough for the night.

Just then, I received the shock of my life. Hayden burst through the door of the warehouse and was greeted by a crowd of vampires who were eyeballing him like he was the tastiest thing they'd ever seen. The lights near us were lit again, so that everyone could better see the newcomer. This had to have been one of the stupidest things that he'd ever done. Chris' words about love making you do crazy things came back to me and suddenly everything made sense.

"Jessi! What are you doing here?"

"I could ask you the same thing!" I shouted back.

"I staked out your house and followed you and your boyfriend here," he explained.

"You really shouldn't have done that," I said, trying to put as much warning into my voice as I could.

"Seeing you last night re-awakened my feelings for you and I realized just how stupid I was to let you get away from me. I came to tell you that I want you back and that I'll change my ways. I'll do whatever you want me to do. I still love you, Jessi!"

"That's nice and all, but when I said that you really shouldn't have come, I mean you *really* shouldn't have come. Look around you: does this look like a good time to try to win me over?" I gestured around the room with my hands.

"What's going on?" he asked, his eyes darting back and forth from me to Chris to the throng of vampires surrounding him.

"Well, it's not a walk in the park, that's for sure. Believe me when I say, walk out of here *right now* while you can."

"What is the meaning of this? Who is this intruder?" Louis demanded to know.

"This is my girlfriend's ex-boyfriend, sir," Chris responded.

"Another human?"

"Yes, sir."

The head of the Council conferred with the black-haired woman and the blond-haired man and they all nodded their heads in agreement. They flashed their fangs as Louis asked, "Ares, if you can control your zombies, would you please have them dispose of the male?"

"With pleasure!" Ares replied. He said something in a language I couldn't understand and then the zombies started shuffling over to where Hayden was standing, stuck in place like a deer caught in the headlights of an oncoming car.

"No!" I cried out, my eyes as wide as saucers. "Don't do it!"

"Too late!" the Councilman cackled in a way that gave me goose bumps up and down my arms. He reveled in seeing the anguish on my face and that pushed me to do something crazy as hell. I guessed that Chris had noticed the change in my expression, because he tried to stop me.

"What are you doing?" he asked, trying to hold me back. "Are you nuts? Do you want to die after everything that's happened?"

"No, but I don't want *him* to die, either," I replied, nodding towards my ex. Before Chris could say more, I took my life in my hands and launched myself at Hayden to push him out of the way of the first few zombies in the horde. Luckily for us, they didn't move very fast, but they still looked very formidable and scary as fuck with those eerie smiles on their faces. I hoped that I wouldn't have nightmares about it later.

"Oomph!" Hayden uttered as he hit the ground and I fell beside him. The both of us landed with a thud, but there was no time to be checking out any injuries. However, I could see that Hayden's suit got a bit scuffed up and I thought that I had seen a small rip on one of the legs. We helped each other up and then backed up as quickly as possible while the zombies clawed at nothing but air.

"I'll hold them off! You guys need to find the way out and escape!" Chris shouted out to us. Not needing to be told a second time, Hayden and I ran as fast as we could and I looked over my shoulder for a few seconds as Chris used his supernatural strength to put some distance between Hayden and me and the zombies.

"Where the fuck is the door?" I shouted in exasperation. I knew approximately where it should have been, but while I panicked I had a hard time thinking straight. I felt around the wall for the doorknob, but Hayden got to it first and opened the door for me. "Thanks."

"No problem." As he shut the door behind us, I caught one last glimpse of Chris defending himself against the zombies and he was unleashing a six-pack of brutality on them. "Are you okay?" Hayden asked me.

"I think so, but my arm might say otherwise," I replied. I looked at my right arm and saw that it was all scraped up and bleeding. It would need to be cleaned properly and very soon to stave off any chance of it getting infected.

"That looks bad."

"And it stings like a mother."

"Sorry, but I don't have any bandages on me. Thanks for saving me back there," he said.

"That's alright, and you're welcome. Who knew that this would happen?" I paused before speaking again. "So, what do we do now?"

"Wait here for him, of course."

"I mean, should we barricade the door or something? If those zombies got out . . ." I didn't want to think of what kind of horror would be unleashed on the world if they were set free.

"No. You saw him, didn't you? He'll be alright. He'll probably be through with them in no time, anyway, so it would be rather pointless to block the door now," Hayden tried to reassure me.

"Maybe you're right, but what if the worst happened and he got overrun?" I asked, the unwanted image creeping into my mind and causing me to begin freaking out. I pushed it out of my head and made myself take a few deep breaths to calm back down.

"Stop worrying, Jessi. Everything will be just fine." Hayden paused and gave me a friendly hug. "Wait a minute, did you just say 'zombies'?"

"Yeah."

"What the hell?"

"Tell me about it," I sighed, thankful to still be alive.

"What's going on here, Jessi? What have you gotten yourself into?"

"You wouldn't believe me if I told you and I'm *not* going to tell you. It's really for the best if you don't know the whole story."

"I nearly died tonight and you saved my life. I think that I deserve to know *some*thing," he reasoned.

"It's complicated and I don't know what I can tell you," I said, shrugging nonchalantly.

"*Try.*"

I took a deep breath, but before I could speak, Chris came running through the door and grabbed Hayden and me with each hand, taking us about a block away. When he stopped, it took me a few minutes to catch my breath. My head spun so fast from everything that had just happened. "Thank goodness, you're okay!" I exclaimed, leaping into his arms to hug and kiss him like there was no tomorrow. Out of the corner of my eye, I could see Hayden averting his eyes and trying to look anywhere else but at our display of affection.

"Thanks, baby. You really shouldn't have saved him like that, though. You should have let me handle it."

"We're all guilty of doing things that we shouldn't have done, but we did them anyway, because it felt like the right thing to do at the time," I replied. "The only thing that I regret is falling on my arm. This shit hurts!"

"May I?" Chris asked and he lifted my arm to inspect it. He held it close to his mouth. As he began to lick the wound, Hayden looked like he was about to puke.

"Thanks." I inspected the wound, and right before my eyes, the blood disappeared and the color was lightening. It wouldn't be long before all physical traces of the injury were gone and only the memories would remain.

"No problem."

"Hayden wants me to tell him about what's been going on. He figures that since he nearly died tonight, he deserves to know the truth."

"And what did you tell him?"

"Nothing yet. I didn't know what to say or even if I *should* say something," I said.

Chris thought for a few moments. "Hayden, what you witnessed tonight is something that you must never speak of again. If I tell you what really happened, you must promise to never tell anyone else about it. Understand?" he asked with utmost urgency. Hayden nodded his head and then Chris did something I'd never seen him do before. He stared intently at Hayden's face and my eyes darted back and forth between the two men, thinking that it was like some sort of Vulcan mind-meld thing ala *Star Trek.*

A few moments later, it was over and Hayden's eyes were closed tight. Chris said, "He'll be fine."

"What did you *do*?"

"It's a vampire thing. I just changed his memory a bit so that he won't remember coming into the warehouse and getting attacked. The last thing that he knows about is that he came to see you at your house, but we'll have to get there quickly before he wakes up." We ran back to Chris' car, hopped in and then sped off back towards town.

"We can put him on the couch," I suggested when we got back home. Chris lifted Hayden onto it and posed him into a sitting position. "He looks comfortable enough now, but how long do we have before he wakes up?"

"I don't know—it could be any time." Within seconds, Hayden's eyes flickered open and I breathed a quiet sigh of relief.

"What happened?" he asked and I exchanged glances with Chris.

"You had a bit too much to drink and passed out for a while," I replied.

"Sorry about that."

"That's okay, but no more Grey Goose for you from now on," I wagged my finger at him in a joking manner.

"Did I do anything embarrassing or break something? I'll pay for it right now if I did," Hayden said, starting to take out his wallet.

"No."

"Oh, good," he breathed a sigh of relief.

"Maybe you should be getting home now."

"What about my car? If I've been drinking, I can't drive it."

"I'll walk you home," Chris offered.

"Thanks."

"I'll drop off your car tomorrow," I said.

"Okay, thanks a lot. Once again, I want to say I'm sorry for whatever I did."

"It's alright, Hayden. Take care!" I called out as I watched the guys go out the back door. That call had been a little too close if you asked me. I locked the door and slumped against the wall, sinking down to the linoleum kitchen floor and sighed in relief. A little while later, Chris knocked at the door and I stood up to let him in.

"He seems fine, but his car is back at the warehouse. I've got his keys so I'll go and pick it up now," he said as soon as I opened the door. I tried to remember in all the confusion and panic if I'd seen it there or not and decided that it must have been since there was no way that he would have walked that far in his usual designer dress shoes. Chris left again and was back in less than twenty minutes.

"Where did you park it?" I asked him.

"Your garage."

"That's fine."

"I figured that it would be less suspicious if we had it stowed away out of view for now," he reasoned.

"Yeah, good thinking. I don't know who would do anything about it, but the less trouble that we can attract and the fewer questions that we have to answer, the better. I'll take the car back to him first thing in the morning and then we can wash our hands of it."

"Are you okay now?" he asked me.

"My arm?" I looked down at it. "Yeah. You can't tell that anything happened to it now. Thanks for helping to heal it."

"No problem."

I opened my mouth to say something and then changed my mind and closed it before changing my mind back again. "How come I've never heard of you being able to do that mind thing before?"

"I've only ever done it a few times in my life and didn't really think it was worth mentioning. Sorry," Chris said.

"You don't need to apologize, but it would have been nice to know of something else that we could use to our advantage. If anyone here needs to apologize, it's me for my daring rescue attempt."

"Do you still have feelings for Hayden and is that why you risked your life to save him tonight?"

"Yeah, I still have feelings for him, but not in the way that I have feelings for you. Hell, if Natalie had come by tonight, I'd have tried to save her, too, but it doesn't mean that I want to bang her, either. I'll help out almost anyone who means something to me," I replied.

A few seconds of silence passed before Chris said, "Okay, then."

"You're not mad at me, are you?"

He shook his head. "No. Where did you get *that* idea from?"

"You just seem a bit, I don't know, subdued and terse right now."

He sighed and exhaled, trying to compose himself. "I suppose I am. It's just that your girlfriend saying that she has feelings for her ex isn't exactly something that you want to hear."

"Well, you wanted the truth," I reminded him.

"I know."

"How about I bang your brains out and then you can see how much you really mean to me?" I grinned, lasciviously.

"That sounds like a good way to end the night," he said, his dour expression quickly replaced by a smile. His fangs protruded as he carried me up to my bedroom for some much-needed fun.

Chapter 10

On Tuesday morning, I woke up feeling pretty sore not only because of what Chris and I had done the night before in my room, but also because I kept tossing and turning in my sleep and I must have accidentally hit a wall. I had been wired from the previous night and had a hard time trying to fall asleep. You'd have thought that all of the drama at the meeting and the aftermath would have made me tired as hell, and it did, but the sex had given me a second wind.

I spent most of the night/early-morning thinking of the meeting and what would happen next. I hated having Hayden dragged into it, although he couldn't remember it thanks to Chris' mind trick, and I hated Chris risking his life, too. I began to wonder if maybe it would have been best for everyone after all if Chris had just turned me into a vampire, because then the Council wouldn't have had as much power over us. I couldn't think of any better way out of the situation.

After breakfast, I got dressed and drove Hayden's car over to his place and then walked back home. At 10 o'clock it was already pretty warm out and making me start to sweat. I decided that I would hop in the shower when I got back, but until then, I popped into a convenience store to get a bottle of ice-cold water to hold against my face and cool down. I took some sips of it and it felt good as it slid down my throat.

I went into work a few hours later and some of my fellow employees asked if I was alright. It seemed that word about my absence yesterday had spread pretty quickly. "I'm fine, thanks," I reassured Natalie and a co-worker of ours named Katie Powers.

"I missed you," Nat said and hugged me.

"I was just gone for a day."

"I know, but I was kind of worried, anyway."

"Thanks for the concern," I smiled, then put away my things in my locker and went to the cosmetics counter. Whenever I had some free time, I thought about the predicament that Chris and I had found ourselves in and I especially thought about the idea of being turned into a vampire. What would it be like? How much would it hurt? Whatever the answers were, I could only assume that anything that the Council would do to me would have been 100 times worse. They wouldn't just make the pain physical, but mental and emotional as well.

At lunch, I was in the break room letting my mind wander and I was so far gone that at first I didn't notice Natalie speaking to me, trying to get my attention. "Jessi! Earth to Jessi! Come in Jessi!" she waved her arms around in front of my face. I shook my head and jolted myself out of my reverie.

"Sorry about that. My mind is somewhere else right now."

"I'll say it is! I've been calling you for the past five minutes. What's going on?"

"I just have a lot on my mind right now."

"Anything that I can help with? Guy troubles?"

"No, sorry," I replied.

"Oh, okay," she said, sounding downcast.

"Maybe," I said slowly, a thought creeping into my head, "we could go out sometime for a girls' night."

"When?"

"Whenever's good for you. How about tomorrow night?"

"Sure, that sounds like fun."

"We'll go out to whatever's the newest, hottest club and check out the scene."

"Sweet," she replied with an eager smile on her face.

"Talk to you later," I called out to her as I went back to work. I tried to keep my focus on what I was doing, but every now and then my mind slipped away and I thought about quitting. My near brush with death made me question my life and I knew that I didn't want to spend the rest of it working at the cosmetics counter of a department store. I began to seriously consider taking Chris' advice and follow my dream of becoming a singer. He seemed to think that I could make it, so what did I really have to lose?

When my shift was over, I couldn't wait to get home. I made a few hotdogs and was just relaxing on the couch with my laptop resting on my legs when Chris appeared in the doorway to the living room. "What are you doing there?"

"Just checking out my e-mail. How was your day's rest?" I asked him.

"Good, but it took me a while to fall asleep."

"Same here."

"Oh *yeah*?" he grinned, probably thinking that my sleeping trouble was related to the satisfaction that he had given me the night before.

"I just kept thinking of stuff. I wish I could shut down my brain sometimes," I replied. He laughed, then sat down beside me and brushed the hair off of my shoulders, stroking them as he did so.

"It's a nice night out, what do you say we go and sit out in the backyard?" he asked me.

"Sure. Let me just shut the computer down and put it away." I closed up the windows on the screen, waited for the device to power down and then slid it back under the coffee table. We went out the backdoor and Chris sat down on the lounge chair that was laid out. I started to go and get another one, but he motioned for me to sit down on the chair with him. I parked myself in front of him and he massaged my shoulders for a few minutes, before working his way down my back and thighs. "Thanks a lot. I really needed that," I murmured.

"Why don't you try to give *me* a massage sometime?"

"Alright, then. How about now?"

"Sure."

"Get up and we'll change places," he suggested. I carefully got up off of the chair and stood aside while Chris gracefully stood up and then we switched spots. He took off his shirt and then I tried to imitate what he did. I gently rubbed every part of his skin that was accessible to me and I could feel him getting more turned on than relaxed. He even moaned a little in pleasure to make sure that I knew what he was feeling.

"Why did you stop?" he asked as I took my hands off of him. "That felt so good." He stood up and put his shirt back on again.

"I need to talk with you," I said, a note of urgency in my voice.

"About what?"

"About us."

"What do you mean?" he asked.

"This whole situation with the Council. I've been doing some serious thinking today and I've come to the conclusion that it makes the most sense for you to just turn me into a vampire," I said before letting out a deep breath that I hadn't realized I'd been holding in. Chris raised his eyebrows at me like I was crazy and if that's what he thought, he was probably right.

"Would you *really* want to be a vampire right now?"

"Well, we can't keep walking on eggshells forever, Chris. Sooner or later, the Council is going to find us slipping up and when it does, I'll be dead before you can count to ten. I don't know what they'll do to me, but it's definitely not going to be pretty. I'd rather take the lesser of the two evils and be done with it already. At least I know that you'll be somewhat gentle with me."

"Are you 100% sure?"

"Yes."

"*Really*?" he asked, doubt evident in his voice.

"Yes," I replied again, my voice faltering this time.

"You don't sound too sure."

"Fuck! I don't know anymore!" I broke down and clutched my head in my hands.

"You don't have to decide right now, baby," Chris said, then sat down and pulled me close to him. "Maybe you won't ever have to decide." I snorted in disbelief. "All right, I guess that's just wishful thinking, but whatever happens, we'll face it together. It's us against the world, alright?" I nodded and sniffed.

"Chris, I'm going out tomorrow night with Nat so feel free to invite someone over if you want. Maybe you can try to make up with Alfonso," I suggested.

"No. It'll take a lot longer than one night for me to want to forgive him. I suppose that I could see if a few of my other acquaintances, Aaron and Tony, can hang out. I haven't seen them in a while."

"Good. Well, have fun."

"You, too. Where are you and Nat going?"

"Out to a club in Munroeville, but we haven't figured out which one yet," I replied.

"That'll be good for you to get out and see how great it is to be human," he said. "Maybe it'll help to change your mind about being turned."

"Clearly, you haven't been to a regular club in a long time. They're usually crawling with creepy jerks who'll hit on almost anything with boobs."

"So then why are you guys going out to one?"

"To dance and let loose a little. Creepy jerks are just an unfortunate part of the whole club-going experience. You can't have a bucket full of apples without catching a few worms, too," I replied.

Chris shook his head and chuckled. "I'll never understand all of the things that you humans do."

"That's okay. I'll never understand all of the things that you vampires do, so I guess that we're even." I smiled and then paused for a moment. "Maybe I should have asked this before, but is it alright for me to be going out? I mean, we've got the Council off of our backs for now, but who knows how long that will last?"

"There's nothing to stop you from going out and living your life now, Jessi. We just have to be a little more careful from now on, that's all. I think that they're going to be watching me more than you, anyway. I'm the one that broke the rules, whereas you were just an innocent bystander caught in the crossfire. I hate to say it, but I'm going to have to prove myself to the Council by killing as many humans as I can and hope that they'll back off completely."

"I understand," I whispered to him, closing my eyes and trying not to think of all of the innocent people who would lose their lives because of Chris' plan to protect us.

The following night, I grabbed a burger from a fast food joint and spent over an hour getting ready to hit the town. I dressed to the nines in a black, strapless dress with a black cropped jacket, white bracelets, white clutch purse, *Poison* by Christian Dior perfume and blue strappy heels. I even styled my hair and gave it a bit of volume so that it was higher than usual. Yeah, I was dressed to kill.

I met Natalie outside of this new club called Exit and together we entered the queue to get in. After waiting for twenty minutes, we stepped inside and I was almost blinded by the color in the room and all of the flashing lights. The music that blared from the speakers was some techno stuff with huge thrumming beats and a lot of bass. I looked at the dancefloor, which was packed with bodies gyrating closely together, and I imagined that it was incredibly hot over there.

I led Nat to an empty booth near the middle of the club and a waiter took our orders a few minutes later. He disappeared almost immediately amongst the other patrons and it wasn't long before he returned with our drinks. I had a Cosmopolitan and she got some drink that I hadn't caught the name of, but it was purple and came with one of those little paper umbrellas and a slice of lime.

Several minutes later, some ugly guy with a large nose, a unibrow and unkempt dark hair came up to our table trying to hit on us. "How are you fine ladies doing this evening?" he asked, thinking that he was being suave. Unfortunately for him, it came off as incredibly desperate and Nat and I had to struggle to refrain from laughing right in front of the poor guy.

"Not interested," I said as calmly as I could. Unibrow looked dejected, but it didn't last for long. He left our table muttering something to himself about how all of the women who turned him down must be lesbians and then moved onto our neighbors behind us. I guessed he figured that sooner or later, someone would take pity on him. As soon as he was out of earshot, Nat and I were finally free to let out our laughter.

"*Wow!*" she exclaimed.

"Yeah. He's got a lot of nerve," I said and she nodded in agreement. We talked some more about him and commented on the guys who we could see in the club. There had been some quality talent there that night, but none of them could compare to Chris in my eyes. Even so, I figured that it didn't hurt to have a little fun and do some window shopping, if you know what I mean.

A while later, a really smoking-hot blond guy came up to Natalie and asked her to dance. She glanced at me to silently ask if it was alright if she went with him and I subtly nodded my head in consent. I sipped my drink while I watched them dance and clapped when they pulled off a crazy dance move. When the song was over, Nat walked back to our booth and sat down. "Woo!"

"That was hot!" I exclaimed.

"You're not kidding me. It's like a sauna over there!" She tried to fan herself with her hand to cool down, but it didn't seem to work very well so she picked up her glass and pressed it against her forehead and cheeks.

"That's not quite what I was referring to," I laughed.

"I know. Why don't you try to pick up a guy and do a little dirty dancing yourself?" she asked. "It's a lot more fun than watching."

"I don't know."

"Chris wouldn't mind, would he? Is he the jealous type?"

"There's no reason for him to be jealous of anyone, but I wouldn't doubt that there are some people who'd be jealous of *him*."

"Then what's stopping you?"

"Nothing," I replied.

"There's got to be some guy that you've been eyeballing since we got here."

"Alright, I'll do it." I gulped down the rest of my drink for some liquid courage and then sashayed around the club to examine the male specimens on display. Most of the guys that were there were already taken, but I eventually stopped in front of a guy with short, jet-black hair who was dressed in a blue, tailored shirt and black jeans. I made a motion with my finger for him to come with me and I led him onto the packed dance floor.

The DJ put on a remix of *Lovegame* by Lady Gaga and, spurred on by the alcohol, I shook my ass like there was no tomorrow. The black-haired guy held onto my waist behind me and we swayed to the frenetic beat together. I turned around to dance closer to him and saw that he had the most beautiful blue eyes that I'd ever seen before. They weren't pale like most people who had blue eyes, but rather they were like the depths of the ocean. We danced through the next song, a remix of *Hot and Cold* by Katy Perry, and by the end, I was sweating up a storm.

I parted from my dance partner to head back to the booth and was delighted to find a new glass of my drink on the table. I sat down and held the cool object against my skin. "I see you had a lot of fun," Natalie commented.

"Yeah. Thanks for encouraging me to do it."

"What's his name?"

"I didn't ask. Why? Are you interested? Because if you are, I could go and talk to him right now."

I could see that Nat was fighting the urge to say "yes" and that she was losing that fight. "Yes, please!"

"Okay, then," I laughed. "I'll be right back." I walked back over to tall, dark and handsome and told him about my friend's interest in him. He wrote down his digits on a napkin and as I walked away, a smile spread across my face. Mission accomplished!

"I love you!" she exclaimed. "Thanks a bunch, Jessi!"

"No problem."

"Wasn't that a great idea after all to ask someone to dance?"

"Yeah, but I felt kind of weird about it at first," I admitted.

"That's where the alcohol comes in handy," she grinned.

"By the way, thanks for the refill."

"It's all good." For the rest of the night, Natalie and I were asked by most of the available guys in the club to dance with them, thanks to our brilliant performances earlier in the evening. Not once during the night, did I think about anything else but having fun. It wasn't until that night that I realized just how much that I enjoyed being human.

When I got back home in the early morning hours, Chris was waiting for me in my bedroom. "Hi. How was your girls' night out?"

"Good, thanks. I had a lot of fun."

"What happened?"

"I had a few drinks and danced with some guys," I replied, slipping off my shoes and sitting down on the end of the bed.

"Oh *really*?" he asked, raising his eyebrows at me. In return, I playfully slapped him on the arm.

"Yeah, and for your information, nothing else happened between us. I even got a little possible love connection going on between Natalie and one of them. Just call me Cupid."

"So you enjoyed yourself enough to change your mind about ever becoming a vampire?"

"Well, I don't know about *that*. It was a great night, but being a human isn't all fun and games as you well know. I doubt that one night is going to permanently change my mind about anything," I said.

"I didn't say that it would, but it's just the tip of the iceberg. There are all sorts of other things to like about being human and there's no way that you could ever experience all of them in your twenty-five years."

"That's true, but as I've said before, not everything in life is something that I want to experience. If I have to become a vampire in order to stay with you forever, then that's what I'll do." As soon as I said those words, I began to doubt the sincerity of them. Was I really ready to give up everything that I'd ever known and every other possible experience that I hadn't had the chance to have yet?

"I don't want you to become one just because of me, Jessi. Think long and hard about what you're saying, because once we start the process of changing you, there's no turning back," he warned and I nodded solemnly, his words weighing heavily on my mind.

There were a few moments of heavy silence until I broke it by asking, "So, how was *your* night?"

"Aaron, Tony and I did a little hunting and then we came back here to hang out. We talked about vampire business and I gave them a tour of the house," Chris replied.

"When did they leave?"

"A little while before you came home."

"Oh. Maybe I can meet them some other time, then."

"Yeah, maybe."

"I've got to go hop in the shower and then off to bed. It was pretty hot in the club, especially on the dancefloor," I said. "I was dancing so much and I'm sure that I reek a bit."

"Want me to join you in the shower?" he asked, waggling his eyebrows suggestively. I was tempted by his offer, but I really wanted to hit the sack.

"Not this time, sweetie. Sorry."

"Oh, okay."

"I'll see how I feel when I've gotten clean. Maybe I'll hit my second wind." I picked up my pajamas and a bathrobe and then walked down the hall to the bathroom. Once inside, I locked the door, shed my clothes onto the floor and ran the water. It felt great cascading down my body, washing away the sweat of the evening.

I lathered soap all over my body, wishing that Chris was there to help me get to the places that I couldn't reach easily. *"Maybe I should call out for him to come in and say that I've changed my mind?"* I thought to myself. When all of my fingers had become slick with water and suds, the bar slipped out of my grasp and fell to the bottom of the shower. As I bent down to grab it, I started to slip and hit my head on the wall. "Ouch!" I cried out. Just then, Chris knocked on the door.

"What's going on?" he asked with deep concern. When I didn't answer, he tried calling out again. "Jessi?"

"Chris! I'm hurt!" He burst through the door, ripping it off its hinges. I clutched at my head and he wrapped me up in the bath towel that I had laid out and then took me back into my bedroom.

"What happened?"

"I dropped the soap, tried to pick it up, slipped and hit my head."

"I'll get you some Aspirin," he said. I moaned in pain as he dashed back into the bathroom to get a pill, a glass of water and my pajamas.

"Thanks," I said as I took the pill and the glass of water, consuming them at the same time. I had no idea how well the pill would work this time, because I had whacked my head pretty good. "A great night followed by a shitty ending. That's being human for ya!"

"It's not like vampires always have great nights, either."

"Yeah, but at least you don't get hurt like this from something as simple as falling down. It feels like someone kicked me with a steel-toed boot," I moaned.

"My poor baby." He carefully helped me get into my pajamas, tucked me into my bed and then lay down beside me, keeping me company. "If there's anything you need, don't hesitate to ask before I have to go to sleep for the day," he offered. I subtly nodded and then winced, hoping that the medication would kick in soon. Chris kissed the top of my head and I went to sleep soon after.

On Thursday, I woke up feeling a bit better. It wasn't like I would be up to running a marathon, but I could make it through the day as long as I didn't do anything crazy. I'd had more than my fill of that sort of action in recent days, so playing it safe was just fine by me.

Throughout the day, Natalie and I regaled our co-workers with stories of the previous night. She embellished some of the details a bit, but I didn't try to correct her. She was in her element being at the center of attention and so I let her have her fun. As we talked about the dances with our respective guys, the other women "oohed" and "aahed". Everyone laughed at the story of the unibrow guy, well, everyone except for Nikki and Ashley, that is. They shot us glances that were as sharp as darts and almost twice as deadly. It was blatantly obvious that they were still mad at us over the confrontation in the break room and I can't honestly say that I blame them.

I couldn't wait until the work day was over and I could relax to try to get rid of the headache that had been throbbing on and off. I took another pill before I left the store, and as I drove, the gentle hum of my car's engine soothed me a bit. Along the way, it all got to be a bit too much for me and I had to pull over onto the shoulder of the road for a few minutes while I closed my eyes and tried to set myself to rights again.

When I got back home, I immediately took a washcloth from the rack in the bathroom, ran it under the hot water tap on the sink and then lay down on my bed with the washcloth on my forehead. It was really boring just lying there, so I turned on the radio by my bed with the volume down low. The pop station was playing the Lady Gaga song that I danced to with the black-haired guy and I smiled at the memory. I decided to ask Nat if she'd phoned him the next time that I saw her.

I didn't know how long I was asleep for, but Chris was by my side when I awoke. "How are you feeling now?" he asked me in a quiet voice. It took me a bit of time to fully wake up and register his words, but he waited patiently.

"I'm a little better now that you're here." Chris looked down at me and smiled. "It still hurts a bit, but I'll live. I've been popping back pills like crazy and they seem to be working."

"That's good to hear." He paused for a moment as he lovingly watched me, probably wishing that he could magically take my pain away. "Have you had something to eat?"

"No. When I came home from work I pretty much just went to sleep," I said.

"You must be quite hungry then."

"Famished."

"I'll fix something for you. What do you want?"

"Just some French fries. When I have a headache, my stomach can't handle anything but basic foods," I replied.

"Alright, then. French fries coming right up," he said. Chris kissed me on the forehead and then disappeared out the door. As I closed my eyes again, I heard him already banging around in the kitchen and before long, the smell of food cooking wafted upstairs. I breathed it in deeply, which made my stomach growl.

A short while later, Chris came back up to my room carrying a plate of fries, a bottle of ketchup and some gravy on a serving tray. "Thanks, Chris," I said.

"I wasn't sure what you'd want so I brought both condiments."

"That's fine. The only thing missing now is something to drink."

"What would you like?" he asked.

"Just some water, please."

"Be right back." He placed the tray on my lap and picked up the glass by my bed, then dashed off down the hall. I carefully tried to sit up without jostling the tray too much and began to dig into the food. "How is it?" Chris asked as he came in and placed the glass back on the nightstand less than a minute later

"Good. I love this whole meal-in-bed thing. Maybe I should hurt myself more often," I joked. "Just kidding," I added when he gave me a look of disbelief.

"Eat up and I'll find something to watch on your TV." Chris flipped through the channels and stopped at an old black-and-white movie featuring actors who had long since died. He cuddled up to me and I looked into his face. I supposed that he could feel my eyes on him or perhaps he saw me in his peripheral vision, because after several seconds, he locked eyes with me.

I asked him, "What did I ever do to deserve you?" A smile and a squeeze of my shoulders was his only response. After I'd polished off the rest of my food, Chris set the tray onto the floor and spooned me while we continued to watch the movie. I wasn't too sure what it was about, because I was just enjoying being with him, wrapped up in his sexy, muscular arms where I felt so safe.

As soon as the movie ended another one began called *High Noon* according to the credits. It was one of those cowboy shoot-'em-up sorts of movies that took place in the Wild, Wild West where the villains were easy to spot because they were dressed all in black. It was a predictable story where the good guy dressed in white, of course, won the girl, but you watched it for the gunfights and bar brawls, which this one had plenty of.

I winced when the White Hat got hit over the head with a bottle and the glass sprayed everywhere. "I can change the channel," Chris offered.

"No, I'm already too into this. I want to find out how it ends," I said.

"Alright." We fell silent again and then a little later Chris said, "Watching this brings back memories."

"Did you ever see a real gunfight?"

"Yeah."

"*Really*?" I asked, amazed. Chris nodded his head. "What happened? Were you hurt? Were you involved?"

"I was just a spectator. When I was only 13 years old, I heard a lot of yelling coming from outside one day, so I stepped out to see what the commotion was. I saw a gentleman about twice my age lay a hand on a whore who couldn't have been more than sixteen. The owner of the brothel was trying to defend her and so he shot at the other guy. Several other people in town had the same idea as me and news of the scandal spread quickly. The man was banned from the brothel for life and I don't know what became of him afterwards," Chris said, shrugging.

"Wow, that's crazy."

"That's what things were like back then or at least how they were in my town."

"It's so weird that you're talking to me about things that happened so long ago. I guess sometimes I forget how old you really are, because you seem so much younger. You're like a sexy history book," I said.

"Well, as long as I'm a sexy one, I don't mind being called a history book," he half-smiled. "You, on the other hand, are my goddess."

"Oh Chris! If I was feeling better, you'd be getting lucky tonight with enough talk like that! I love you."

"I love you, too," Chris murmured, kissing me on the lips. I returned the kiss and then sank deeper into the covers to go to sleep. I could feel his arms around me, and then after some time, I had a vague sense of him slipping his arms out from under me to leave me alone to rest. The only thing that I truly despised about being in a relationship with a vampire was the problem of conflicting schedules, but we tried our best to make it work.

Friday was a killer day at work. We had another big promotion on and so I was busy for most of the day. Thanks to the heavy-duty pills I had been taking, all that remained of my headache was an occasional twinge. I rushed about serving customers, answering questions and selling tons of merchandise. My feet had hurt badly by the end of my shift, but at least it had been a payday and with my day's sales factored in, I would be taking home a pretty hefty sum.

On the way home, I stopped off at a Pizza Hut to treat myself and celebrate. Almost as soon as I set foot into the restaurant, I was greeted and seated by the hostess. I perused the menu for several minutes before a server finally came by to check on me. "Are you ready to order?" he asked, pen and pad in hand poised to write it down.

"Yeah. I'll have a medium Meat Lover's and a pitcher of Pepsi, please."

"Is there anyone else joining you?"

"No."

"I'll put in your order now, but it may take a while because we're getting very busy."

"That's alright. I'm not in a rush." He walked away and I could tell that he thought I was a pig for ordering that much food for just myself. How rude. "*Well, fuck* him!" I thought to myself and smiled as I imagined how Chris could tear him limb from limb if he knew what this guy had thought of me. He wouldn't really do it, of course, but the idea amused me nonetheless.

Speaking of Chris, I checked my watch and saw that it wasn't time for him to be up yet. While I waited on my order, I used my cell phone to check my home voicemail and found no new messages on it. Although I had planned to be back before he'd get a chance to hear it, I left one for him saying that I wouldn't be coming straight home from work so that he wouldn't be worrying about my whereabouts.

Over an hour later, I left the restaurant with my box of leftover pizza and got in my car. Instead of singing along to the radio like I usually did, I hummed and got so into it that I nearly didn't see a black SUV changing lanes and trying to cut me off. I slammed on the brakes, nearly jolting me out of my seat even though I had on my seatbelt, rolled down my window and began cursing up a storm. "Hey asshole! Who the hell do you think you are? Where did you learn how to drive—playing *Grand Theft* fucking *Auto*?"

Just then, the SUV started backing up and I stayed in my idling car. A broad-shouldered man built like a pro football player clambered out of the vehicle and walked towards me. I had no intention of running away and just watched as he came closer and closer. "Come out of your car and repeat what you yelled to me," he commanded.

I looked him over and thought that Chris could give him a good run for his money in a fair fight, but of course, if Chris fought him, it wouldn't *be* a fair fight. This guy looked a little bigger than Chris, but he didn't have the supernatural strength, speed and healing powers that the vampire had.

I got out of the car, looked the guy straight in the eye and repeated the words I'd just yelled out like he told me to. There was a pause where I thought things would come to blows and just when he started to walk away, he turned back around and punched me in the face with a fist the size of a ham.

Blood dripped down my nose and as I touched it, my rage got the better of me. I looked around for something to throw, but all I could see besides the vehicles was random garbage that careless people had thrown out of their windows. A bunch of discarded drink cups from fast food joints and chocolate bar wrappers couldn't do any damage, which left the SUV as my only viable option.

I focused on the vehicle and, rather than floating it because it was too heavy, I was able to make it drive forwards to hit the guy from behind, knocking him backwards. He tumbled over the roof and landed with a thud on the other side. It wasn't quite what I had in mind, but I was happy enough with it. Maybe he'd think twice the next time he wanted to cut someone off or try any other douchebag maneuver.

When I got back to my car, I rooted around in my glove compartment for some Kleenex, found some and held a tissue to my nose. It was bleeding profusely and I hoped that it wasn't broken. I didn't hear the crunch of any bones, but that didn't necessarily mean a thing. With one hand on the wheel and the other trying to stanch the bleeding, I peeled away from the scene of the crime.

I glanced through my rearview mirror at the body of the SUV driver lying motionless on the road and laughed. It served him right and seemed like some sort of justice or perhaps just plain old irony that he had gotten hit by the same vehicle he almost hit me with. A second glance in the mirror showed a small crowd gathering around the man and a few emergency vehicles approaching with their lights flashing.

On the drive back home, I went back to humming to the radio as if nothing had ever happened. Right after I walked in the door, I deleted my voicemail message. Just as I was checking to make sure that it had worked properly, Chris came into the kitchen. "What are you up to?" he asked.

"I deleted a message that I left for you. Now that I'm home, it doesn't matter."

"What did it say?"

"Just that I had decided to stop off somewhere for supper instead of coming straight home," I said, taking off my jacket to put it on the hook by the backdoor.

"What else did you do today?"

"Worked my ass off and got into a fight."

"What happened? Are you okay?" he asked, deeply concerned. I told him everything about the near-accident and he couldn't contain the anger on his face. "I'm glad you're fine."

"Except for my nose," I said.

"It could have been worse and you really shouldn't have put yourself in that position."

"Don't you think I knew that? Of course it was stupid, but I handled myself well. Anyway, what's done is done so let's move on. Besides, if it wasn't for me doing stupid things, I never would have met you."

"True enough, but I think that there's also a lot to be said for taking caution," Chris said, taking the tissue from my nose and examining my face. I couldn't feel the blood anymore and he licked my nostrils, which I guess still had some of the red stuff on display, although it was probably dried after so much time. When he was done, I went to the bathroom on the main floor to look in the mirror and saw no trace of a wound anywhere on my face. I did still feel some pain in the area, though, and hoped that I wouldn't have any bruising.

"What am I going to do with you?" he asked, exasperated, when I re-joined him.

"Love me?" I fluttered my eyelashes at him in a flirtatious way, causing him to smile despite himself.

"Come here you!" He enveloped me in a big bear hug and whispered sweet nothings in my ear. We kissed so passionately that I thought I was going to end up being bent backwards over the dining table, but before it got to that point, Chris pulled away from me.

"What is it? Why did you stop?" I asked, confused by his hesitance.

"I have something to tell you," he replied, a grave expression on his face.

"Uh, oh. Lay it on me and get it over with."

"You know how I hung out with Aaron and Tony the other night?"

"Yeah. What about it?"

"I wasn't entirely truthful about what happened that night. While we were out hunting, we came across Alfonso and he threatened to kill you. He planned to track you here so I ripped out his throat before he could come to the house. I tried to talk things over with him, but it didn't work out and we ended up having a big fight instead. I sent Aaron and Tony to the house just in case something happened before I could kill him. They were meant to ambush him, but it wasn't necessary in the end," Chris said.

"That's good, isn't it? I mean, it sucks that you lost him as an acquaintance or whatever, but if he was threatening my life, then that's one less vampire to deal with."

"Yeah, but now the Council is going to be after us again."

"I don't really understand," I said.

"It's a grave offence for one vampire to kill another unless it's done in self-defense. As I understand it, humans have a similar law."

"Yeah. If you kill someone, you usually get arrested and go to jail for several years."

"It's much worse in the vampire community since there are so few of us compared to the human population. Anyone found guilty is punished by extreme torture or staking. In this case, both of us will face certain death," Chris explained.

"I still don't get it. Wouldn't what you did be considered self-defense?" I asked.

"No. I killed Alfonso to protect *you*, not myself."

"So, what you're saying is that we're basically fucked."

"Yeah."

"What if you were to turn me into a vampire *now*? Would that change things? Maybe I could be spared after all and figure out a way to keep you from dying. When are we supposed to see the Council about this?" I asked.

"In a few days," Chris replied.

"We don't have much time to wait, so let's do this if we're going to."

"Are you sure about it this time?"

"I don't think I have much choice, do I?"

"You always have a choice no matter the situation. Sometimes the choices are shitty, but they're there," he reasoned.

"I'll never be ready for this. Then again, how *do* you prepare to become a vampire? It's not like there are books on the subject like: *So You Want To Be a Vampire?* by Barry D. Live and Yul B. Sory," I said, trying to inject a little levity into the conversation.

"I agree that you can't ever truly be ready, but at least you know more than I did when it happened to me all those years ago."

"I guess so."

"Alright then, here goes," he said. Chris leaned in to me and slowly lowered his mouth until his fangs broke the skin on my neck. I closed my eyes as I waited for him to bite me and bring the answer to all of my problems. My life flashed before my eyes and I realized that I didn't want to end it so soon no matter what the consequences were. There just *had* to be something else to do—some other way out.

I opened my eyes abruptly and pushed Chris away before he could go too far to turn back. "Chris, I'm sorry for being such a fang tease, but this really can't happen. You're right that I *do* have a choice and I'm choosing to live—whatever I have to do to make that happen."

"I'm glad to hear that."

"I won't go down . . . without . . . a . . . fight," I said slowly, a new idea forming in my mind. *"Of course!"* I thought to myself. It was so simple that I didn't know why neither Chris nor I had thought of it sooner. "That's *it!*"

"What do you mean?" he asked, confused. A beat of silence passed during which, it seemed to dawn on Chris what I was now thinking about doing. "Are you seriously planning to fight the Council?" I nodded my head, a mix of excitement and terror etched on my face. "That's *insanity!* Please re-think this plan. They have a large number of fighters at their disposal. We don't stand a chance against the odds."

"Then we'll have to celebrate when we beat them," I beamed, trying to appear more confident than I felt. "We'll have a better chance if you can round up people you're still on good terms with like Aaron and Tony. Would they be willing to help us out?"

"I'll ask around."

I nodded again and said, "The more, the merrier. If it helps get them on our side, tell them that I'll owe them a favor."

"What if they want you to do something sexual?" Chris asked, displeased with such a vulgar possibility.

"We'll cross that bridge when we come to it."

"I don't know if this is a good idea, Jessi. Even if I get the two of them to join us, it'll still be only four against who knows how many."

"Then we'd better hope that we can do enough damage between us."

"I'll head out now and see what I can do, okay? Maybe I can even convince them to bring along their mates."

"Good luck!" I called out as he headed out the back door. When I heard Chris' car pull out of the driveway, I locked the door, slipped into my nightgown and watched some TV in bed. I changed channels until I found a late-night talk show that I hoped would be a good way to lift my spirits after the day's craziness.

While I ate breakfast the next morning, I browsed the newspaper until I came upon a small article about the accident that I'd caused the day before. Thankfully, there was no mention of me in it so it looked like I was in the clear. When I was done, I went to the bank to cash my check and then ran some more errands. I bumped into Hayden and he still had no recollection of what had happened on Monday night, except for the getting drunk part. Chris had done a really good job with the memory alteration. We exchanged a little small talk and I asked him how he was doing after his "hangover".

As I walked away from him, I glanced back over my shoulder and saw him staring at me with a longing in his eyes that I hadn't seen in ages. My ex was proof that all of that stuff about not knowing what you've got until its gone was true. I prayed that hopefully history wouldn't repeat itself. The next Council meeting would be hard enough as it was without Hayden crashing the proceedings again.

I spent a few hours of the afternoon lying outside on one of the lounge chairs reading a book and turning over once in a while so that I didn't burn. Once I had my fill of fresh air, I went back inside and started making supper just to have something else to do. I made two types of salad and then put them in the refrigerator to keep until I was ready to eat. I thought that it would take longer to make all of that, so I unlocked my bike from the shed and went for a ride around town to work up an appetite.

Later that night, the first thing that Chris said to me was, "I have some good news. Aaron and Tony will help us and so will Tony's mate Serafina, but no one else that I talked to would give a damn even after I told them about your offer."

"Oh well, thanks for trying. At least we've got five instead of just two now," I said.

"Do you know how to fight?" he asked.

"I can throw some punches and kicks, but that's mainly by pure luck."

"I'll teach you how to do it the right way. Under my tutelage, you'll soon be a lean, mean, fighting machine." I laughed at how cheesy that sounded and Chris was confused. "What?"

I shook my head. "Nothing. Never mind. Let's do this thing." For all of Saturday and Sunday night, he showed me a plethora of moves—some simple and some fairly complex—that we practiced over and over until I could almost do them in my sleep. I felt like I was in one of those 80s movies with a training montage set to a song full of inspirational lyrics about chasing your dreams, following your heart, having the eye of the tiger and stuff like that.

Chapter 11

When I went into work on Monday, I was sore as hell. Katie Powers joked that it was because I had spent the weekend having a big sex marathon with my boyfriend. I tried to tell her that I had just been doing a lot of exercising, but she didn't seem to believe me. If she only knew . . .

The mood at work was considerably lighter than it had been on Friday. The store wasn't anywhere near as busy, in fact there were only about 20-30 customers at any given time, so everyone talked about their respective weekends and upcoming plans for the next one. I took some more good-natured ribbing from other co-workers and got to dish out a little in return. While the conversations went on, it hit me how their lives were so much different from mine. They were worried about making plans for their futures whereas I was planning how to make sure that I was even going to *have* a future.

During the long drive home, it occurred to me that there were only a few hours left before my fate would be sealed, for better or worse, and I'd be carrying out my plan with Chris and our cohorts. I suddenly felt bile rising up in my throat and I pulled my car over to the side of the road, opened the door and then threw up. I waited a few minutes and, feeling that I was done, I locked the door and drove off.

When I got home, I made something for supper, but I had a hard time trying to eat. I knew that I had to keep my strength and energy up, especially since I'd need all the help I could get, but my stomach was all tied up in knots. I forced myself to chew and swallow every last bit of food, but I went pretty slowly so that there wasn't as much need for my body to rebel on me. "Are you ready?" Chris asked when he entered the kitchen and pulled up a chair to sit beside me.

"As ready as I'll ever be."

"If you remember everything that I taught you, you'll be fine."

"Then why do I feel like I'm about to face a firing squad and this was my last meal?" I gestured to the remains of my fettuccini Alfredo.

"If it helps, I don't feel much better about this than you do. My existence is hanging in the balance, too," Chris admitted.

"That didn't really help, but thanks for trying anyway, baby," I said, sighing.

My mind wandered around wondering what I could do to stall going to the meeting. "Can we have some last-time sex before we go?"

"It won't be the last time. Besides, would you really be able to concentrate on enjoying it? I can tell that you're already extremely tense."

"Of course I am! At least if we had sex, I could channel it into something positive and have a good memory to hold onto for however long I still have left to live."

"I don't like this negative thinking. You have to change your attitude or we may as well give up now," he scolded me.

"You're right, I'm sorry. I'm really scared, Chris," I sobbed and hugged him.

"You want incentive to get through this?" he asked and I nodded my head. "How about this?" He whispered in my ear of all the kinky things that he would do to me later and they were so raunchy that I blushed a few shades of red.

"Oh Chris, you sure know all of the right things to say to a girl!" I exclaimed, wiping away what little tears that had fallen. "I'm ready now to do some serious damage, but before we go, you should take some blood to make sure that you're at full power, too."

"Alright," he agreed and bit my neck. Since I'd gotten used to him biting me there, the pain wasn't as sharp as it usually was, but it still managed to give me an ice-cold chill up my back. When he was done feeding, Chris licked the wound and put on a fresh bandage. "I'm ready now."

We hopped into Chris' car and sped off into the night towards whatever fate awaited us. We arrived at the warehouse early and met up with Aaron, Tony and Serafina outside. "Hey," Tony called out to Chris.

"Hey," Chris replied.

"So this is your girlfriend—the reason that we're here?" Tony nodded towards me.

"Yeah. Tony, Aaron and Serafina, this is Jessica," Chris introduced us.

"Nice to meet you all," I said. There were a few moments of silence where the trio of vamps stood and stared at me, sizing me up, and so I tried to break the ice a bit. "Serafina is a pretty unusual name. I mean, it's pretty and unusual," I amended, not wanting to offend my potential ally.

"Thanks, I think," the female vampire replied drily. She had long, raven-black hair and dressed like a Goth girl. Perhaps it was a tribute to the era that she died in or else she aspired to fit in with the modern vampire stereotype. In any case, she was very elegant with flawless skin like a china doll. Her mate Tony was almost her polar opposite. He had short, blond hair that was so light it was almost white, a complexion that was close to the same shade and was dressed very preppy like he'd just stepped out of a J Crew catalogue.

Rounding out the trio, Aaron had reddish-brown hair that he wore tied back in a ponytail and leather-studded clothes that befitted someone in a biker gang. Perhaps that was where he had gotten them from, but I didn't dare to ask and find out. It wouldn't have done to piss off these vamps right when we were about to head into a battle where my life and Chris' hung in the balance.

"I can see why you're going to so much trouble, Chris," Serafina said and leaned into me, then sniffed at my neck. "She smells delightful like a mix of strawberries and peaches."

"Thanks, I think," I said, giving her an uncomfortable half-smile.

"Shall we head in?" Chris asked me, offering his elbow. I hooked my arm into his like we were headed into a fancy costume ball instead of a battle royal and I wished that I wouldn't ever have to let go.

There were more vampires at the meeting this time so I guessed that word must have gotten around about the big event. *On a very special meeting of The Council—my possible death*! There must have been at least 200 there all waiting for my blood to get spilled. "Quite a turnout tonight," I remarked.

"Yeah, but don't let that bother you. We're all great fighters and we've got your secret weapon."

"I call to order a meeting of The Council of the Night," Councilman Louis declared loudly.

"The only order of business scheduled for tonight is the case of Chris and his human versus the Council," the blond vampire second-in-command called out.

"Christopher Sinclair, you are guilty of the murder of Alfonso Parks. What do you have to say in your defense?" the head of the Council asked.

With his head held high, Chris replied, "Alfonso was threatening to go to my girlfriend's home and kill her. I was simply doing what I had to do to protect her."

"You know the laws concerning vampires committing acts of murder against one another, yet you did it anyway to protect a lowly human. I think I speak for everyone in this room when I say that I will enjoy watching justice be served. Say your goodbyes now before we carry out your respective punishments."

Chris and I turned to look at each other, embraced and pretended to kiss as if we really were doing as we were told. It was all an excuse for Chris to whisper last-minute instructions into my ear. Just as I made the tiniest nod signifying that I understood, he made a gesture meant for Aaron, Tony and Serafina and then shouted out, "*Now!*" Everything after that happened so quickly that my head began to spin or maybe it was just the speed at which the vampires moved. In any case, all around me I saw almost nothing but blurs of movement.

I had no time to figure out anything that was going on as a group of human men was approaching me menacingly. The one in front of the pack—he had short, dark brown hair and a face like a model—would have been kind of hot if it weren't for the horrible sneer on his face and the fact that he was attempting to kill me. It was stupid of me, but I sort of felt bad for him as I used my telekinesis to throw him into the red-haired guy several feet behind him. Model Guy flew through the air like a rag doll and I watched as he hit Red before they both went down in a tangle of arms and legs.

The next people in the group approached me with trepidation. Now that they knew what I was capable of, they would have to re-think their attack strategy. "Show me what you've got!" I goaded them. "Bring it on! Or are you not man enough to try me?" "*That ought to get their goat!*" I thought to myself.

While they secretly debated what to do next, I seized the opportunity to check out what Chris was up to. I could see him whaling on some ugly gray-haired male vampire with a hook nose and then move onto a female with bright green hair styled in a Mohawk. With rapid-fire speed, he alternated between punching and kicking her in the stomach and head until she crumpled to her knees.

Chris caught my gaze and quickly nodded at me before taking on his next opponent. Turning back to my own situation, I saw that the humans had finally sorted themselves out. I watched my new adversary stroll up to me with an air of over-confidence, probably thinking that I didn't have any more tricks up my sleeve. Oh boy, would he *ever* be wrong!

I took a deep breath and let loose on him, letting my fists and legs do the talking for me. I landed blow after blow and unfortunately took a few myself, but each time that I was hit, I came back harder than ever. At one point, I kicked him straight into the rest of the group and they all went down like bowling pins knocked over by a giant ball. I would have found it very comical if I hadn't been fighting for my life.

I risked another glance at Chris and he was steadily working his way through the vamps, a pile of dust and severely injured bodies accumulating nearby. Aaron, Tony and Serafina were doing similar business and before long, half of the attackers were disposed of in some fashion. When Chris said that they were all good fighters, it was quite clearly an understatement. I'd never seen anything like it before. They had become a force to be reckoned with like a tornado leaving nothing but destruction in its path.

I kept fighting and threw everything that I had into it. I became a whirlwind of arms and legs myself, moving with a combination of a ballerina's grace and a ninja's deadly power. Anyone who fucked with me would soon be sorry that they had! I left the rest of the world behind and focused on defeating my enemy. The sounds of the fighting going on around me became the soundtrack as I dealt out my own brand of ass-kicking. I took what Chris had taught me and combined it with things that I'd seen from various shows and movies. Who says that you can't learn anything from TV?

I was doing really well, taking down one foe after another, until I tripped on something on the concrete floor. As someone else tried to attack me, I thought that I would finally be done for, but then all of a sudden Chris was at my side to help out.

He bashed in the guy's head with a wet smacking sound, then sucked at his neck, blood dripping down his fangs and chin before dropping him onto the floor like an empty candy wrapper.

I wasn't sure if it was ironic or not, but what I had tripped on and nearly cost me my life was one of the first guys that I'd killed in the melee. I had gotten so into the heat of battle that I hadn't been watching where I was stepping. I couldn't afford another near-accident and so I decided that I would have to be more careful for the rest of the fight. I was lucky that Chris had been able to help me, but I knew that I probably wouldn't be so lucky again.

I moved to another space while keeping an eye on the humans and by this point there were only about a dozen left. When I was finished with my share of the Council's army, I planned to help out with the others if I still had any energy left. I didn't know how much longer I could go on for, but I had no intention of stopping until there was absolutely nothing left in me.

I carried out more rage on the rest of the human fighters, continuing to use a combination of my telekinesis, moves that Chris had taught me and some dirty tricks that I'd picked up here and there. I used my supernatural power to throw the body that I'd tripped over and it hit a black-haired guy square in the stomach, which knocked the wind right out of him.

When another guy got to within a few feet of me, I lifted up my shirt to reveal my bare breasts and the guy just stared at them like I knew he would. He had never seen my right leg moving to give him a roundhouse kick and send him flying backwards. He hit the solid ground with a thud and a crunch of bones. A pool of blood gathered around the spot where he had landed, marking another casualty in the battle.

Out of the corner of my eye, I could see the vamps staring at my still uncovered chest, including Tony. I don't like to brag, but even the Council members were mesmerized by my assets. If Tony had been a cartoon character, his eyes would have been bugging out of his head. Serafina saw what he was doing and nudged him harshly in the ribs and then the four of them took advantage of their momentarily stunned opponents.

I pulled my shirt back down a short time later and after another ten minutes I had taken down the rest of my guys. I was panting and sweating profusely as I surveyed the damage that I'd done. The floor around me was littered with dead and broken bodies. I felt sorry for whoever had to clean up this mess; then again, maybe they'd just torch the place instead and find another venue for the meetings.

While I tried to catch my breath, I watched how things were going with the others and saw that they were nearly finished. Chris struggled with a young man who must have only been turned recently as he had an excessive amount of energy and a more feral nature compared to the rest. As a new vamp, he also wouldn't have a good control on himself, which we could take advantage of.

I stepped in to help my boyfriend gain the upper-hand by presenting myself to the young vamp and he followed me wherever I went, desperate for my fresh blood. Chris flashed me a look that said, "*What the fuck are you doing?*" I flashed him one back that said, "*Trust me, I know what I'm doing,*" and gestured to him to come over and get into position.

I led the young vamp over to a fallen body, which went unnoticed by him and he tripped over it, stumbling to the ground. Right when the vamp hit the cement, Chris plunged a stake in and a cloud of ashes erupted. The particles floating in the air caused me to cough and Chris clapped me on the back. "Thanks," I said.

"Anytime, baby." We worked together on the last few vamps and destroyed them all in a matter of minutes. As the others were finishing up their tasks, Chris asked me, "Are you okay?"

It took me several seconds for me to catch my breath enough to respond with any sense of coherence. "Yeah. I feel like I've just run a ten mile race, though. I'll be sore for over a week, but at least I won't have to exercise anymore for a while."

He gave my shoulders a squeeze and a victory peck on my left cheek.

Just when we had thought that it was all over, a couple of big goons came out of the shadows. It seemed like the Council had yet another surprise for us and it came in the form of four vampires built like tanks. I guessed that they had probably been bodybuilders or linebackers in their previous lives.

I watched as Chris and our allies rushed the tanks and bounced off of them like rubber balls. I had no idea of how we were going to take these guys down, but I supposed that they would have to have some kind of weakness. As I watched the failed attempt, it occurred to me that perhaps we could use their enormous sizes and weights against them after all as the saying went, "*The bigger they are, the harder they fall.*"

After Chris, Aaron and Tony tried and failed several more times, I said to Chris, "I'd like to test a theory."

"The floor is all yours," he gestured.

"Okay, but you might need to stand by in case something goes wrong." He nodded his head and I approached the giant vamps. They looked at me with contempt as if I were nothing but a mere fly buzzing around their heads being a pathetic nuisance. I focused on the one closest to me and knew from the experience with the SUV that I couldn't float him because he would be too heavy, but there had to be something else that I could make him do.

Just as the vamp was about to try to squash me like a bug, he was pushed sideways by the invisible force that I projected with my power and crashed into a wall where he made a massive dent in it before slumping down. The other vamps stepped up to try to accomplish what the first one couldn't, and not only did I push them out of the way, but I made them collide with each other and they plummeted to the ground unconscious. It looked like the old saying was right. When I was done, I also collapsed to the ground because of all of the effort that I'd just expended on the giant vamps.

"Are you going to be alright?" Chris asked me with concern. "I'll give you some of my blood if you think it will help."

Just as he was about to rip open his wrist, I shook my head and replied, "Just let me lean on you and support my weight until I can get myself back under control, okay?" Chris easily lifted me up with one arm and I clutched onto it for dear life, leaning against him somewhat uncomfortably.

Councilman Louis clapped his hands and it sounded like thunder in the echo of the now mostly empty chamber. "Well, well, that was quite a performance."

"Glad you liked it," Chris snapped, sarcasm dripping from his voice.

"Come up here you two," Louis commanded. Chris and I walked up to the dais and stopped several feet away from the Council. "That was a performance definitely worthy of a reward. So much blood, death, broken bones and you even managed to incorporate a little sex." He leered at me and I felt incredibly dirty, like the kind of dirty where you'd need to shower at least a dozen times to get rid of the feeling. "I must commend you and your allies on a job well done. Bravo," he said, clapping again.

"Does this mean that you'll let both of us live?" Chris asked him, anticipating that the head vampire would not change his mind about our respective punishments.

Louis thought about it briefly and deliberated with the other members of the Council. "Yes, but you must not ask for another favor of us until *she*," he pointed at me with his bony, white finger, "is no longer a human."

"No problem," Chris replied and we left the warehouse with Aaron, Tony and Serafina trailing along behind us. When we got outside, we stopped just beside the door to talk a bit and gather ourselves together.

"That was something else, huh?" Aaron asked with a grin on his face so wide that his fangs were showing. The sight made me feel even more unsettled than when I'd first met him earlier in the night. I could already tell that he was definitely not a guy to get on the wrong side of, but because he'd helped me and Chris out of a very tight situation, I couldn't really say anything bad about him.

"I don't think that I've ever had so much fun before," Serafina said, a little more friendly and lively than she had been earlier.

"What about that time in Rome?" Tony asked her.

As she thought about the memory, she got this dreamy look on her face. "Oh, yeah. That was great! How could I forget?" She exchanged glances with Tony and they smiled at each other. "*That* was definitely the most fun that I've ever had! I suppose that tonight comes in a close second, then."

"Thank you all so much for your help. Chris and I couldn't have done it without you," I said, trying to put as much sincerity into my words as possible as I looked around at our allies.

"You're very welcome," Tony said. "Just remember that you owe us a favor now."

"Don't worry, I will," I replied.

"I never worry." He paused for a moment, probably to measure his next words carefully. "You know, Jessica, if you ever do decide to become one of our kind, you'd make a pretty good addition to our community. You put up a hell of a fight."

"You're only saying that so you can get more chances to see her tits!" Serafina accused her mate and punched him in the arm. Aaron grinned lasciviously at the idea of seeing my chest again, his tongue caressing his fangs, and Serafina smacked him, too.

"Speaking of which, what compelled you to do it?" Chris turned to ask me.

"I saw it on a TV show. One of the female characters flashed a male character in order to distract him. I thought it was a good idea so I tried it and it worked," I replied.

"Maybe next time you could tell me ahead of time if you're going to try something like that."

"I only thought of it on the spur-of-the-moment. I guess you could call it a desperate measure."

"I'm just not comfortable with the idea of other people seeing your naked chest like that. I want it all to myself."

"Are you jealous?" I teased.

"No, of course not," Chris replied, trying rather unsuccessfully to hide his true feelings.

"We should go now and let the lovebirds work out their problems alone," Serafina said to Aaron and Tony. "Goodbye," she called out to us.

"Goodbye," I replied. "Nice meeting you guys."

"Uh, yeah," she said, reverting back to her reserved demeanor.

"We'll be in touch soon," Tony said and then they all melted into the shadows.

Chris turned his attention back to me and asked, "What do you say that we go home now and call it a night?"

"That sounds like a great plan. I've had enough of this place to last me a few lifetimes." As we began walking away from the building and towards Chris' car, I looked over my shoulder at the old warehouse that I hoped to never come back to for as long as I lived.

As soon as we got home, I was hungry as hell and ate a bunch of the cookies that I'd made the previous week. I didn't care that they weren't healthy; I just needed some sort of food to give me back part of what I'd lost during the big fight. "I'm so proud of you," Chris said to me while I ravenously devoured the treats. "I didn't get to see much of what you did tonight, but like Tony said, you really put up a hell of a fight from what I did see. Those guys didn't stand much of a chance against you."

"Thanks. My feet are hurting like hell and so is pretty much every other part of my body," I groaned.

"Yeah, I saw you take a few good blows."

"So you caught that, huh?"

"It looked like you had gone down pretty hard," he replied.

"And it felt even worse," I said.

"Let me take a look." I lifted up each leg of my pants so that he could inspect them and, sure enough, there was some bruising. They were fairly light-colored, but I had no doubt that they'd get darker with time. I pulled the waistband of my jeans away from me to check out my upper thighs and the bruises there were even bigger and the color was already getting dark. Chris touched the spots and I winced in pain, sucking in air through my teeth.

"It's pretty bad, isn't it?"

"Yeah," Chris replied. He checked out my arms and then licked the scrapes and open wounds that covered them. Although a few of them were fairly deep, they all healed within a matter of seconds. He touched my face and I winced again. The skin was so tender and I felt like someone had pulverized me. I imagined that I looked like someone who had gone a few rounds with Mike Tyson without protective headgear on. I looked at myself in the bathroom mirror and my fears were realized.

"I guess that it wouldn't be a good idea to go into work tomorrow looking like this, huh?" I asked, pointing to my badly beaten face. Just looking at my injuries was enough to make me ill, never mind the pain that had spread all over my body.

"I could give you some blood, but even with that you'd still have some slight bruising and pain for a day or so. You took one hell of a beating, Jessi. I don't think that you can cover this with makeup," he reasoned.

"Me neither. I guess I'll have to phone in sick first thing in the morning."

"Good idea."

"I can't really move well, though," I said. I stood up and tried to walk around the bathroom to prove my point and almost fell down. Well, I would have fallen down if Chris and his lightning-fast reflexes hadn't been there to catch me. "See? How am I going to get by tomorrow if you're not around to nurse me?"

"I'll take care of you for as long as I can, alright?" he offered and I nodded. "The sun won't be up for about another five or six hours so I'll do what I can until then."

"I love you, Chris."

"I love you, too, Jessi." He carried me up the stairs to my bedroom, pulled the covers back, laid me down on the bed and covered me up with the linens. He went back downstairs, brought up some DVDs to watch, went to the bathroom to get me some medicinal cream for aches and pains and then joined me on the bed. Chris popped in one of the DVDs, and as we watched it, he rubbed the cream all over my body. Between his hands and the cooling sensation of the cream, I felt tingly all over and eventually fell asleep in his arms.

Just before I finally drifted off, my mind wondered about what Aaron, Tony and Serafina would ask of us. I wouldn't have had a problem with helping them out, after all, it was only fair to return the favor, but I wouldn't be looking forward to the possibility of risking my life again. I decided to put the whole ordeal out of my thoughts again until the day when they'd come calling and hoped that it wouldn't be any time soon.

Chapter 12

On Tuesday morning, I called in to work and told Kathy that I had to take the week off. "What's the reason *this* time?"

"I've been badly hurt," I replied, wincing a little as I sat up straighter in my bed.

"Are you alright? Never mind, that was a stupid question."

"I'm in a lot of pain and it's really hard for me to even get out of bed."

"I'll report this in the system as an injury. Is it work related?" she asked.

"No."

"Alright then." I heard her typing something into the computer.

"Thanks," I said.

"Off the record, can I ask you what happened?"

"I fell off the ladder when I was trying to re-paint my house yesterday," I lied. It sounded like a pretty legitimate excuse to me. My co-workers, especially Nat, knew how much I'd wanted to get the task done.

"Ouch! I hope you get well soon," Kathy said.

"Believe me, I'll be trying to," I replied and then hung up the phone. *"Whew! That was close!"* I thought to myself. *"I'll be so happy when I can quit that place and not have to worry about calling in sick anymore."* I lay back down on the bed and flipped through the channels on the TV, but there was nothing on that I wanted to watch. I grabbed my latest romance novel from a pile that Chris had assembled on a chair next to my bed and read that for a while. I got through 50 pages before I set it aside and decided to try to hobble downstairs to eat.

I winced again as I carefully got out of bed and then I slowly made my way down the stairs. When I got to the kitchen, I pulled out a chair and sat down while I figured out what to make and how to go about doing it. I stood up, walked over to the refrigerator, pulled out a bunch of ingredients and then set about making a salad and a ham sandwich.

After lunch, I checked the mail and slowly went back upstairs carrying my laptop and its charger so that I could check on my e-mails and watch some DVDs while lying down. Before I slid back into the bed, I went to the bathroom and spread some of the pain cream all over my body. The cooling sensation made me tingle again and I remembered how Chris had put it on me the night before. I wished that he could have still been with me to help me out, but I thought that I was doing pretty well by myself, all things considered.

By 3 o'clock, I was getting bored and began to think about what I was going to do once I was back in working order. I thought of how Chris had complimented me on my singing and how I had wanted to do more with my life than just working at the makeup counter. I decided that maybe I should give a singing career a serious shot, after all what else was there to stop me now that I didn't have to worry about the Council trying to kill me?

I had no idea how I would go about such an undertaking, but like Chris had said, Natalie might still have contacts in the business and that would be a step in the right direction. It occurred to me then that I would have to go to a big city like Nashville and leave Chris behind in Hollingsford unless he wanted to make the move with me. On the other hand, Nashville wasn't so far away that I couldn't come back once in a while for a visit.

I had no idea how Chris would feel about this new plan, but I figured that he only wanted the best for me and he'd support me no matter what. It would be tough going for a while, but I had no doubt that we'd make it work somehow. I tried to reassure myself that it was a great idea, but I also felt some measure of guilt about making plans without consulting with him. At the end of the day, it was my life and I would follow my dreams wherever they would lead. I resolved that if Chris couldn't see that, then I would go it alone without him, but I had no intention of letting him hold me back.

I decided that while I was incapacitated, I would work on figuring out my plan in more detail and when I knew for sure what was going to happen, I would give my two weeks' notice to the store. In the meantime, I started to get worried and excited about giving Chris my big news.

Satisfied that I had some sort of course of action planned, I smiled to myself. My stomach began rumbling and I looked over at the alarm clock on my bedside table to see that it was already 6PM. I struggled to get out of bed and nearly got myself caught up in the bed sheets. Just call me klutzy! Once I was out of the danger zone, I went downstairs to cook a chicken burger, but it ended up setting off the fire alarm and Chris raced into the room to make sure that everything was okay.

"What are you doing? Trying to burn the house down?" he said as he swiftly turned off the alarm.

"Of course not! The alarm is just a bit too sensitive sometimes. What are you doing up already? The sun isn't down yet."

"It's down far enough that it won't hurt me now. Let me get that." Chris turned off the stove, picked the burger up off of the frying pan and placed it on the bun that I had ready, then he brought it over to the table. "Sit," he commanded and I obeyed. "How are you feeling today?"

"About the same as last night," I said as I carefully eased myself down onto a chair. "I put some more of that cream on a while ago and I think it's starting to lessen the pain a bit."

"That's good to hear." I smiled and took a bite of the burger. "How did you get along without me today?"

"I'm still alive, aren't I?"

"But you're better now that I'm here?" he asked and I nodded my head. "I'll take you back to your room when you've finished eating and then we can play 'nurse' again." Chris watched me as I ate and I wondered whether I should tell him about my new career path or save it for another day after I'd done some more thinking and soul-searching. He leaned in to me to whisper in my ear and what he said had made up my mind. My plan could wait for another day—that night would belong to us.

Chris carried me up the stairs and laid me on the bed, then climbed onto it himself to lie down beside me. He spooned me and as I stared up into his eyes, he stared back into mine. There was a twinkle in his eyes as he began to touch me intimately. "Just let me know if I'm hurting you too much, Jessi. We didn't really get to celebrate our victory last night, but I'd rather not wait for a week or more to get to do anything physical with you."

"What? Putting the pain cream on me didn't get you all hot and bothered? Technically, that was getting physical," I joked and he laughed a deep throaty laugh.

"No, that wasn't my idea of sexy."

"It wasn't mine, either, especially since it kind of smells like ass."

"Charming," he said sarcastically.

"It's just an expression."

"I'd rather see you have a different one." Chris grinned slyly and then slid his hand down my body, searching for the waistband of my panties. When he found it, I could feel his hand making its way underneath towards my private area. His fingers inserted themselves into the opening, wiggling around trying to find my special spot. I sucked in my breath at the cold touch and my body jerked against his.

I both loved and hated it when Chris touched me like that. It drove me crazy and my body felt like it was on fire, but at the same time, it felt so good. I couldn't see his face from my position, but I guessed that he enjoyed my reaction and he kept going until my whole body convulsed with desire and longing. It had been so long since we'd done anything like it and I wished that I could have frozen the moment so that we would have done nothing else until the end of time.

"Am I hurting you?" he asked.

"No," I moaned and panted. "Keep going." He did as I said and moved his fingers in and out of my opening as well as all around inside, trying to keep me on my guard. After a few more minutes, I couldn't take it anymore and begged him to stop. I found my release and Chris removed his magic fingers from me, wiping them on a tissue from the box on my nightstand. I struggled to twist my body so that I could look him straight in the eyes and said, "I want to give *you* a treat now."

"You really don't have to do this if it'll be too much for you, Jessi," Chris said. "I'd rather that you focus on recuperating."

"I'll try to be careful." I lifted up his shirt to caress his well-toned chest and then I undid his belt before sliding my hand under his pants. I slowly moved down past his underwear until I was holding his manhood in my right hand. I gently moved my hand up and down the shaft and stroked the skin, which was more delicate than I had imagined. I took great pride in having aroused Chris so much that he made a sound sort of like a mix of growling and moaning.

As I continued to stroke his genitals, I carefully moved my other hand and slid it down the back of his pants and jostled him a little bit, although he didn't seem to mind much. Next, I moved my hand down past his underwear and grabbed one of his ass cheeks. I didn't know how he'd react to a two-handed attack like that, but the way that he writhed around and tried to buck against me told me pretty much the same thing that I had told him when he fingered me.

When he'd signaled that he'd had enough, I wiped my hands off on a tissue and we both lay back down on the bed, feeling pretty spent for the time being at least. "That was wonderful," I beamed.

"You're not so bad yourself."

"*Not so bad*? You frigging loved it, didn't you? Come on and admit it already! I saw and felt how turned on you were. Either you're a really good actor or a horrible liar."

"Alright, you caught me. I can't get one by you, can I?" he asked, grinning.

"Not when I could feel you getting hard right in my hand! It's true what they say, '*The body never lies.*'" I laughed and Chris joined in a few seconds later.

"What do you want to do now?"

"Lots of things, but unfortunately, they'll have to wait until I'm feeling a lot better, if you know what I mean?" I asked, waggling my eyebrows suggestively. "For now, I'll settle for another round of pain cream graciously applied by my loving vampire boyfriend."

"No problem," he replied.

"And a massage," I said.

"Coming right up." Chris scooped up some of the cream from the plastic jar and smeared it all over my legs, but rather than cooling me down as it had before, it just numbed me. I supposed that I had gotten so used to the sensation that it didn't have the same effect anymore or else the pain had finally begun to die down. In any case, it probably wouldn't be much longer before I knew whether or not all of the effort had been worth it.

When he had finished and wiped off his hands, Chris massaged my shoulders and my body gently rocked along to the motion. I closed my eyes and let the feeling of his busy hands take me away to another world where nothing existed except for the two of us and we were free to do whatever we wanted for as long as we wanted.

In this world, I imagined that we were naked and exploring each other's bodies in the most intimate of ways. We were in a large bathtub filled with bubbles and over a dozen white candles ringed the outside of the tub as we kissed and fondled each other in the suds. The scene suddenly changed and we were making wild, passionate love on a king-size bed with a canopy overhead and red rose petals were scattered all over the place.

I moaned with pleasure at my daydream as I vividly imagined his hands all over me and then I was brought back down to reality when I remembered that he actually *did* have his hands all over me. He had moved from my shoulders down to my lower back and then to my thighs.

"What were you thinking about?"

"Huh?" I asked, confused as I came out of my little dreamland.

"Just now. I saw that you had your eyes closed and it looked like you were thinking of something very pleasant. I also heard you moaning. Was that because of the massage or was it because of whatever you were thinking of?" he asked.

"Both," I replied.

"So are you going to tell me about it?"

"You really want to know?"

"Yeah," he replied, continuing to rub my skin.

"Alright, then." I told him about my daydream and watched the expression on his face, but found that I couldn't really decipher the look on his face. "So, what do you think?" I asked.

"That's interesting to say the least. Would you *really* want me to do that for you?"

"I think it'd be nice to try sometime. It's very sexy and romantic."

"I guess so. I'm probably not the best authority on stuff like that, though," Chris admitted.

"Stick with me kid and I'll teach you a thing or two," I joked.

"Oh, I've no doubt about that. So, what else did you do today besides try to burn down the house?" I playfully swatted him on the arm and he chuckled.

"I brought up my computer so that I could check some e-mails, watched a few DVDs and I read another 50 pages in my book. I'm nearly finished it now."

"Good."

"I also called in to work to tell them that I'll be out for a week," I said.

"What did they say to that? Did they give you a hard time about it?" he asked.

"No, not really. I just said that I had a bad injury from falling off a ladder because I was trying to re-paint the house."

"If I didn't know what really happened, I think that I'd buy that excuse."

"*Really*? That makes me a feel a lot better," I said, breathing a sigh of relief.

"Yeah. It makes a lot of sense to me. The bruises on your face and legs look like you could have gotten them by falling from a good height," Chris explained.

"Exactly. I just hope that everyone else buys it, too."

"How do you feel now? Did the massage help?"

I twisted my body around, trying it out and touching the various spots where I ached. "Yeah. Maybe it's just temporary, but I feel better now. Thanks a lot."

"I feel so guilty about being the cause of all of this," he admitted. "I hate seeing you all bruised and banged up like damaged goods."

"Chris, didn't I tell you before that you have nothing to feel guilty about? *I* chose to be with you and that means that *I* chose all of the risks that go along with it. No one needs to feel guilty here. Shit happens and I love you too much to let you go over a few bumps and bruises. It might take a while, but the injuries will fade. I couldn't imagine living without you forever, even if it meant that I would get the crap beaten out of me less," I said.

"That's oddly romantic."

"I thought that you didn't really know much about romance or was that just a half-truth?" I raised my eyebrows at him questioningly.

"I think I'm starting to catch on a bit," he said and wrapped me up in his arms, smothering every inch of my body with kisses.

"Yeah, you are!" I giggled and kissed him forcefully on the lips. He reciprocated the gesture and then climbed on top of me. I sucked in a breath and he lifted himself up on his arms.

"Are you okay? Maybe this is too much too soon."

"Quit worrying, alright? I'll let you know when it gets to be too much," I reassured him.

"Okay," he said. Chris settled himself back on top of my body and we stared into each other's eyes so intensely that it felt like he was trying to mesmerize me or drill holes into my head. His eyes were so gorgeous and brown that I could have easily let him just lie on me, looking into them all night and I'd have been as happy as a cat in a tuna factory.

Without warning, Chris shifted his body and his hands found the waistband of my panties again, then he slid his body inside of mine. *"God, how I missed this!"* I thought to myself. The feeling of his body so close to mine that you couldn't fit a piece of paper between us was very comforting and natural and I loved feeling his sweet breath on my skin. I trembled beneath him, screaming out his name and many of the usual phrases that accompanied sex like "oh god", "harder", "oh baby" and "don't stop".

He kissed me while he worked his magic on me and I tousled his wavy hair, running my fingers through it. After some time, he began thrusting harder and harder and I ended up pulling on his hair, trying to hold on before I exploded. I bucked against him, pushing my body even closer to his and we moved together in perfect synchronization.

It seemed like hours later that it was all over and I was left a panting, sweating mess on the bed with Chris lying beside me, trying to catch his own breath. "That was great," I said. "Well, actually, 'great' is an understatement. I think that was some of the best sex that we've ever had and we've had some pretty damn good sex."

"And I didn't hurt you?"

"Did you hear me complain?"

"No," he replied.

"Then there you go." We lay in bed in silence for a few moments and Chris just stared at me, raised up on one arm. "What?" I asked, suddenly self-conscious.

"Nothing. I'm just amazed by you, that's all."

"Uh, okay," I said, not sure how to respond to that. "I think I need a shower now. Can you help me out?"

"Sure. Maybe I should take one, too," he said.

"It couldn't hurt," I teased him. Chris leapt up onto the floor and then helped me off of the bed. He put his hands around my waist and we walked a short way down the hall to the bathroom. I thanked goodness that it had already gotten so dark outside otherwise the neighbors would have had quite an eyeful seeing two naked people walking around the house.

Chris helped me into the shower and then locked the bathroom door, ensuring our complete privacy and keeping as much sound as possible in the room. As he turned the water on, it splashed over us and I couldn't help but stare at his wet chest and the way that the water droplets glistened on it. He lathered soap all over his body and then did the same to me, rubbing the suds into every one of my private crevices. Who knew that washing up could be so hot and sexy?

He put the bar of soap back on the little shelf on the wall and then fingered me again with one hand, while rubbing my back with the other. I gasped a little and closed my eyes, willing him not to stop. Between the warm water and the way that he had felt me up, I melted like putty in his hands and I gave a release that was instantly washed away in the shower. I didn't know how I still had more to give, but there it went down the drain.

Chris gently led me to the wall directly underneath the showerhead and fucked me up against the wall, while I gripped onto the top of the shower door with my right hand. The floor was slick with water and I silently prayed that I wouldn't slip and fall down again. Although the water had made the act so much better, it had also made it a bit trickier. When we were through, he washed me again and kissed my neck before washing himself.

Thoroughly cleaned and physically satisfied, I turned off the water and Chris opened the shower door, then helped me onto the bathmat and passed me a towel. "I've never done that before," I remarked.

"Neither have I."

"Well, you certainly have seemed to pick up a knack for it."

"So you wouldn't mind if we did it again sometime?" he asked, giving me a lascivious grin.

"Just name the time and place," I beamed. "I am definitely spent now."

"Me too."

"I think I'll sleep well tonight."

"Good. I love to watch you sleep." Chris paused and thought about his words. "That sounds kind of creepy, doesn't it?"

"A little," I admitted. As we walked back to my room, I had found a little spring in my step and forgot about the pain that I still had. Chris helped me back into my nightgown and then almost as soon as I had carefully climbed back into the bed, I fell asleep in his arms.

Despite the joy of that night, I hadn't forgotten about my newfound career plans and began to spend a lot of my time surfing the internet to look for apartments for rent in Nashville. I had found several that were within a decent price range, but after I thought about it for a while, it began to occur to me that perhaps they were so cheap because either they were in a bad part of town or there was something else wrong with them. I had only been to the city once or twice in my life, so I wasn't really sure about anything.

On the other end of the quality spectrum, I had found some places that went for over $1000 a month. Unfortunately, it would have been impossible for me to live in one of them unless I could either get Chris to help me out or I got a job in Nashville while trying to pursue my new career. All that I knew was that I definitely didn't have enough money in my bank account to afford it all on my own.

I made a note of my top apartment prospects, scribbling down the addresses and phone numbers of the contacts. I decided that as soon as I was mobile again, I would drive out to Nashville and check out the places in person before I handed over any money. I also did some research of various prospective record labels that I would check out while I was there. Nashville had some lesser-known ones like Pacific, Royal and Control Records just to name a few that were home to rising stars like Tiffany Derling and Susie Welling as well as bands like Chain Mail and Dead Before Dawn.

I figured that if I could get in the door to one of those labels, I would be pretty lucky and if I was even luckier to get signed, there was a chance that I could use them as a stepping stone to be recognized by an even bigger label and be well on my way to true superstardom. In any case, I wanted to shoot for the stars and see where it got me.

I knew that I was getting completely ahead of myself thinking about how I was going to get discovered and make tons of money like all of those other artists when I didn't even have a demo or an agent yet. I made a mental note to check out that last aspect another day, but in the meantime I tried to think of what I could do for my demo. Perhaps a little Mariah or Whitney?

I started typing up a list of pros and cons for my idea, trying to think of every angle that I could such as what I'd miss and what I'd gain if I went through with my grand plan. By Thursday night, I had come up with this much:

Pros

1. Get a chance to be famous and make loads of money.
2. Get a chance to leave Hollingsford and make a better life for myself.
3. Won't have to see The Bitchinator ever again (even though we don't have a beef with each other anymore).
4. Won't have to see Ashley Rogers ever again.
5. Won't take long to travel back to Hollingsford to visit whenever I want.
6. Won't take long for Chris to visit me in Nashville whenever he wants.
7. Won't have to give makeovers anymore.
8. Won't have to run into Hayden as much anymore and fear that he'll do something crazy to try to get me back.

Cons

1. Won't be able to see Chris and Natalie as much (I can still phone them, though).
2. Won't know anyone in the city and will be lonely.
3. It'll take a lot of hard work and luck to get discovered.
4. Will go from living in a big house to a small apartment.
5. Will probably be expensive to live in Nashville unless I can get a new job there.

It was a good sign that the pros had outweighed the cons, but it wasn't by much. I studied the lists carefully, trying hard to think of anything else to add and I couldn't, so I guessed that I had covered all of the bases. I saved the lists on my laptop and as I continued to stare at the words on the screen, the enormity of it all came crashing down on me.

It hadn't occurred to me until then to take Natalie's feelings into consideration. She was my best friend and I would be dropping this huge bombshell on her. I hoped that she would understand and support me just like I hoped that Chris would, but I really needed to talk to her as soon as possible before things got any further. I decided to talk to her in person after I had talked to Chris about it.

Almost as if he'd read my thoughts, I sensed him coming up the stairs and so I closed the file with my lists. "Am I interrupting something?" he asked, poking his head into my room a few seconds later.

"No."

"Okay, good. Have you eaten yet?"

"No," I replied.

"I'll make you something, then," he said.

"You really don't have to, Chris. I'm not in as much pain now and I think that I can make it downstairs in about half the time that I used to."

"I'm still faster."

"Yeah, I know you are," I smiled. "You'll always be faster than me for as long as I'm human."

"Okay, fine. How about I carry you downstairs and you can watch me cook?" he suggested.

I sighed and relented, "Alright." Chris scooped me up in his arms and we flew down the flight of stairs, then he sat me in a chair. I was amazed to see him work so fast, gathering the ingredients, chopping them and mixing them with the skill of a highly trained chef.

There was still so much that I didn't know about him, so I wondered if maybe he had spent a lot of time studying the culinary arts somewhere like France or maybe he had simply drunk the blood of a chef and the talent had transferred itself to him. Then again, maybe Chris had just been naturally good at cooking. Wasn't there some sort of saying about chefs being good in bed? If so, my boyfriend was a great example of it.

When he was done showing off, he served me a mouth-watering dish of his own creation or so he said. "It looks so good that I almost hate to destroy it," I admitted.

"If you don't eat it, it'll just go to waste, because I won't be having any," he said.

"Yeah, yeah, I know the drill." I dug my fork into the concoction and it tasted like a little slice of heaven. I thought that it was too bad that Chris was a vampire, because with his talent, we could have opened a four-star restaurant and made money hand over fist with cuisine that good.

"While you enjoy the meal, I'm going to go out and get something of my own to eat. I haven't had anything in a few days."

"Sure thing. See you in a little while." Chris left the house and I continued to savor the food, whatever it was. I thought that I could taste a hint of cinnamon or nutmeg and apricots. It looked sort of like angel hair pasta mixed with grilled chicken, but tasted more exotic somehow.

When Chris came back twenty minutes later, I was just finishing off my dinner and about to put the dish and cutlery in the sink. "Let me get that for you," he said, taking them out of my hands. "What did you think?"

"It was really good. Did you put cinnamon in it?" I asked.

"Yeah."

"I thought so. That gave the pasta an interesting flavor. My compliments to the chef."

"It was a little something that my mother used to make. She called it 'The Sinclair Special', except that I've added my own little twists to it."

"So maybe now you can call it 'Pasta a la Chris' or something else not so lame," I said and laughed.

"Yeah," he replied, smiling.

I sat back down. "Chris, we need to talk."

"Uh, oh. I haven't been human for a long time and even *I* know what that means."

"I'm leaving you."

"What? What did I do wrong? I'll give you anything you want if you stay here with me. What do you want? A diamond necklace? Something from Tiffany's? Designer bags?" I laughed at his puzzled and worried expression. "*What*? Why are you laughing?"

"I didn't mean that I'm leaving you as in *leaving* you. Obviously, that wasn't a very good way of starting off things, but you should have seen the look on your face! That was priceless!" I exclaimed, laughing some more.

"Then what *did* you mean?" he asked, a look of confusion etched all over his face.

"Do you remember how you told me that I had a good singing voice?"

"Yeah," he said, slowly drawing out the word unsure of where the discussion was going.

"And do you remember how you asked me if I wanted to do something more with my life?"

"Yeah."

"Do you see where I'm going with this?" I asked, gesturing a little with my hands, hoping that he'd put two and two together.

"Not really."

"Then I'll break it down for you. I want to try to go to Nashville and make it as a singer. I'm going to quit my job as soon as possible and move to the city." I waited a moment for Chris to say something in response, but nothing came out. I supposed that it had been a lot of information to take in without any warning.

"*What*?" he said in disbelief. "When did you decide this?"

"This week. I did a lot of thinking while I was lying in bed and bored out of my mind. This whole business with the Council made me realize that life is too precious to be stuck in a dead-end job. I want to be able to go out and try to chase a dream. I suppose I should really thank the Council and that battle the other night for lighting the fire under my ass and being the catalyst to get me to finally change my life. So what do you think?" I asked with a hopeful expression on my face, eager for his approval.

"I . . . I don't know. It's all so sudden."

"I know that it's a lot to take in, but I'm dead serious about this. I've already done a lot of research trying to find places to live there and record labels that I want to try to get signed by. Tomorrow, I'm going to start looking up people who can help me do a demo and see what agents and managers are out there. It would really mean a lot to me if you'd back me up on this and support me."

Chris opened his mouth as if he was about to say something, then he seemed to think the better of it and closed it again. At least one minute passed before he finally spoke. "Of course I'll support you, but I'm not so sure that all of this is a good idea."

"Why not? I know that it's so crazy, but if I don't at least try it, I'll always be wondering '*What if . . .?*'"

"I get that, but what if you run into trouble out there with some other vampires? I can't always be your knight in shining armor and rescue you. Just because the Council and their assassins aren't a threat to you anymore, it doesn't mean that you're completely safe, Jessi. The Council doesn't control every vampire," Chris said.

"I can't live my life worrying about what may or may not happen to me, Chris. I appreciate your concern, but I feel that I need to do this no matter what," I said.

"If you really want to do this singing thing, I'll support you. I'll miss you a lot, though."

"I'll miss you too, but Nashville isn't that far away from here so I figure that I can still see you at least once a week."

"If Nashville isn't that far from here, then why are you talking about moving there? How far away is it, anyway?" he asked.

"About forty minutes," I replied.

"That's not much longer than your commute to Munroeville and you have no problem with *that*," he reasoned. "Forty minutes isn't that much. If it was four days away, then I would completely understand needing to move out there."

"I guess I can't really argue with that kind of logic. Dammit Chris, why do you have to be so smart and convincing?" I grinned, wrapping my arms around him.

"Some of us are just born with it," he joked. "Seriously though, why were you thinking of moving?"

"I just thought that it would be easier to live there than having to drive back and forth everyday. Also, it would help me out a lot to get noticed if I was constantly around the city, trying to mingle with people, going to clubs and stuff like that."

"Can't you still do all of that? Maybe just hang out there on some weeknights?"

"Yeah, I guess," I said slowly, realizing that Chris was right. It seemed that with all of the fantasizing that I'd done, I hadn't thought everything through as thoroughly as I thought I had.

"How much would it have cost you to live in Nashville?" he asked.

"At least $450, but some of those places might have ended up being a real hole-in-the-wall."

"I love you too much to see you live in squalor. I believe that you deserve the finer things in life and I'd do anything to give them to you," he said with complete honesty. As his words sunk in, they nearly brought tears to my eyes and I hugged him for being so sweet.

"I didn't want to see myself living like that, either, believe me. I would have liked to try to get one of the more expensive apartments, but I wouldn't have been able to afford it by myself," I said.

"Well, that doesn't really matter now, does it?"

"No."

"I would have hated not being able to see you everyday," Chris said, wrapping his arms around me and looking deeply into my eyes.

"I know. I was resigning myself to the idea of having to settle for phone sex."

"Like where you talk about what you're wearing and what you'd do to your partner if you were together?" he asked.

"Yeah. Or we could have tried having cybersex on the internet or do some sexting on our cell phones," I replied.

"You humans and your crazy technology!" he shook his head in amazement. "Even though you're not moving away now, I'd still like to try out that whole phone sex thing sometime."

"We'll see." There was a brief pause as I figured out how to word what I was going to say next. "Do you really think that I might get attacked while I'm out in Nashville?"

"I can't say for sure, but it's always a possibility. As I said, the Council doesn't control every vampire and so not every vampire would know about our deal with them," he replied.

"Oh. Well, I'll just have to do my best to be on my guard, then. Chris, I think that I've proved that I can handle myself and I'll try to make sure that I'm not alone for long, anyway," I reassured him and squeezed his hand.

"It's not much of a promise, but it's a start, I guess," he relented. For the rest of the night, we cuddled up on the couch downstairs and he read from some old book of short stories that he'd had since he was a young child. By the time that he was about halfway through it, I had begun to fall asleep.

I called up Natalie at lunchtime on Friday to ask her if she could come over that night. "Hello?" she answered the phone.

"Natalie?"

"Jessi?"

"Yeah, who else would it be?" I joked.

"Sorry, I just wasn't expecting to hear from you. How are you?" she asked.

"Steadily recovering, thanks. What's been up with you?"

"Not much, just the usual."

"Work, work and more work?" I asked.

"You know it!" she laughed.

"I need to talk to you about something. When can you come over? Would tonight be fine?"

"Yeah, sure. What is it about?"

"I can't go into it over the phone. I really need to talk to you face to face," I admitted. We made a little more small talk and then Nat agreed to come over around seven.

"Okay then, take care and I'll see you later. And Jessi?" she asked.

"Yeah?"

"If there's anything else you need, don't hesitate to call, alright?"

"Sure thing. Thanks, Nat. See you tonight," I said and then hung up the phone. I wondered for a brief moment if there might have been some sort of hidden meaning behind her offer, but then shrugged it off as nothing more than simply a good friend showing concern. If our situations were reversed I would have made the same offer because that's the kind of thing that friends do.

Natalie meant so much to me because she was one of the first people that I had met when I began working at STARS and we bonded instantly like it was fate that had brought us together. I dreaded having to tell her about my new career plans, because it felt like I would somehow be breaking her heart.

I spent the rest of the afternoon searching on the internet to find people who could help me make my demo. I phoned up a few who sounded very professional and charged a pretty hefty sum for their services. Although I had found people that were much cheaper, they didn't have any qualifications or references listed on their websites so I had been pretty wary about them.

I had been heading down to the kitchen to make myself a salad when Chris appeared at the top of the stairs. "How are you today?" he asked, walking over to me.

"I'm better than yesterday if that's any indication."

"May I take a look?"

"Sure," I said, shrugging. He lifted up each leg of my jeans to inspect my injuries and then checked out my thighs.

"The coloring is much lighter now, so that's a good sign. How much do they still hurt?" he asked. Chris pressed lightly on my left thigh, applying a little more pressure every few seconds or so and looking up into my eyes.

"Just a little tender and sore," I replied.

"You're healing remarkably well."

"Thanks. By the way, we have a guest coming over soon."

"Natalie?"

"Who else?" I asked, thinking that the answer was kind of obvious.

"Why? She shouldn't see you like this," Chris said.

"I'm going to break the big news to her."

"Do you want me to leave so that you can have some privacy while the two of you talk?"

"No. I want you to be here to give me some support," I said. As I ate my salad, Chris went around the house making it look presentable for our company and then I tried to cover the bruises on my face with a bit of foundation and concealer. Thankfully, it didn't take as much to cover them up as I thought it would because they had been fading away quite nicely.

"Hi!" Natalie exclaimed when I answered the door a short while later.

"I'm so glad that you could come," I said as I carefully hugged her.

"Nice to see you again," she said to Chris who had just entered the kitchen.

"Likewise," Chris replied.

"So what's this you needed to tell me so desperately?" Nat asked me. I glanced at Chris, who gestured for me to get on with it and Natalie looked back and forth between us wondering what was going on.

"Maybe we should sit down first," I suggested and led Chris and Nat into the living room. I sat down on the couch and Chris joined me, while she sat on the armchair opposite.

"Okay, spill it now."

"I've been doing a lot of thinking this week while I've been laid up in bed," I said to her.

"Thinking about what?" she asked and then a slow smile spread across her face. "Are you thinking about getting married?" I shook my head. "Having kids?" I emphatically shook my head again. "Then what else could it be?"

"I wanted to let you know that I'm planning to quit my job," I replied.

"*Why?*" Natalie was really confused now and I could tell that she had a million questions kicking around in her head that she was dying to get out.

"I want to do something more with my life than just give makeovers so I'm going to try to make it as a singer in Nashville."

For once in her life, she was rendered almost speechless. "*What?*" she said, not quite sure that she had heard me correctly.

"I want to be a singer," I repeated. "Chris told me that I had a good voice, so I thought that I'd give it a try. I realize that it'll be a lot of hard work and take a lot of luck, but I'm really serious about this. I'm going to need you to support me. I love you as a friend and almost like a sister, Nat."

"Of course I'll support you, but this is just a lot to take in. Are you going to move out to Nashville?"

"No. I thought that I would have to, but Chris pointed out that I could just make the commute there. Nashville is only about 10 minutes further away than Munroeville is so not much should change."

"Wow. This is all so sudden and I had no idea that you'd felt this way. I just hope that you won't forget all about the little people like me when you get rich and famous. I don't want you to go and get a big head," she said.

I chuckled, "How could I forget you?"

"I *am* pretty hard to forget, aren't I?"

"And you take a lot of pride in that. I promise that if I ever get a big head about my fame, then you can call me up and put me in my place. Deal?"

"It's a deal. So, when are you quitting?" Nat asked me.

"As soon as I can come back into work," I replied.

"And when's that?" she asked.

"I was hoping to come in for Monday, but I'll have to see how things go."

"Okay."

"You're taking this remarkably well," I commented. "I thought that maybe you'd be making a big scene about it, crying and pleading for me not to go."

"Yeah, well, later I might break down," she admitted. "I'm happy for you, but at the same time, I won't get to see you around as much."

"Nat, I'm going to try my hardest to stay in touch with you. You've got my phone number and my e-mail address, so it's not like we can't still talk."

"Yeah, but it's not the same as getting to talk to you in person and just hang out."

"I'm going to miss working with you so much, but this is all going to be for the best," I said, trying to reassure myself more than anyone else.

"Same here."

"Have we ever taken a picture together?" I asked, an idea forming in my head.

"I don't think so," Nat replied.

"I'll be right back." I hobbled upstairs to my room to get my digital camera and when I came back down, Chris and Nat were still in the same positions as when I'd left them. "Do you know how to use one of these?" I asked him and he shook his head. I told him how to hold the camera, how to get us in the frame and which buttons to press to take the picture. Nat and I posed together, hugging each other and making cheesy smiles. Within seconds, we checked out the results on the camera's small screen and then took a few more pictures for good measure.

"Can you e-mail them to me soon?" Nat asked.

"Sure thing."

"Whey didn't you ever tell me about this singing thing before?"

"I think that everyone has secret ambitions, but they're too scared to admit them aloud to anyone. Something happened recently that made me aware of how precious life is and that you should never let it go to waste," I replied.

"What are you talking about?"

"Let's just call it a near-death experience and leave it at that. I'd rather not go into further detail about it."

"Oh, okay," she said, knowing that it was time to back off. There was a moment of uneasy silence while we thought of what else to say. "Tell me more about your plans." I told her about everything that I'd been researching and what songs I had been thinking of doing for my demo. In turn, Nat told me about a childhood dream that she had of becoming a dancer in a professional company. I suggested that she take some dance lessons and see what happened, but she laughed it off and claimed that she was too old to give it a try. Despite what she had said, I knew that she would end up giving it some thought.

At the end of the night, Natalie hugged me and wished me good luck. "I love you, Jessi. Be careful."

"I will," I promised.

"Remember to keep in touch with me. I want to know everything that you're doing." She winked at me and Chris. "Well, maybe not *every*thing."

I chuckled and blushed a little. "Believe me when I say that there are some things that you *don't* want to know about."

"Alright, then. Goodbye," she said as she began to walk away.

"Goodbye," I called out back to her and then watched her walk down the path to her car. I stood in the doorway until she drove off into the warm night and waved at the car even though she probably couldn't have seen me.

"That went well," Chris commented.

"Yeah," I agreed. "Maybe a little *too* well. I can't help thinking that she wasn't being completely honest with me for some reason."

"I guess that only time will tell."

"Yeah."

On Monday morning, I was feeling almost back to normal and went to the manager's office at the store to hand in my two weeks' notice. It was one of the most nerve-wracking things that I'd ever had to write, but there I was, standing in front of Leon Kowalski and being told how I was such a valued employee and how they would be sad to see me go.

Over the next two weeks, practically every co-worker asked me about my future plans and speculated on what had happened to me to cause me to spend a week from work. It seemed that Kathy, from the store's administrative offices, had kept the information under lock-and-key. On the last day of work, I was given a surprise party in the break room complete with a chocolate cake, punch and streamers. I wasn't surprised that Nikki and Ashley were absent, but I thought that maybe they could have swallowed their pride just for the occasion.

After my last ever shift at the store, I decided to celebrate the new chapter of my life at this restaurant called Ben's Roadhouse that boasted the world's biggest hamburger and I ordered one of those bad boys. It was three pounds of grade-A beef, topped with almost every fixing that you could think of. I couldn't eat the whole thing there, so I took about half of it home in a box.

"How did your last day at work go?" Chris asked me as soon as I saw him later that night.

"Fine," I replied.

"Did they throw you a farewell party?"

"Yeah. I think Natalie pulled some strings to make it happen."

"That was really nice. Wish I could have been there," he said.

"We can celebrate whenever we want and isn't that much better? I prefer our own little private parties," I winked suggestively.

"So do I." He grinned and wrapped his arms around me, carefully whirling me around the living room.

"I feel like going to a movie. I haven't done that in ages, but I'm not sure what's playing."

"Well, if there's nothing worth watching, we could always rent or watch something you own," Chris suggested.

"I'll check out what's playing in Munroeville first," I said and he gently placed me back down on the floor. I went upstairs to get my laptop and then when I came back down, I placed it on the coffee table so that the both of us could take a look. There were a few romantic comedies playing that had just been released, a horror movie, a children's animated film and some documentary about the environment.

"What do you think?" he asked me.

"I'd like to go to one of the comedies, but I don't know if you'd be into that. It's sort of girly stuff about love and romance."

"I don't mind, well, as long as it doesn't get *too* mushy."

"If it does, then let's say that I owe you one," I said.

"Owe me one what?" he asked, a suggestive glint in his eyes.

"Whatever you want."

"You're on, but we'd better leave now if we're going to make it to the 9 o'clock show."

"Yeah, just let me get changed first. I've been wearing these jeans and this old shirt all day and I'm sure that they stink like crazy by now."

"Good idea," Chris agreed. I jogged up the stairs as quickly as I could and put on a fresh pair of black jeans, a red tank top, the most floral smelling perfume that I had and black sneakers. I stashed my keys, wallet and cell phone in my little black clutch purse and grabbed a jacket just in case it was cool when we got out of the theater.

We drove to the city in Chris' flashy car and I laid my head back against the headrest to enjoy the ride. It was so nice not having to drive somewhere. I changed the station on the radio and began singing along with the song that was playing. Chris glanced to his right to see me, but I didn't care. I needed to practice as much as possible and I think that he just enjoyed listening to me.

The theater was packed when we got there so we ended up sitting near the back row which was fine with me. I just thought that it was so good to get out of the house for a reason other than going to work or trying to talk someone into not killing me. As we watched the movie, Chris wrapped one of his arms around my shoulders and I leaned in close to him just as many of the other women in the theater were doing with their significant others.

By the time the show ended, it had gotten chilly outside and I was glad that I'd brought my jacket. Although I had slipped it on when I stepped outside of the multiplex, I still shivered a little. It seemed that Chris had seen me in his peripheral vision, because he pulled me close to him to try to give me some extra warmth and I couldn't help thinking again about how good he smelled.

"What did you think of the movie?" Chris asked me as we drove back to Hollingsford.

"It was alright. Honestly, I wasn't really paying all of my attention because I was thinking of you being so close to me. It just felt nice to be like other couples, you know?

What did *you* think of it?"

"The acting and the storyline were okay and there were some pretty funny bits. You were right that it would be pretty girly."

"But not too mushy?" I asked.

"*I* thought it was so you owe me now."

"Okay, but hopefully it'll be a treat that we'll *both* enjoy."

"Oh, we will," he grinned and put the pedal to the metal so that we could get home as quickly as possible to indulge in our favorite pastime. Instead of the bed or the shower, this time we chose to christen the new carpet in the basement. The fabric was luxurious and felt so good on my skin that I knew I'd definitely picked the right one.

To top the night off, Chris and I went back to that sleazy bar in town to have a few drinks and do a little dancing. Some random guys checked me out as I moved to the music, but I tried to ignore them. Almost as soon as we got home, I went right to sleep still dressed in my clothes. It had been a hell of a long day, but what a way to celebrate!

Chapter 13

I woke up on Saturday morning feeling like a weight had been lifted off of my shoulders and replaced with an even heavier one as the enormity of my new situation descended upon me. I hadn't been unemployed since my teenage years and suddenly I was looking at a very uncertain financial situation unless my boyfriend stepped up to help me through my transitional period. I felt like I was on the brink of something amazing yet scary as hell and I hated not knowing how it would all turn out, but it was exhilarating at the same time.

As I thought about my situation, I wondered how Natalie was dealing with my news. I had spoken to her at my party, but even then she had only talked about the decorations and food that she'd had everyone chip in for. I supposed that she needed more time to absorb everything that was going on and I couldn't blame her so I decided that I would give her a few days before I tried to check in with her.

I got out of bed, testing my body to see how much I still had of my aches and was pleased to find everything was continuing to fade away nicely. I still had some tenderness so I'd have to keep being careful, but I figured that I would be almost as good as new in a few more days. Unfortunately, I also found that the margaritas that I'd had the night before were a mistake. I nearly fell over and so I climbed back into bed for a while longer while I waited for things to calm down.

I eventually got up to change into a blue, denim mini skirt that I hadn't worn in ages and a cute purple v-neck top with a cat on it that said "I ♥ pussy" and then made myself some French toast. Afterwards, I went to the Stop-n-Shop to get a few things and then went online to check out some chat rooms.

I spent the afternoon phoning some more studios that I'd found online and in the phonebook. I had a long list of possible options and as I called, I made some notations to help me narrow down my choices. Occasionally, I would find some people who wouldn't quote me anything over the phone and I'd cross them off.

After a lot of consideration and fancy talk, I eventually decided on this guy named Brett LaSalle. He sounded very knowledgeable, very professional and was very patient with me while I asked him about a zillion questions. When he told me how much it would cost to work with him, I let out a low whistle. He assured me that, although the price was a bit steep, I would be getting great service catered to my personal needs and use of state-of-the-art equipment.

I agreed to meet him on Monday afternoon and he gave me an address that I scribbled down on a scrap piece of paper. "I looked you up in the phonebook and it's got a different address printed there," I said.

"We just moved recently," he explained.

"Oh, okay." While his answer seemed pretty plausible on the surface, the way that he replied and his tone of voice made me think that he wasn't being entirely truthful. I wasn't in the position to be calling him a liar, so I just let it slide and made a mental note to be extra cautious around him.

"So, I'll see you on Monday at 3 o'clock. Thank you for choosing me, Ms. Winters. I look forward to meeting you."

"Goodbye, Mr. LaSalle," I said and then hung up the phone. I was happy that the wheels were finally being set in motion, but the joy was quickly offset by the enormous cost. It would cost me $1500 to make my demo and I didn't have much more than that in my bank account. I hoped that the studio would have some sort of payment plan where I could pay a small chunk of the cost each month, but I doubted it. I decided that I had no choice but to bite the bullet and ask Chris to give me some quick cash.

I rummaged around in the kitchen to find something suitable to eat for supper and came across some old boxes of various pastas that had just a small amount of stuff left in each of them and a package of sauce mix. Twenty minutes later, I was sitting down to an odd-looking, but delicious meal.

As soon as I saw Chris, I talked to him about my financial situation. "How much money do you need?" he asked.

"$1500. Now, I know that it's a lot of money, but I swear I'll pay it back whenever I can. Even if I can't give you the money, I'm prepared to do other things to make up for it," I offered.

"I know you are. I'll give you the money with no strings attached—consider it a gift."

"No joke?"

"No joke, but if you still want to make it up to me, I won't try to stop you," he grinned.

"I know you won't," I teased him.

"How are you feeling now?"

"Almost back to normal."

"Good. So, when are you going to see this guy about the studio?"

"On Monday afternoon."

"That soon?" he asked.

"I know that it feels like everything's happening so fast, but I'd rather think of it as making up for lost time," I replied.

"I really hope you know what you're doing, Jessi."

"I'm a big girl, Chris, I can handle myself."

"I know *that*, but I also know that there are some pretty shady people in the music business and I just don't want to see you get hurt and taken advantage of," he said.

"That's really sweet of you, but I think I'll be fine. I'll have my cell phone on me in case of an emergency and I'll leave you the address and phone number of the place I'm going to, alright?" I tried to reassure him.

"Thanks."

"How do you know so much about the music business, anyway?"

"When you've been around for as long as I have, you pick up on these things. Vampires have to keep tabs occasionally on the human world in order to fit in and check out our prey. Plus, I've fed on a few record execs here and there."

"Ah," I said nodding my head.

"What do you want to do tonight?"

"I don't know."

"I'm getting sick of staying in. Let's go for a drive up the state," Chris suggested.

"Like where?" I asked him.

"Nowhere in particular. It's all about driving for the sake of driving and who knows what we might come across? I feel up for a little adventure. Are you game?"

I hesitated for a few moments, considering all sorts of crazy scenarios that could happen and then I reined in my wild imagination and shrugged. "Sure, why not?"

"Great! Get a few things together and we'll leave in five minutes." Chris laughed as I animatedly ran around the house trying to gather up my handbag and a few things to take with us on our little trip. "*I* could have been done in less than a minute."

"Yeah, well, not only do I not have your speed, there's also the fact that I'm still trying to get over some bad injuries. You just want to be a little show-off, you know." He laughed at my accusation and I playfully swatted him on the arm, then we left the house and got into his car.

We drove for I don't know how many miles past Munroeville and a few other towns and I watched the scenery change from concrete buildings to trees and farmland at lightning speed. I rolled my window down, but my hair was blowing around my face too much for my liking so I rolled it back up most of the way. Before I knew it, I saw a large sign declaring that we were two miles from the Kentucky state line.

"Holy crap! We're almost in Kentucky!" I exclaimed.

"I know," he smiled.

"That's so crazy. How fast are we going?"

"About 120 miles an hour."

"I stand corrected—*that's* crazy!"

"What can I say? What's the point of owning a car like this if you can't drive fast? I can't do it out on the city streets, but we're out here practically in the middle of nowhere with no one around so I don't see the harm," he replied. I wouldn't say it to his face, but I supposed that Chris had a point although I still thought that it was insane to drive at that kind of speed.

After a while, we stopped off at a tourist center where he checked a map of the area and I was able to go to the bathroom. When I came back out, he informed me that there was a park nearby about a few miles away that had a gorgeous man-made waterfall and so we climbed back into the car and sped off in that direction.

The park was nearly deserted so Chris and I were free to roam around in privacy, which had been fine by me. I thought that it was pretty romantic to walk around under the stars and kiss him in the moonlight where his face glowed in an otherworldly fashion, highlighting his gorgeous features.

We followed the paved path through the trees and eventually we came to the waterfall which was quite obviously the centerpiece of the park. It was surrounded by multicolored flowers and small lights that created a sort of spotlight in the darkness making it a beautiful sight to behold. I imagined that in the daytime it was even more spectacular when you could see the full color of the flowers. The rest of the park, while quite pretty, couldn't hold a candle to the scene in front of me.

"It's not as pretty as you," Chris whispered to me as if he had read my thoughts.

"You're just saying that because you want to get in my pants, don't you?" I joked.

"You know I don't need to work hard for that!" he teased. I considered his words and thought about how easy that made me sound. I knew that he didn't mean it that way, but it still didn't sit right with me.

"It's not like you're all that hard to convince, either." It made me feel a bit better to say that. As much as I loved to be intimate with him, I had been starting to get a bit tired of having most of our relationship being based around that and I promised myself that I'd try to make it into something deeper. There was still so much that we didn't know about each other and that we hadn't experienced together and I wanted to change that.

"I know." We walked around for a while longer and then began heading home. It would be at least a few hours back to Hollingsford, even going as fast as Chris had been driving earlier. I fell asleep on the ride back, somewhere around the state line and hadn't woken up until he nudged me to tell me that we were home.

"What?" I asked, groggily.

"We're home, Jessi," he said.

"Oh, okay." My eyes closed again and I felt his arms lift me out of my seat and then slam the car door closed just before we went up the path to the back door. The last thing I remembered about the night was being bounced as he carried me up the stairs to my room.

I spent Sunday sleeping in until noon and then I made myself a brunch of sorts with hash browns, scrambled eggs, leftover pasta and fresh fruit. After I ate, I finished the rest of my book and started on a new one about a woman who was a door-to-door salesperson. She got abducted by a man whose house she had visited and, in a bizarre twist, she ended up falling in love with him.

At night, Chris and I cuddled up on the couch in the living room to watch a horror movie that was playing on TV. It was one of those movies where a bunch of beautiful teenagers find an abandoned house, not realizing that there's a serial killer on the loose and that he's locked inside the house with them. Axe and chainsaw-wielding fun ensue. There was a point where the violence and gore got a bit too much for me and I hid my face against his chest.

"Are you ready for tomorrow?" he asked.

"I hope so."

"I still haven't given you the money yet. I'll leave it out for you in the kitchen later."

"Thanks again, Chris," I said.

"It's my pleasure."

Just before I was about to head out early on Monday afternoon, I wrote out the studio's address and phone number for Chris and picked up a credit card that he had left for me. A little note was attached to the card, which read:

> *Good luck, Jessi! Break a leg!*
> *You'll knock 'em dead!*
> *Use the card to treat yourself to a new outfit.*
> *A superstar like you deserves to look like a million bucks.*
>
> *Much love,*
> *Chris*

I felt tears starting to sting my eyes, but I wiped them away before they could do damage to my perfectly painted on mascara. I quickly went to the bathroom to check myself out in the mirror and touched up my makeup a little bit, then spritzed some more perfume on and straightened my outfit a bit. I wanted to make a great first impression so I wore my best pair of black jeans, a red sleeveless top, a pair of white hoop earrings and my black, open-toed strappy sandals.

I pulled up to the address that Brett LaSalle had given me, but I checked it again to be sure. He had told me that it was 1405 Church St., but the place didn't look like it was home to a recording studio. The outside of the building looked like it was in desperate need of repair. The brick was crumbling, the paint was peeling and the sign above the doorway seemed like it could fall at almost any second.

I glanced up and down the street for any sign of life, anything that would signify that I was indeed in the right spot, but there was nothing to be found. It seemed weird to me that any place of business would have no advertising in the immediate area. Just as I was about to drive off in search of a gas station to get some information, a man with short, dark-brown hair popped his head out of the entrance and gestured for me to come inside. I supposed that this was Mr. LaSalle, but when I hesitated in my car, he walked over to the passenger-side window and I rolled it down a little.

"Are you Jessica Winters?"

"Yes," I replied, glancing nervously around me. I figured that if I was wrong about this guy, then I could peel away from the curb before he had a chance to try anything against me.

"Come on in, Ms. Winters. You're a little early."

"I wasn't sure how long it would take me to find the place so I made sure that I had plenty of time just in case."

"I hope it wasn't *too* hard to find," he said. I cautiously exited the car and followed him towards the entrance. Before we went in, I quickly scanned the street again and found nothing but some bungalows with well-maintained front yards just like a typical neighborhood.

As I entered the building, I glanced around and it looked pretty legit to me. There was a reception desk complete with a female receptionist who was filing her nails and a small waiting area with a handful of comfy chairs and a stylish coffee table piled with magazines. The walls were lined with neatly framed gold records and pictures of various recording artists who had used the studio. There were even certificates from the Better Business Bureau and various recording industry organizations hung up on the wall behind the desk.

"Wow!" I remarked.

"Never been in a recording studio, eh?" he asked and I shook my head. "Well, hopefully you'll get to see more of them from now on. I have a feeling that big things are going to happen for you." I walked with him down the hall towards one of the several studios that the building housed and he held the door open for me. As I entered, I felt a hard blow to the back of my head and the last thing I saw was the floor rapidly coming up to meet me.

When I eventually came to, I found myself chained up to the floor in what looked to be a basement. I assumed that I was still in the building of the recording studio, but that was the only thing I could be sure of. "What the hell is going on here? Why did you hit me?" I asked, barely containing my rising anger.

"Maybe I shouldn't tell you, but since you're about to die, I'll go easy on you because I like you," he replied and I rolled my eyes.

"Just spit it out, *already*!"

"I've been hired by some vampires to kidnap you and hold you hostage until they can get here to deal with you themselves. You might be wondering how I got involved in this. Well, it seems that the vamps found out that you were planning to become a singer and so they went around trying to contact everyone in town to look out for you. I don't know how they knew anything and I was smart enough not to ask. By the way, this shit hole isn't my real studio. The vamps killed the real owner and asked that I pretend it was mine as part of the elaborate ruse. It's quite genius, when you think about it."

"How much are they paying you?" I asked as calmly as I could.

"$50,000 in cold, hard cash. That's a lot of money to do some babysitting so I guess they must really want you dead. What'd you do, anyway?"

"I don't know. Who are they?"

"They didn't give me their names, so I couldn't say. Well, since they won't be up for a while yet, I'm going to have a little fun with you myself," he said, rubbing his hands together and staring at me in the sleaziest way that I'd ever seen. I tried to back up as far away from him as I could, but the act was made almost impossible by the fact that my legs and wrists were chained to a ring in the floor. I didn't have much length, but what I did have, I made full use of.

"Get away from me!" I shouted, trying to put as much menace into my voice as I could muster.

"It's nothing personal, sweet cheeks," I shuddered when he called me that, "but just consider it something to do while we wait. Besides, what they're going to do is a lot worse than what I'll do to you." Tears started to fall down my face. "Aw, look at that! She's crying!" He wiped the tears away from my cheeks and I winced at his touch. "That'll make it *so* much sweeter!"

"You won't get away with this!" I cried out.

"Oh, but I think I will! Who's going to stop me?" he sneered.

"My boyfriend will notice that I've been gone for too long and he'll hunt you down. I've told him where I am so it's just a matter of time before you're screwed."

Although some of that was an overstatement, I figured that I might be able to call his bluff.

"You mean your *vampire* boyfriend? His name is Chris, right?" Although it probably shouldn't have, it surprised me that he knew so much. "Somehow, I doubt that he's going to be able to save you now. By the time that he gets here, my employers will have had their way with you, but if he's lucky, maybe he'll get to take home a few of your fingers as a keepsake. It's such a shame to let such a pretty girl like you go to waste," he said, caressing my face and stroking my hair. I cringed at his touch and turned my face away.

He proceeded to kick me in my ribs and I curled up into a ball, trying to reduce his target. The chains were beginning to cut into my skin, but I couldn't give a damn. After a few minutes, he moved on to whipping my legs and back with a metal chain that stung me and I was sure that my body would be covered in bright red marks. I cried some more and thought only of Chris until I could barely feel what was being done to me.

I don't know how much time had passed while I was being tortured and abused, but it had felt like an eternity. The battle at the warehouse was like a walk in the park in comparison to this beating. A few punches to the face and a few knocks to the ground weren't that big of a deal, especially since I hadn't been alone and I could move around freely whereas I had been chained up in the basement with no way to run and no weapons to defend myself with. It wasn't a fair fight in any sense of the word.

"Let me go!" I whimpered.

"No. Why would I go and do *that*? You'll just call the cops or get your boyfriend to kill me when the sun goes down. I'm not stupid. What I *will* do though, is leave you alone in the dark for a while and you can get all of that crying business out of your system," he said and begun to walk back towards the stairs. As he climbed them, he took one last look at me over his shoulder and grinned lewdly before locking the door behind him.

I fell into a pit of despair when Brett had gone and felt so despondent. I knew that he was probably right that there was nothing Chris could do to save me. He'd either burn in the sun trying or come too late and all that would be left was my corpse. I scanned the room for anything that could possibly be used as a tool. I thought that if I could get a hold of something, I could break free from the chains or at least get them loosened up a bit, but I had a hard time seeing in the darkened room.

I struggled against the chains hoping against hope that with enough movement and strength maybe I could loosen them that way or find a weak link that I could use to my advantage. After several minutes, it had become apparent to me that my theories weren't panning out well and that I had just been wasting some much-needed energy.

I felt like a caged animal waiting to be slaughtered and there wasn't anything I could do about it except scream. He hadn't put anything across my mouth to prevent me from making noise, which I chalked up to either forgetfulness or a lack of expertise. In any case, I was grateful for the little bit of hope that I'd been given.

Deciding on a new course of action, I took a few deep breaths and screamed like my life depended on it, which it pretty much did. "HELP ME!! SOMEBODY PLEASE HELP ME!!" I waited for about twenty seconds, but despite the volume that I tried to project in my voice, no one came to check on me. As soon as I had refilled my lungs with enough oxygen, I tried my tactic again. "I'M DOWN IN THE BASEMENT! I NEED HELP! PLEASE SOMEBODY RESCUE ME!"

I looked around the room again and kept randomly willing something to move, hoping that my telekinesis would hit upon a useful object. I tried several times to no avail, but eventually I saw a large unknown object hit the basement door with a resounding thud. I aimed my thoughts at it again and it hit the door repeatedly until it opened.

The light that streamed in from the hallway upstairs was enough for me to see not only the tool box that I'd been using, but something so unexpected that my mouth just opened in shock. Hayden was standing there, peering into the darkness at me, although I'm not sure if he actually could see me. "Hayden?" I asked, my voice hoarse.

"Jessi? Is that *you*?"

"Yes, it's me!"

"What are you doing down here?" he asked as he ran down the stairs.

"Oh, you know, just hanging around," I said sarcastically. "I'm chained up and that LaSalle guy kidnapped and beat the hell out of me."

"You don't have to worry about him, anymore."

"I don't?"

"No. I've just called the cops on him. They should be on their way shortly," Hayden said as he unlocked my cuffs and freed me from my temporary prison. "I heard someone screaming, but I couldn't get through the door to come and see who it was until just now."

"What are you doing here?" I asked, feeling incredibly grateful and rubbing my newly-freed wrists.

"I came by to do a consultation with Mr. LaSalle. If I'd known it was you that was making that racket, I would've tried harder to find a way to get through. Your voice sounded so strangled and desperate that I couldn't recognize it. In any case, I managed to get his keys."

"How'd you get them from him?"

"I punched him in the face and stole them. My associate, Luke, is holding onto him until the police arrive," he replied.

"*You* actually punched someone?" I asked in amazement.

"Yeah. You'd be surprised by some of the things that I'm capable of."

"Thanks a lot, Hayden. I guess I owe you one now."

"We can talk about that another time. For now, let's just get you home," he said.

"On second thought, maybe I should go to the hospital first," I said, looking at the indentations on my wrists.

"Better idea." Hayden drove me to the hospital and held my hand while I was attended to. A lot of pain cream was slathered all over me and then bandages were applied to help heal the various cuts and scrapes that I'd acquired. I had also been given a prescription for some painkillers that I planned to get filled out as soon as possible.

After we left, Hayden took me back to the scene of the crime so that I could retrieve my car. I decided that I would drive ahead while he followed me home to make sure that I got there without too much trouble. If it looked like I couldn't handle it, he'd be there right behind me to help me out.

When we got to the studio building, twilight was settling in and just as we were about to leave, a black car with tinted windows pulled up. A group of vampires emerged from the vehicle and strode purposefully towards the building. It dawned on me all of a sudden that I'd seen these guys before. I remembered them from the vamp nightclub that Chris had taken me to on our second date.

My eyes widened in shock as an even bigger revelation hit me. They had been the ones that ratted us out to the Council. It was *their* fault that my life had been threatened by assassin attacks and why I'd had to endure the battle at the warehouse. Although I hadn't remembered seeing them during the fight, it seemed that they'd gotten word about our deal with the Council and were so pissed off that they wanted to carry out some sort of vigilante justice and ensure that I would finally be dead.

I slammed my foot on the gas pedal before the vamps could stare at me long enough to figure out who I was. I watched them in my rearview mirror and saw that they had paid me no mind, thinking that I was just some random woman. I assumed that they were more concerned with the torture they wanted to perform and I smiled to myself as I thought about how mad they would be if they ever found out that their quarry had slipped by right under their noses. I even felt somewhat sorry for Brett for having to face the wrath of a bunch of angry vamps, but that feeling dissolved as I thought of what he had done to me.

I was filled with adrenaline and my heart raced as I drove back to town. I had never felt such a rush before and hopefully never would again. Unlike my previous near-death experiences, I had no doubt in my mind that I would die in the basement and that the vigilante vampires would have made it more painful than anything I could have ever dreamed up. I thanked my lucky stars that Hayden was somehow in the right place at the right time to rescue me. Maybe it had been yet another sign of his crazy, love-struck behavior that I was warned about, but I didn't care; I was just so happy to still be alive.

When I arrived home, I ran into the house as fast as my legs would carry me, ignoring the pain, and I nearly collapsed at Chris' feet. Thankfully, he caught me in time and tried to set me back on my own feet, but when I nearly went down again, he scooped me up in his arms. "What happened?" he asked, his eyebrows knitted together in confusion and anger. "Why are you hurt?"

I tried to calm down and slow my breathing to respond as coherently as I could. "The guy at the studio kidnapped me and chained me up in the basement." Chris' mouth dropped open in shock and then in an instant his face switched to a look of fury. He gritted his teeth, making sure not to show off his fangs in front of Hayden. It scared me to see Chris so full of anger and he tried to stroke my arm to calm me down.

"Do you know why?"

As I whispered to Chris about everything that Brett LaSalle had told me, I watched the expression on his face slowly become more savage. "Bastard!" Chris muttered. I burst out in tears and he rubbed my back. The word caught Hayden's attention, but he turned away again as Chris continued to console me, uncomfortable at the display of affection. For a few moments, Chris and I just stood there holding each other, forgetting that we weren't all alone.

"If Hayden hadn't been there I would be dead by now," I said as I turned to my ex and smiled at him through my tears. "Thank you so much for saving me. I don't know how I can ever repay you."

"I'm sure that I can figure out a way," he replied, returning my smile.

"I'm sorry that I wasn't there to save you," Chris said as I turned my attention back to him. "I've only been up for an hour. When you weren't back by the time I awoke, I called the number that you'd left me and got no answer except for a voicemail message telling me what their business hours were.

I tried phoning police stations and hospitals in the area to see if you'd come in and one of the hospitals told me that you had already left so I just decided to wait here."

"Thanks for trying, anyway," I said, reaching out to touch his hand.

Chris murmured to me, "You don't need to worry about those vampires anymore. No one will ever try to hurt you again like that."

"Oh? Why's that?"

"If there's one thing that the Council hates more than humans, it's vampires who go behind their backs and undermine their authority."

"So what will happen to them?" I asked.

"Do you really care?" he said and I shook my head. "Needless to say, it will be horrific." Chris turned his attention to Hayden and said in a normal volume, "Thank you very much for saving her. Even if we haven't seen eye to eye, I feel that I owe you a debt of gratitude."

"I didn't save her for *your* sake," Hayden snapped.

"I realize that, but I also believe in giving credit where credit is due."

"Let's not ruin the moment with fighting, alright guys? Besides, I've got a prescription that needs to be filled," I said, interrupting before the conversation could bloom into a full-on argument.

"I know of an all-night pharmacy in Munroeville. I'll head over there now for you," Chris offered and I handed him the slip of paper that I had been given at the hospital. Chris kissed me on the cheek, handed me over to Hayden and then climbed into his car, disappearing into the darkness.

"Let me help you up to your room," Hayden said and grabbed my waist, putting most of my weight on him. I hobbled up the stairs and was relieved when I dropped onto the bed.

"Thanks," I said. I tried to put some pillows behind my back so that I could sit up against them, but I couldn't get them right. Hayden understood what I was trying to do and I leaned slightly forward so that he could fluff them up and position them properly. "Thanks again." I leaned back on them and let out a sigh of relief.

"No problem. Jessi?"

"Yeah?"

"Can I ask you a question?"

"Of course," I replied.

"Even though I've saved your life, I still have no chance of getting back together with you, do I?" Hayden asked, a hint of disappointment coloring his voice.

It seemed to take me ages to figure out how to word my answer without hurting his feelings. "No. I'm sorry, but I love Chris with all of my heart and soul. I loved you, but this is different in a way that I can't really explain. It's like he's my soul mate if such a thing truly exists. Maybe we look weird to people on the outside, but we make perfect sense together and that's all that really matters."

"I'm really sorry about everything that went wrong with our relationship, Jessi."

"I am, too, but if it helps, what we had was great while it lasted."

"Yeah, it was," Hayden agreed, nodding his head. "If I could do it all over again, I would do what I should have done in the first place and you'd still be with me."

"I'm sure you would, Hayden, but what's done is done and we just have to make the best of it," I said, trying to reassure him.

"I know. Can I ask you a personal question, Jessi?"

"I guess I don't really see the harm in it."

"Are you going to marry him?"

"I don't know. Maybe one day," I said with a dreamy expression on my face. The two of us sat together in a comfortable silence for a while, reflecting on the good times that we had shared and wondering what the future held in store for us. I didn't realize how much time had passed and before I knew it, Chris had appeared in the doorway to my bedroom.

"Hi, baby. I've got your pills so you can take one now if you want."

"Thanks a lot, Chris." I turned to Hayden and said, "You don't have to stay here any longer if you want to get some sleep or if you've got other things to do."

"Yeah, I should probably be getting home now. I've got to get up pretty early in the morning," Hayden said.

"Thanks again," I said, trying to pour as much sincerity into my voice as possible. "I don't want to think of what would have happened if you hadn't come along when you did."

"Neither do I. Good night, Jessi. Good night, Chris."

"Good night to you, too," I called out as Hayden left the room and began making his way back down the stairs.

"I guess I get to play nurse with you again," Chris said, grinning.

"Yeah, I guess so."

"Do you want a painkiller now?"

"Yes, please," I replied.

"I'll go and get you some water first, then." Chris went to the bathroom and was back with a glass of water within seconds. I drank everything as quickly as I could and lay down to wait for the pill's effects to kick in.

"So, what were you guys talking about while I was gone?" he asked.

"Just about how much I love you and how sorry that Hayden and I were about our relationship not working out. He also asked if I was going to marry you."

"And what did you say?"

"Maybe one day," I replied.

"You think so?" Chris asked.

"Stranger things have happened." With that, I cuddled up to him as close as I could, then shut my eyes to go to sleep as he wrapped his muscular arms around me. The last thing I felt before I drifted off was his lips kissing my hair and the sweet smell of his breath on my skin. Pleasant dreams.